JAPANESE FOR BUSY PEOPLE III
The Workbook

JAPANESE FOR BUSY PEOPLE

Revised Edition

III

The Workbook

Association for Japanese-Language Teaching

KODANSHA INTERNATIONAL
Tokyo • New York • London

PHOTO CREDITS　写真協力

ドラキュラの花 (p. 9) © 宇田川芳雄
象の足 (p. 9) © 財団法人東京動物園協会
酒造り (p. 9) © 世界文化フォト
おもちゃの医者 (p. 10) © モーターマガジン社、協力松尾達也氏
聴導犬 (p. 10) © DCカード、THE CARD、古軸泉
カモ猟 (p. 65) 朝日新聞社提供
鳥人間コンテスト (p. 88) 津田雄一氏提供
東京ドーム (p. 93) © 世界文化フォト
サッカーボール (p. 98) © 世界文化フォト
ふじみ野駅周辺 (p. 111) 富士見市勝瀬原特定土地区画整理組合提供
洋服で働いている今の女性 (p. 115) © 世界文化フォト
田舎の遊園地 (p. 116) © 世界文化フォト
和太鼓 (p. 150) Susan Merron 氏提供
千羽鶴 (p. 184) © 世界文化フォト
新人研修 (p. 207) 日本マクドナルド株式会社広報部提供
七人の侍 (p. 211) © 東宝株式会社
用心棒 (p. 211) © 東宝株式会社東宝株式会社

Illustrations for lesson title pages, reading sections, and pages 39 and 70 by Andrew Boerger.
All other illustrations by Akiko Kajikawa.

Distributed in the United States by Kodansha America, Inc., 575 Lexington Avenue, New York, New York 10022, and in the United Kingdom and continental Europe by Kodansha Europe Ltd., 95 Aldwych, London WC2B 4JF.

Published by Kodansha International Ltd., 17-14 Otowa 1-chome, Bunkyo-ku, Tokyo 112-8652, and Kodansha America, Inc.

Printed in Japan.
ISBN 4-7700-2331-6

First Edition, 1999
99 00 01 02 03 10 9 8 7 6 5 4 3 2 1

CONTENTS

INTRODUCTION

Japanese for Busy People is, as the title suggests, a concise course for "busy" students who want to learn natural, spoken Japanese as effectively as possible in a limited amount of time. Three main texts—*Japanese for Busy People I*, *Japanese for Busy People II*, and *Japanese for Busy People III*—with related workbooks, cassette tapes, CDs, teacher's manuals, and videos make up this fully integrated three-level series. The overall learning objective of Book III—the final level of this series and the last stage of what is often called "beginner" Japanese—is the ability to communicate naturally and effectively in Japanese. To do so, students must be able to understand a speaker's intent, to choose the most appropriate expression from several possible expressions, and to adopt a speech level and style that is appropriate to the social context of any conversation. This fully illustrated workbook has been specially designed to help students develop and practice these three basic skills and also provide motivation and encouragement for those making that difficult transition from beginner to intermediate Japanese.

Japanese for Busy People III: The Workbook can be used both for self-study and as an effective preparation and review resource in the classroom. A set of audio tapes (available separately) has also been prepared to provide the learner with recordings of natural, spoken Japanese. Use the tapes to practice listening skills and to support your reading. The directions printed in English throughout this workbook tell you when and how to use the tapes. Note that at the back of this workbook we have appended a full tape script so that students can use this workbook even without the audio tapes. Repeated playback of the tapes, however, can genuinely accelerate learning progress as well as providing an authentic guide to spoken Japanese.

1. The Structure of Japanese for Busy People III: The Workbook

The workbook is divided into twenty lessons in parallel to the lessons in the main text. A typical lesson is centered around the following three sections.

1 SENTENCE PATTERN AND PRACTICE

This section includes the key learning objectives of each lesson and provides a selection of drills and exercises for the student to practice the sentence patterns illustrated by the Key Sentences introduced in *Japanese for Busy People III*. The activities presented in this section include "structure drills," "skit drills," and "discourse drills" and aim to maximize accuracy.

2 COMMUNICATION

As its name suggests, this section focuses on improving communication skills, with an emphasis on fluency over accuracy. Accordingly the exercises in this section include listening comprehension, role-playing activities, and other similar practice that will ultimately encourage students to apply the sentence patterns and forms they have learned in the main text to more productive usage of Japanese.

3 READING

Reading comprehension is an important part of intermediate and advanced Japanese language acquisition. At the end of each lesson, students will find a reading passage that has been written in natural, flowing Japanese. All of these passages are based on real-life newspaper and magazine articles—selected on the basis of their content, rather than their grammatical structure—and rewritten to be readily readable by students of this level. (A list of these sources appears at the end of this volume.) All the reading passages have been recorded on the audio tapes (available separately) to provide extra support to students without access to a native Japanese speaker. An idiomatic English translation of each passage appears on the page immediately following the original Japanese.

This workbook also features five review sections which we have labeled Check 1 through Check 5 and appear after Lessons 4, 10, 13, 16, and 20 respectively. Where possible we have tried to include here those sentence patterns which students tend to find more difficult to understand in dialogue form based on a clear and readily understandable context. Students are encouraged to tackle these Check sections as they progress through the workbook, referring to the main text whenever they find something that they fail to understand.

At the back of this workbook, students will find suggested answers to all the exercises together with English translations of some of the more difficult sections, a full tape script, and a Japanese–English glossary of all the new words that appear in this text.

Immediately after this introduction, we have included a special section in Japanese that offers teachers advice and practical tips on how to use this workbook in the classroom.

2. How to use Japanese for Busy People III: The Workbook

Knowing exactly where to focus attention is a common difficulty in learning a second language at this level. We have tried to address this problem by presenting material as consistently as possible throughout this workbook. Below, we offer some basic tips on tackling the three types of drills found in the Practice sections and typical activities in the Communication section.

1 VISUALIZATION

At this level of Japanese, the meaning and usage of many sentence patterns are quite difficult to analyze and explain in a way that is readily understandable to students who are not language experts. To try and overcome this problem, we have given each lesson an English chapter title that will help the student focus attention on the sentence patterns covered in that lesson. Furthermore, on the first page of each lesson, the sentence pattern is introduced with a humorous cartoon or thought-provoking photographs. This visual element should help students identify with the situation in which the sentence pattern is being illustrated and lead to a better understanding of the language. Self-study students, in particular, will also find the short English commentaries at the bottom of these pages helpful in getting a clearer idea of how these sentence patterns actually work.

2 PRACTICE: "STRUCTURE" DRILLS

The point is to understand the meaning and structure of the sentence patterns presented in the lesson. In a typical drill (see page 26), a series of short interesting questions in the form of a check list or questionnaire illustrate the usage of the sentence pattern.

Tips:

1. Read the questions and check the ones that apply.
2. Put the questions to other students in your class.
3. Report their answers.

3 PRACTICE: "SKIT" DRILLS

The point is to understand how the sentence pattern is used in context. A simple dialogue (see page 3) is typically presented as a short skit or cartoon, in which the key elements of the dialogue have been left blank.

Tips:

1. Try to figure out the missing expressions. Discuss with fellow students.
2. Listen to the audio tape and write in the missing parts.
3. After making sure that you have fully understood the dialogue, practice alongside the tape.

4 PRACTICE: DISCOURSE DRILLS

The point is to form written or spoken sentences by using the sentence patterns presented in the lesson. A typical drill (see page 42) begins with two or more short anecdotes and ends with a "Talking" part in which students describe an experience of their own in the same style of the original anecdotes.

Tips:

1. Read the anecdotes.
2. Using the pictures and key words as a guide, retell the stories that you have just read.
3. Listen to another anecdote on the audio tape.
4. Talk about a similar experience using your own words and expressions. A list of suggested topics is provided in most cases.
5. Retell your own anecdote using the same style and sentence patterns introduced in the anecdotes at the beginning of the drill.

5 COMMUNICATION

The aim is to apply the sentence patterns that you have learned and use them in spoken and written Japanese. In a typical section (see pages 9 and 10) we have divided the process into two activities, "preparation" and "evolution."

Tips (Preparation):

1. Look at the photograph(s) and discuss what you see.
2. Listen to a conversation about the photograph on the audio tape.
3. Answer the questions to check that you have understood.

At this stage, you should now have a clearer idea of how to express yourself in the next part.

Tips (Evolution):

1. Look at the photograph(s) and discuss what you see.
2. Read the passage that provides background information to the photograph.
3. Using this information, explain the photograph to another student.

3. New Vocabulary

Most of the vocabulary used in this workbook has been based on the main text. Additional vocabulary has been marked with an asterisk and English equivalents have been supplied. A glossary of these additional words has been appended.

4. Japanese Script

Throughout this workbook, all Japanese has been rendered in the kanji covered in the *Kana Version* of the main text (and some others to make up compounds) and kana. Furigana pronunciation guides have been added above each kanji on its first incidence on any page. The quiz answers and tape script at the back of this workbook have been entirely written in kana.

ACKNOWLEDGMENTS

This textbook was written by seven AJALT instructors, Mss. Yoko Hattori, Akiko Kajikawa, Haruko Matsui, Akiko Nagao, Mihoko Ozeki, Itsumi Sawa, and Yoriko Yoshida. Many other AJALT instructors are also to be thanked for all their support, advice, and encouragement during the development of these learning materials. Special thanks are due to Andrew Boerger who drew the illustrations for the lesson title pages, the reading sections, and the illustrations on pages 39 and 70. The authors would also like to thank Paul Hulbert and other editorial staff at Kodansha International for translating and compiling the glossaries, as well as the usual editorial tasks.

先生がたへ

「Japanese for Busy People」は、初級の最終段階として自然で効果的なコミュニケーション力を目指しています。自然で効果的なコミュニケーション力を身につけるために、学習者は、1.話し手の表現意図を理解すること。2.多様な表現の中から最も適切な表現を選択すること。3.社会文化的に適切な表現スタイルを選択すること。を学習しなければなりません。

学習者からみれば、この段階の難しさは既習表現で意味の疎通が可能であるにもかかわらず、新しい表現をさらに学習することにあります。忙しい社会人がこの段階を乗り越えるためには、各課に十分な達成感が必要となります。本ワークブックは、学習者に達成感を与えるため、話す練習を中心に据えました。積極的にかつ無理なく発話練習ができるように各課を構成しましたので、自動化を目指して楽しく練習をすすめることが可能でしょう。

■ワークブックIIIの構成列

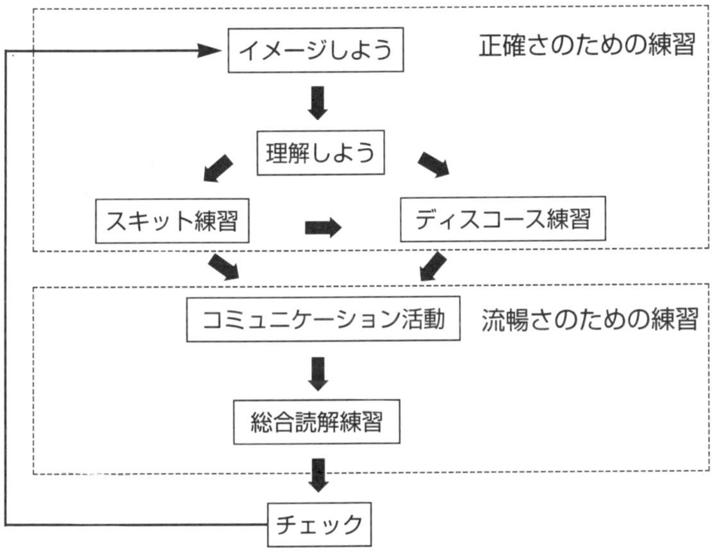

その他に「Background Information」として文化的な情報を紹介するスペースを適宜設けました。また、テープ教材が準備されているプラクティスにはテープのマークがついています。スクリプトが巻末にありますので、テープがなくても練習をすることは可能ですが、聴解力開発練習や発音練習のために、テープの使用をお勧めします。なお、このワークブックの対訳部分は、特に独習者の助けとなることを考え、ここの例文や会話の内容や状況にふさわしいと思われる英語を使用しました。文型理解のための直訳ではないことをご理解の上、参考にしていただきたいと思います。

■主な練習の使用例

イメージしよう　(P.1)

言葉による説明だけでは意味が理解しにくい文型を、絵の中の登場人物の気持を感じとってもらうことで、理解を深めてもらおうというページです。絵の中の登場人物がどのような意図を伝えようとしているのか、学習者が臨場感を持ってイメージできるよう指導してください。絵は、学習者が興味を持って新しい学習事項に臨むことができるようにユーモアのある楽しいものを準備しました。英文による状況説明や社会文化的な情報も紹介してありますので、独習者でも理解しやすいでしょう。

PRACTICE

◆文型の意味理解を深め、形に慣れるための練習です。目標文型がチェックリストの形式で提示されていますので、以下のような手順で活動を発展させると、何度も目標文型を使うことになり文の形に慣れることができるでしょう。

指導例　(P. 26)

1. 学習者はチェックリストの文を読み、自分に当てはまるもの　にチェックする。
2. 学習者間でチェックリストの質問をし合う。
3. 他の学習者の答え（行動や嗜好など）を報告する。

学習者間で質問をしあうときは、お互いにどんな傾向があるか興味をもって質問ができる雰囲気を作っておくと、活発な活動になりさらに効果があがります。

◆スキット練習

漫画形式のスキット練習です。登場人物の会話がところどことろ空白になっていますが、この空白部分が最終的に覚えてもらいたい目標の部分です。

指導例　(P. 3)

1. 会話の抜けている部分で登場人物たちが何を言っているのか　考え、話し合う。
2. その後テープを聞き、目標部分を書き取る。
3. 会話全体が理解できたら、テープにあわせて話す練習をする。

（テープと同じ速度、イントネーションで話せるようになるまで何回か練習する）

この練習では気持ちを込めて練習することが大切ですので、学習者が登場人物になりきって演じられるよう指導してください。発音やスピードに自信をもって発話できる表現の数が増えれば、実際に日本語を話す自信につながっていくはずです。

◆ディスコース練習

3～4行の長さの体験談を読んだり聞いたりして、最終的には学習者が自分の経験を段落のまとまりで語れるようになることを目指します。体験談は3つ、あるいは4つあり、同じ文章構成になっています。

指導例　(P. 42)

1. 体験談をふたつ（あるいは3っつ）読む。

2. 絵やキーワードを助けに今読んだ体験談をもう一度自分で言ってみる。

3. もうひとつの体験談を聞く。（テープのみ。本文なし）

4. 自分にも同じような体験があるかどうか、それはどうだったかを自由に話し合う。

5. 初めに読んだ体験談と同じ文章構成で自分の体験談をまとめる。

理解した話を再生するという行為は、長期記憶につながると言われています。学習者によっては単純な練習と感じる人もいますが、そのような場合は「間違えなく正確に人に伝えなければならないような状況」を設定して再生の練習をすると、より効果があがるでしょう。まとまった形で話す力がつけば、日常の会話場面である程度長い時間話続けることができるようになり、発話力が飛躍的に伸びたと感じられるはずです。

コミュニケーション

内容伝達を中心とした練習です。正確さよりむしろ流暢さの養成を目指していますので、学習者が間違いを気にせずのびのび話せるよう指導してください。ディスカッションにつながる聴解練習、インフォメーションギャップを中心にしたロールプレイ、自由な会話を促すための活動などを作成しました。課によっては学習者が無理なく発話できるよう、「準備一発展」という段階を踏んだ練習が用意してあります。

指導例（P. 9）

① 準備練習

1. 写真を見て、何の写真か話し合う。

2. その写真について会話しているテープを聞く。

3. 質問に答える

この段階で、学習者に次の発展練習でどのように話したらいいのかポイントを理解してもらいます。

② 発展練習

1. 写真を見て、何の写真か話し合う。

2. 写真の説明文を読む。（写真、説明文は複数用意してある）

3. 今読んだ説明をもとに、写真の内容を他の学習者に教える

独習者の場合は、相手を想定して練習してみてください。シュミレーションをしておけば、いざというときに自信を持って発話ができるようになるでしょう。

総合読解練習　(P. 12)

中上級につなげることを目標とした読解練習です。できるだけ自然な日本語で書いてありますので、文法事項に注目するのではなく、読むことの楽しさが感じられるように指導してください。

社会人の興味を惹く話題が選んであるので、自由な話し合いに発展させることができるでしょう。独習者でも確認ができるよう、全訳つきにしました。

チェック　(P. 48)

使い方の紛らわしい文型、表現を確認するためのクイズです。「総合チェック」は会話形式になっているので実際の場面での自然な使い方も確認できるでしょう。ある程度学習が進んだ時点で振り返って確認できる形にしました。自分で理解が不十分だと感じたら、導入の課に戻って復習するようにしてください。

本書で一貫して心がけた点は、学習した日本語をできるだけアウトプットさせようしたことです。話して使ってみる過程を経ることで、学習者の理解は深まり話すことへの自信につながるでしょう。なお、ここに上げた使用例は一例に過ぎません。学習者に応じた適切な使用を試みていただければと思います。

LESSON

1 Apparently a Famous Star Is Staying Here

SENTENCE PATTERN 1-1

〜ようです

A：すごい人(ひと)ですね。　Wow, what a crowd!

B：だれか有名(ゆうめい)な人が泊(と)まっているようですね。
Someone famous seems to be staying here.

What do you do when you see a crowd of people? Do you wonder what might be going on? Do you go and have a look for yourself? Do you try and guess for whom or what the crowd might be waiting?

PRACTICE

I

1. Look at the pictures below and read what Bijii-san is saying.

① 事務所にだれかいるようですよ。まだ電気がついています。

② 何かあったようですね。ビルの前に人がたくさんいるし、けいさつの車もとまっています。

③ あの犬はだれかを待っているようですよ。今朝からずっと駅の前にすわっていて、駅から出てくる人を見ているんです。

④ いい*におい！この近くにイタリアレストランがあるようですね。

⑤ *背中に何か*ついているようなんですが。

におい　*smell, aroma*
背中　*back*
〜につく　*is stuck on …, is on …*

PRACTICE II

1. Listen to the tape while following the pictures below. Write the missing parts ①, ②, and ③ in the spaces provided.

2. Practice the dialogue while listening to the tape. Take special care with your pronunciation and speak at the same speed as the tape.

A SURPRISE BIRTHDAY PARTY

Bijii-san has been told to deliver some documents to Mr. Green's house by six o'clock this evening. He has gone with Ms. Kobayashi. It's now exactly six, but ...

① ＿＿＿＿＿＿＿＿＿＿＿＿＿＿＿＿ね。

② やはり＿＿＿＿＿＿＿＿＿＿＿＿＿ね。

③ ＿＿＿＿＿＿＿＿＿＿＿＿＿＿＿＿ね。

PRACTICE

III

1. Read the following passages.

いつもとちがいます
Odd Behavior

① 最近、むすめの様子がちょっとかわったんです。急に、*おしゃれになって、きれいになりました。週末はよく朝から*二人分のおべんとうを作って出かけているんです。だれか*好きな人ができたようです。

---

② 最近、Xさんの様子がちょっとおかしいんです。仕事の*ミスも多いし、会議にもよく遅れて来ます。いろいろな人にお金を借りているし、ときどき*クレジットカード会社から電話もあるんです。何か問題があるようです。

おしゃれ *stylish, dressed up*	ミス *mistakes*
二人分 *for two people*	クレジットカード会社 *credit card company*
好きな人ができる *find a boyfriend/girlfriend*	

2. Using the pictures as a guide, retell the two stories that you have just read.

① 最近、むすめの様子がちょっとかわったんです。

急に

週末はよく朝から

二人分のおべんとう

① 最近、Xさんの様子がちょっとおかしいんです。

仕事のミス

会議

SENTENCE PATTERN 1-2

～ようです

A：きれいですね。　Isn't she pretty?

B：ええ。花(はな)のようですね。　Umm, like a flower.

BACKGROUND INFO
Women of exceptional beauty are often said to be "as pretty as a flower" in Japanese.

PRACTICE

Fill in the blanks with よう, ように, or ような, as shown in the example.

ex.

A：おもしろい*ヘアースタイルですね。
B：ええ。*鳥(とり)のようですね。

①

A：*へびの＿＿＿ヘアースタイルです。
B：すごいですね。

②

A：今日(きょう)はいい天気(てんき)ですね。
B：ええ。春(はる)の＿＿＿あたたかいです。
A：今日はコートがいりません。

③

A：これは*本物(ほんもの)の (a)＿＿＿ですが、
　食(た)べられないんですよ。
B：ええ！そうなんですか。
　本物の (b)＿＿＿見(み)えますね。

ヘアースタイル　*hairstyle*
鳥　*bird*
へび　*snake*
本物　*real*

SENTENCE PATTERN 2

～そうです

A：今朝(けさ)の地震(じしん)、大(おお)きかったですね。

This morning's earthquake was big, wasn't it?

B：ニュースによると、新幹線(しんかんせん)がまだ止(と)まっているそうです。

According to the news, the Shinkansen is still not running.

PRACTICE

I

1. The following words and pictures describe what was reported on this morning's TV news bulletin. Explain what was in the news to someone who didn't see the broadcast for themselves. Fill in the underlined parts to complete the sentences. The example has been done for you.

ex. 午前(ごぜん)7時(じ)ごろ東京駅(とうきょうえき)で*火事(かじ)がありました。けがをした人(ひと)はいませんでした。

① 北海道(ほっかいどう)で地震がありました。くわしいことは、まだわかっていません。

② 明日(あした)は飛行機会社(ひこうきがいしゃ)がストです。飛行機は朝(あさ)からとびません。

③ 九州(きゅうしゅう)の近(ちか)くに台風(たいふう)が来(き)ています。天気(てんき)は悪(わる)くなります。

火事 *fire*

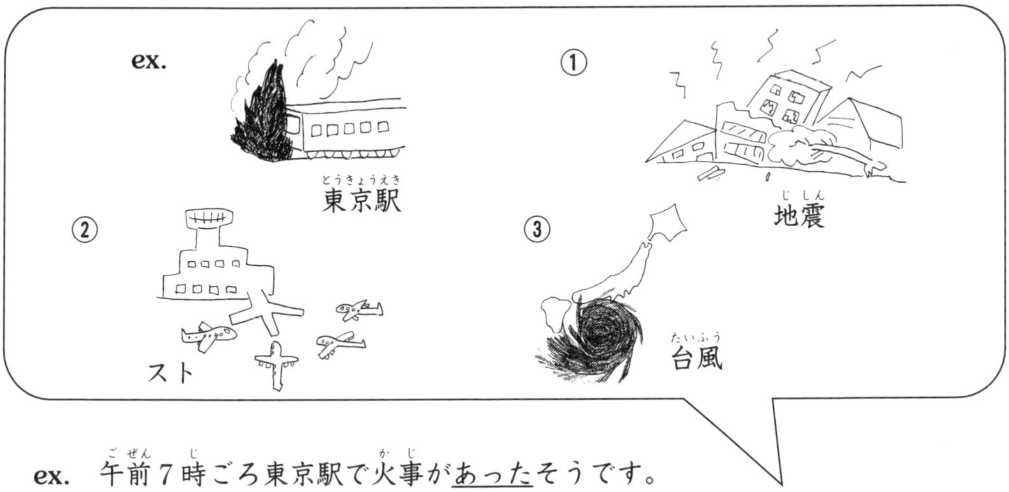

ex. 午前7時ごろ東京駅で火事があったそうです。

けがをした人はいなかったそうです。

① 北海道で地震が(a)____________そうです。

くわしいことは(b)__________________そうです。

② 明日、飛行機会社が(a)__________そうです。

飛行機は朝から(b)____________________そうです。

③ 九州の近くに台風が(a)______________そうです。

天気は(b)______________そうです。

2. Make a single sentence from each of the sentence pairs above as shown in the example.

ex. 午前7時ごろ東京駅で火事がありましたが、けがをした人はいなかったそうです。

① ____________________________、__________________________そうです。

② ____________________________、__________________________そうです。

③ ____________________________、__________________________そうです。

PRACTICE

II

Listen to the tape and report what you hear to a friend by completing the following sentences.

① A friend wants to know JBP Store's opening hours. Listen to the store's recorded information and then tell your friend.

友だち： ＪＢＰショップは日曜日も開いていますか。

あなた： いいえ。(a)__________________そうです。

友だち： 何時から何時までですか。

あなた： (b)__________________そうです。

② The train for which you are waiting with a friend doesn't seem to be coming. A station announcement is made explaining the delay. Tell your friend what the announcement said.

友だち： アナウンスは今、何て言ったんですか。

あなた： となりの駅が (a)__________そうです。

友だち： 電車はいつ来るんですか。

あなた： (b)______________________そうです。

③ Next it's the weather forecast. A friend is planning to go to an "o-hanami" party tomorrow. Tell your friend how the weather is supposed to turn out.

友だち： 明日はあたたかいでしょうか。お花見に行くんです。

あなた： *天気予報によると　明日は (a)________________そうです。

友だち： 雨はどうでしょう。

あなた： 夜になってから (b)__________そうです。夜、出かけるなら
(c)_______________________________そうです。

天気予報　*weather forecast*

Communication 1

1. What do you think the picture is? Below there are four different descriptions. Mark the one that you think is most accurate with a ○. Or if you don't agree with any of them, add your own description in ⑤.

① (　　) *こうもりのように見える。
② (　　) *さるのように見える。
③ (　　) *人間のように見える。
④ (　　) *ドラキュラのように見える。
⑤ ________________のように見える。

こうもり *bat*
さる *monkey*
人間 *human*
ドラキュラ *Dracula, vampire*

2. Bijii-san and Ms. Kobayashi are talking about the above photograph. Listen to the tape and answer the questions.

① このしゃしんは何のしゃしんですか。
② ビジーさんは日本語がわからないとき、何と言いましたか。

3. What do you think is shown in the two photographs below?

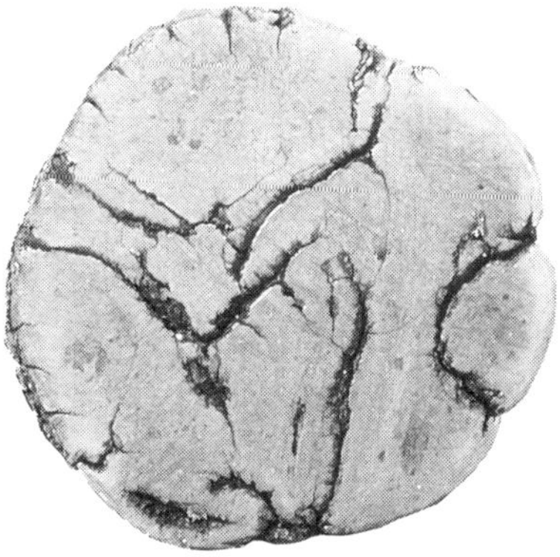

何のようですか。

何をしているようですか。

Communication 2

1. Look at the pictures with a partner and discuss what you see. What kind of work does the man in picture ① do? What do you think the dog in picture ② is doing? Use the strategies presented in the previous drill (～って日本語(にほんご)で何(なん)て言(い)うんですか。～はえいごで～ですか。) to get around vocabulary that you do not know in Japanese.

①

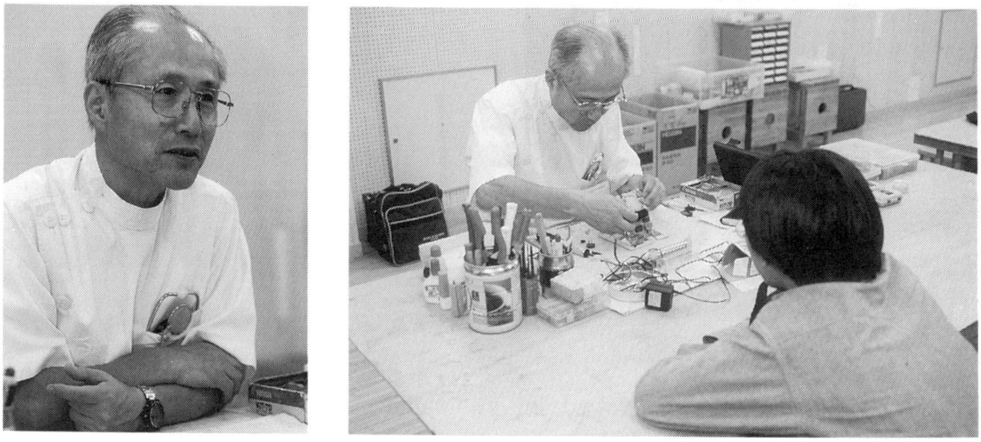

②

2. Students work in pairs. First decide who is A and who is B. Next read the following explanation of the pictures. Finally, tell your partner about the pictures. Feel free to use your own words when talking, but make sure that you communicate all the information that is supplied.

STUDENT A

①の写真の人は*おもちゃのお医者さんです。古くなったおもちゃや、*こわれたおもちゃを直します。最近はおもちゃがこわれたら、すぐ新しいのを買う人が多くなりましたが、おもちゃ*ドクターによると、毎日、たくさんの子どもたちがこわれたおもちゃを持って来るそうです。こわれたおもちゃにはいろいろありますが、ほとんど*ハイテクおもちゃなのだそうです。

おもちゃ *toy*
こわれる *break*
ドクター *doctor*
ハイテク *high-tech*

STUDENT B

②の写真は「*ちょうどう犬」の写真です。「ちょうどう犬」は*耳の不自由な人を *たすける犬です。耳の不自由な人は時計のベルの音が聞こえません。玄関にだれか来たときも、ベルが聞こえないのでわかりません。そんなとき、「ちょうどう犬」は、ベルがなっていることを主人に教えます。主人の耳になることが、ちょうどう犬の仕事です。

ちょうどう犬 *hearing dog*
耳の不自由な人 *hard of hearing, deaf*
たすける *help, aid*

READING

BUSY新聞

ちょっと変わったゴルフ

Are you a golfer? Did you know that golf is even played on desert courses where not a blade of grass is to be seen? So how do they do it?

*中東の国で仕事をする外国人ビジネスマンの間でゴルフはとても人気があるそうです。しかし、夏は気温が四〇度以上になりますから、暑い国でゴルフをするのはなかなか大変なようです。

*バーレーンの*アワリ・ゴルフクラブには自然の*芝生がありません。白い*砂の上でゴルフをします。砂の上でボールを*打つのはとても難しいので、ゴルフをする人は三〇センチぐらいの*人工芝の*マットを持って*コースをまわります。このマットの上にボールを置いて打ちます。*グリーンは砂と*石油を*かためてつくりますが、これは「ブラウン」と呼ぶそうです。この「*ブラウン」はボールがよく*ころがるそうです。

中東　*the Middle East*
バーレーン　*Bahrain*
アワリ・ゴルフクラブ　*Awari Golf Club*
芝生　*grass*
砂　*sand*
打つ　*to hit*
人工芝　*artificial turf*
マット　*mat*
コース　*(golf) course*
グリーン　*green*
石油　*crude oil, petroleum*
かためる　*to harden*
ブラウン　*brown*
ころがる　*to roll*

QUESTIONS

1．バーレーンのゴルフ場ではどうして３０センチぐらいの特別のマットを持ってコースをまわるのですか。

2．あなたの国にもちょっと変わったスポーツがありますか？それはどんなスポーツですか？

A Strange Round of Golf

Golf, we are told, is very popular among foreign businessmen working in the Middle East. Since summer temperatures often exceed 40°C (104°F), playing in such blisteringly hot countries is—as we shall see—not such an easy thing to do ....

In Bahrain's Awari Golf Club there is no real grass. Instead you play the game on a course of white sand. As it is extremely difficult to hit a ball directly off the sand, players have to carry a mat of artificial turf about 30 cm (12 inches) long around the course. They then place the ball on this mat and hit it. The greens are made by hardening the sand with oil, and are actually called "browns." Apparently golf balls travel very smoothly across these "browns."

L E S S O N

2 He Ought to Be Here By Now

SENTENCE PATTERN 1

～はずです

A：ホバートさん、遅いですね。先に行きましょうか。

Mr. Hulbert is late, isn't he? Shall we go ahead?

B：会社を５時に出たと秘書が言っているので、もう来るはずですよ。

His secretary said he left the office at 5:00, so he ought to be here by now.

ホバート：待ち合わせはここのはずですが……。

Hulbert： This is where we're supposed to be meeting ....

How do you express qualified conviction about something about which you do not know for sure in your language?

PRACTICE

I

1. Fill in the blanks as shown in the example.

ex.

A：コーヒーはもうできているでしょうか。

B：10分ぐらい前に*コーヒーメーカーの*スイッチを入れましたから、もう<u>できている</u>はずです。

①

A：東京デパートの駐車場は、いつでも車がとめられますか。

B：午後は込んでいますが、午前中に行けば＿＿＿＿＿はずですよ。

②

A：東京の*インターナショナルスクールに日本人の子どもも入れるでしょうか。

B：ええ、山田さんの息子さんが行っていますから、＿＿＿＿＿はずですよ。

BACKGROUND INFO
Tokyo—and indeed many other cities in Japan with expatriate communities—is home to numerous "international schools" which provide formal education at all levels for children in English. The majority of schools follow an American-based education program, with courses similar to those taught at schools in the United States.

③

A：年賀状は*元旦に着いたほうがいいと聞きましたが、今出せば間に合うでしょうか。

B：今日は12月24日ですから、今出せば＿＿＿＿＿はずです。

BACKGROUND INFO
To ensure a January 1st delivery for *nengajō*—the Japanese New Year greetings card—the Japanese postal services generally require that all cards be mailed by December 25th.

コーヒーメーカー *coffeemaker*　インターナショナルスクール *international school*
スイッチ *switch*　元旦 *New Year's Day*

2. Fill in the blanks as shown in the example.

ex.

ビジー：　会議室にだれかいるようですね。

吉田：　おかしいですね。今日は会議がないので、だれもいないはずですが。

①

吉田：　ビジーさん、どこに行ってきたんですか。

ビジー：　駅の前のスーパーにサンドイッチを買いに行ったんですが、閉まっていました。

吉田：　おかしいですね。あの店は9時までですから、まだ＿＿＿＿＿＿はずですが。

ビジー：　今日は特別なんでしょうか。

②

吉田：　さっき駅の前で*人事部の山田さんを見ましたよ。

ビジー：　え、山田さんなら、今ロンドンに行っていますよ。

吉田：　そうですか。

ビジー：　ええ、吉田さんが見たのは山田さん＿＿＿＿＿はずですよ。

③

ビジー：　ブラウンさん、来月ホンコン支店に転勤するそうですね。

ブラウン：え、だれに聞いたんですか。だれにも言っていないので、だれも＿＿＿＿＿＿はずですが。

人事部　*personnel department*

PRACTICE

II

1. Listen to the tape while following the pictures below. Write the missing parts ①, ②, and ③ in the spaces provided.

2. Practice the dialogue while listening to the tape. Take special care with your pronunciation and speak at the same speed as the tape.

GETTING LOST

Bijii-san is going to a concert with Linda. Despite having a map, they can't find the concert hall.

① ______________________________

② ______________________________

③ ______________________________

PRACTICE

III

Read the following passage and then complete the dialogue below.

夏の夜のミステリー
A Midsummer Night's Mystery

吉田さんは海の近くに古い*別荘があります。週末によく家族とその別荘に行きます。かぎは吉田さんとおくさんしか持っていません。今週は吉田さんのおくさんと子どもたちは外国に行っているので、吉田さんは佐藤さんとビジーさんを*さそって、その家に来ました。家の前で車からおりると……。

佐藤：　あれ、家の中で何かが動いた！
　　　　だれかいるようですよ。

吉田：　いいえ、________________
　　　　はずですよ。

ビジー：くらくてよく見えませんが、カーテンが
　　　　動いているようですよ。だれか来ているんじゃないですか。

吉田：　いいえ、________________はずです。かぎを持っているのは
　　　　私と家内だけですから。

佐藤：　じゃ、きっとおくさんですよ。

吉田：　いいえ、________________はずです。今、子どもと海外に行っているんです。へんですね。

ビジー：おかしいですね。

佐藤：　ちょっと*こわいですね。

三人は*そっと家のドアを開けました。
急いで電気をつけると、ねずみが
テーブルの下にいました。

ねずみ

別荘	*country house*
さそう	*invite*
こわい	*frightening, scary*
そっと	*quietly, softly*

SENTENCE PATTERN 2

～で

停電(ていでん)でエレベーターが動(うご)きません。

Due to a power failure, the elevator is out of order.

PRACTICE

I

Study the pictures and then fill in the blanks with the words provided.

ex. こしょう

① 台風(たいふう)

② 火事(かじ)

③ 満員(まんいん)

④ インフルエンザ

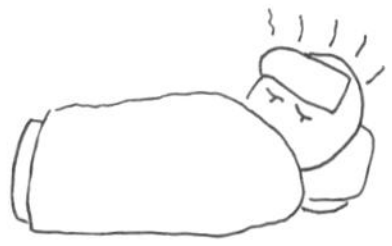

ex. こしょうで車(くるま)が動(うご)きません。

① ＿＿＿＿＿で野球(やきゅう)の*試合(しあい)ができません。

② ＿＿＿＿＿でたくさんの人(ひと)がけがをしました。

③ ＿＿＿＿＿で中(なか)に入(はい)れません。

④ ＿＿＿＿＿で会社(かいしゃ)を休(やす)みました。

試合　*game, match*

PRACTICE

II

1. Listen to the tape. A secretary receives calls from four colleagues and makes a note of their messages as shown in the table below. Make notes for the other three messages.

person	**subject**	**reason**
ex. 川田	朝の会議に遅れる	事故で電車が動かない
① 小林	(a)	(b)
② ビジー	(a)	(b)
③ 佐藤	(a)	(b)

2. Pretend that you're the secretary and report the messages to your boss as shown in the example.

ex.
部長、川田さんから電話がありました。
事故で<u>電車が動いていない</u>ので、<u>会議に遅れる</u>そうです。

Communication 1

1. Bijii-san, Ms. Kobayashi, and Mr. Sato have arranged to go to a concert together. Ms. Kobayashi and Mr. Sato are waiting in the agreed meeting place, but Bijii-san has yet to arrive. Listen to the tape and mark the most appropriate statement with a ○.

① (　) 佐藤さんは早くコンサートに行きたいと思っている。

② (　) 小林さんはビジーさんが来ないだろうと思っている。

2. Ms. Kobayashi is trying to persuade Mr. Sato to wait a little longer for Bijii-san. What does she say to overcome Mr. Sato's objections to waiting? Write your answers in the spaces provided. The first one has been done for you.

佐藤		小林
ex. ビジーさんは来ないかもしれない。	→	**ex.** ぜったい来るはず。 きのう来ると言っていた。
① 場所がわからないのであきらめたのかもしれない。	→	①
② 今日は残業かもしれない。	→	②

Communication 2

Students work in pairs. First decide who is A and who is B. Read the following role-playing cards and practice the conversation as shown in the example.

B has arranged to introduce an old college friend to A, a colleague. A and B have been waiting for more than half an hour, but B's friend still hasn't turned up and A is getting a little impatient.

STUDENT A

OBJECTIVE: Persuade Student B that you should both go home without waiting any longer.
REASONS:

- Student B's friend may have forgotten about the appointment.
- Student B's friend may be unsure of the meeting place.
- Student B's friend may simply be reluctant to meet Student A.

STUDENT B

OBJECTIVE: Persuade Student A to wait a little longer.
REASONS:

- Student B's friend said on the phone yesterday that he/she would come.
- Student B has met the friend at the same place on a previous occasion.
- Student B's friend said on the phone only yesterday that he/she was looking forward to the meeting.

ex.

A：遅いですね。どうしたんでしょう。今日の約束をわすれたのかもしれませんね。

B：いいえ、電話で________________________________

R E A D I N G

BUSY新聞

*方向オンチの話

In Japanese we call a person who gets lost easily "hoko onchi," which literally means "direction tone-deaf." What do you call such people in your country?

病気で入院している友達を車で訪ねたときの話です。車で行くのは初めてだったので、地図で道を確かめてから出かけました。*高速道路をおりて二つ目の交差点を右に曲がるとその病院があるはずでした。でも、同じような建物がたくさんあって病院はなかなか見つかりませんでした。近くの*コンビニで道を聞きました。店の人は次の角を右に曲がると病院が見えるはずだと言いました。しかし、次の角を右に曲がるとまたわからなくなって、同じ道を行ったり来たりしました。すぐそばにまたコンビニがあったので、もう一度道を聞こうと思って中に入りましたが、店員の顔を見てびっくりしました。さっき道を聞いたコンビニだったのです。

私のようによく*道に迷う人を日本語で「方向オンチ」と言います。後でタクシーの運転手から聞いたのですが、道に迷ったときはなるべく*大きい道に出るといいそうです。大きい道には道の名前を書いたサインがあるはずだからです。それに、近くのバス乗り場のサインや店の*かんばんを見れば自分が今いる*場所の名前がわかるはずなので、それを地図でさがせばいいと言っていました。

方向オンチ　*(person who has) no sense of direction*

高速道路　*expressway, motorway*

コンビニ　*convenience store*

道に迷う　*lose one's way, get lost*

大きい道に出る　*get onto a big street*

かんばん　*shop sign*

場所　*location*

QUESTIONS

1. タクシーの運転手は道に迷ったときはどうすればいいと言いましたか。

2. あなたも道に迷って困ったことがありますか。そのときどうしましたか。

No Sense of Direction

This is a story about me visiting a friend who was in hospital. Since it was the first time I had gone by car, I had checked the route on a map before setting out. Turning right at the second crossing after coming off the expressway should have brought me to the hospital, but since there were lots of buildings that all looked the same, I just couldn't find the place, so I dropped into a convenience store to ask the way. The clerk said that if I turned right at the next corner, I would be able to see the hospital, but when I turned the corner, I couldn't see it and just kept driving up and down on the same street. As there was another convenience store there, I went in intending to ask for directions again, and got quite a surprise when I saw the clerk's face. I was in the same store where I had just asked the way!

People like me who easily get lost are called "hoko onchi" in Japanese. Afterwards a taxi driver told me that when lost you should get onto the biggest road you can find—the reason being that there are likely to be signs indicating the name of the road. If you then look at bus stop and shop signs you should be able to figure out the name of the place where you are, and you can then look up your location on a map.

LESSON

3 I Haven't a Clue When We'll Be Able to Go

SENTENCE PATTERN 1

～か／～かどうか

A：いつ、うちゅう旅行(りょこう)に行(い)けるでしょうか。
I wonder when we'll be able to go on a space trip?

B：さあ、いつ行けるかわかりません。 I've got no idea when we'll be able to go.

A：*２１世紀(せいき)の終(お)わりには行けるでしょうか。
I wonder if we'll be able to go at the end of the twenty-first century?

B：さあ、行けるかどうかわかりません。I've got no idea if we'll be able to go or not.

Do you ever wonder what life will be like at the end of the twenty-first century? Do you think that we will be able to go on space trips? Or do you think that the world will have become a barren planet—wasted by nuclear war and environmental disasters?

２１世紀　*twenty-first century*

PRACTICE

I

1. Do any of the following statements apply to you? Fill out the following questionnaire, answering each question with the most appropriate response from A through F. See the key below. Now ask someone else the questions.

What do you do when you leave home?

出(で)かける前(まえ)に

- ❑ 電気(でんき)をけしたかどうか*かくにんする。
- ❑ *るす電をセットしたかどうかかくにんする。
- ❑ さいふを持(も)ったかどうかかくにんする。
- ❑ くつがきれいかどうかかくにんする。
- ❑ 服装(ふくそう)が*似合(にあ)っているかどうか*かがみを見(み)て、かくにんする。

出かけてから

- ❑ かぎを閉(し)めたかどうか*気(き)になる。
- ❑ エアコンやストーブをけしたかどうか気になる。
- ❑ まどを閉めたかどうか気になる。

KEY

A いつも　B よく　C ときどき

D たまに　E めったに　F ぜんぜん

かくにんする　*make sure, check*
るす電　*answering machine*
似合う　*suit (one), go together*
かがみ　*mirror*
気になる　*worry (about)*

2. Fill in the blanks as shown in the example.

ex. A：21世紀(せいき)の終(お)わりに*せきゆがまだあるでしょうか。
B：さあ、あるかどうかわかりません。

① A：21世紀の終わりに*タイムマシンがつくれるでしょうか。
B：さあ、____________________わかりません。

② A：21世紀の終わりに世界(せかい)の人口(じんこう)は今(いま)よりふえているでしょうか。
B：さあ、____________________わかりません。

せきゆ　crude oil
タイムマシン　time machine

PRACTICE

II

1. Fill in the blanks by changing the underlined parts as shown in the example.

ロンドン支社のジョンソンさんが出張で日本に来ます。東京支社の人がジョンソンさんについて話しています。

ex. A：ジョンソンさんは 何時に成田空港に着きますか。

B：何時に着くか聞いていません。

① A：ジョンソンさんはだれと取引先をまわりますか。

B：＿＿＿＿＿＿＿＿＿＿＿＿＿＿聞いていません。

② A：ジョンソンさんはどこにあいさつに行きますか。

B：＿＿＿＿＿＿＿＿＿＿＿＿＿＿聞いていません。

③ A：ジョンソンさんはどんな料理が好きですか。

B：＿＿＿＿＿＿＿＿＿＿＿＿＿＿わかりません。

2. Fill in the blanks with appropriate phrases.

① A：ジョンソンさんといっしょに食事をするそうですね。

B：ええ、日本料理のレストランに行こうと思っているんですが、＿＿＿＿＿かまだ決めていません。

A：「すしまさ」はどうですか。静かでおいしいすし屋ですよ。

② A：ジョンソンさんの通訳をだれかにたのむんですか。

B：ええ、たのむつもりなんですが、＿＿＿＿＿＿＿＿かまだ決めていないんです。

A：スミスさんはどうですか。日本語がとても上手ですよ。

PRACTICE

III

Use the following sentences to make dialogues as shown in the example.

ビジーさんは先月、中国旅行の*ツアーに申し込みました。かくにんしたいことがあるので、今からたんとう者の田中さんに電話をかけます。

ex.

ビジー：	もしもし、JBPコンピューターのビジーですが、田中さんをお願いします。
旅行会社の人：	申しわけございません。田中は今*席をはずしておりますが。
ビジー：	**ex.** ツアーに行く人が全部で何人になったか聞きたいんですが。
旅行会社の人：	さっそくしらべて、ごれんらくします。

ex. ツアーに行く人は全部で何人になりましたか。

① 今からホテルの*グレードはかえられますか。

② 一人部屋を申し込むとどのぐらい高くなりますか。

③ *ほけん料はツアーの費用に入っていますか。

④ *当日何時までに空港に行かなければなりませんか。

ツアー	*tour*	ほけん料	*insurance premium*
席をはずしております	*be away from one's desk*	当日	*(on) that day*
グレード	*grade, level*		

PRACTICE

IV

1. Read the following passages.

心配しています
I'm a little worried

① 吉田さん：	私は明日から家族全員で北海道にスキーに行く予定です。つまも子どもたちも北海道に行ったことがないので、楽しみにしています。でも、3日前からストで飛行機がとんでいないので、旅行に行けるかどうか心配しています。
② ビジーさん：	私は12月に日本語の試験を受けようと思っています。先生は、よく勉強したので、合格するだろうと言っています。でも、私は、漢字をあまりおぼえていないので、合格するかどうか心配しています。
③ 佐藤さん：	私は明日からアメリカ支社に出張します。今までは部長といっしょに行っていましたが、*今回は一人で行って*プレゼンテーションしなければなりません。プレゼンテーションをするのは初めてなので、うまくできるかどうか心配しています。

今回　*this time, (on) this occasion*
プレゼンテーション　*presentation*

2. Answer the following questions to check that you have fully understood what you have just read.

① (a) 吉田さんは明日から何をする予定ですか。
(b) 吉田さんはどうして旅行に行けるかどうか心配していますか。

② (a) ビジーさんは12月に何をしようと思ってますか。
(b) ビジーさんはどうして合格するかどうか心配していますか。

③ (a) 佐藤さんは明日どこに行きますか。
(b) 佐藤さんはどうしてプレゼンテーションがうまくできるかどうか心配していますか。

TALKING

3. Have you ever experienced anxiety or apprehension about doing something? Listen to another person's experience on the tape. Choose a topic from the list below and talk freely about it. Finally summarize your story as shown in the table below.

EXPLAIN THE CIRCUMSTANCES ______________________________。
______________ので______________かどうか心配(しんぱい)しています。

TOPICS

日本語(にほんご)でスピーチをする

転勤(てんきん)する

新(あたら)しい会社(かいしゃ)に入(はい)る

日本人(じん)のうちに行(い)く

SENTENCE PATTERN 2

～ように言(い)いました

部長(ぶちょう)はビジーさんに明日(あした)までに資料(しりょう)を作(つく)るように言いました。

The boss told Bijii-san to put together the reference materials by tomorrow.

PRACTICE

1. Rewrite the sentences as shown in the example.

ex. 部長はビジーさんに「会議室(かいぎしつ)を予約(よやく)してください。」と言いました。

→ 部長はビジーさんに<u>会議室を予約するように</u>言いました。

① 部長はビジーさんに「明日の会議に遅(おく)れないでください。」と言いました。

→ 部長はビジーさんに________________言いました。

② 部長はビジーさんに「出張(しゅっちょう)の費用(ひよう)がいくらかかるかしらべてください。」と言いました。

→ 部長はビジーさんに________________言いました。

③ 部長はビジーさんに「大阪支社(おおさかししゃ)に着(つ)く時間(じかん)をれんらくしてください。」と言いました。

→ 部長はビジーさんに________________言いました。

2. Read the following dialogues and answer the questions.

① 佐藤さんは、今外出中です。ビジーさんにれんらくしたいことがあるので、会社に電話をします。

佐藤：　佐藤ですが、ビジーさんお願いします。

小林：　今、電話中ですが……。

佐藤：　じゃ、明日の会議の前に打ち合わせをしたいので、少し早目に来るように伝えてくれませんか。

小林：　わかりました。そう伝えます。

(a) だれがだれに明日少し早目に来るように伝えますか。
(b) だれが明日少し早目に来ますか。

② グリーンさんは、今出張中です。ビジーさんにたのみたいことがあるので、会社に電話をします。

グリーン：　グリーンですが、ビジーさんお願いします。

近藤：　今、食事に行っています。

グリーン：　じゃ、明日の会議に必要な資料を今日中に*そろえるように伝えてください。

近藤：　わかりました。そう伝えます。

(a) だれがだれに会議に必要な資料をそろえるように伝えますか。
(b) だれが会議に必要な資料をそろえますか。

そろえる　*sort out*

Communication 1

Listen to the telephone conversation on the tape and mark the statements that most accurately describe the conversation with a ○.

①

(a) (　) ビジーさんが落合さんに資料を送る。

(b) (　) 落合さんがビジーさんに資料を送る。

②

(a) (　) 佐藤さんがビジーさんに見積書を送る。

(b) (　) ビジーさんが佐藤さんに見積書を送る。

③

(a) (　) 大阪支社の人がビジーさんの送った資料がとどいたかどうか佐藤さんに聞く。

(b) (　) 佐藤さんが大阪支社の人にビジーさんの送った資料がとどいたかどうか聞く。

Communication 2

Students work in pairs. First decide who is A and who is B. Read the following role-playing cards and practice the conversation in pairs. Use the dialogue on page 33 as a guide.

1

STUDENT A	STUDENT B
You make three calls to your office and leave the following three messages for your colleague, Mr. Sato.	You receive three calls for a colleague, Mr. Sato. After explaining each time why Mr. Sato isn't able to talk to the caller, you take a message.
☎ ① The meeting will start at 3:00.	① Mr. Sato is not in the office.
☎ ② You want to know whether or not the documents for the meeting are ready yet.	② Mr. Sato is away from his desk.
☎ ③ You need to have the documents before the meeting, and want Mr. Sato to deliver them by 2:00.	③ Mr. Sato is on another line.

2

STUDENT A	STUDENT B
Your name is Yamada and you make three calls to your spouse at the office and leave the following three messages.	You receive three calls for a colleague, Yamada, from a member of Yamada's family. After explaining why Yamada isn't able to talk to the caller each time, you take a message.
☎ ① Your child is ill and you are going to the hospital.	① Yamada is on another line.
☎ ② You want to know whether or not your spouse can come to the hospital right now.	② Yamada is away from his or her desk.
☎ ③ You want your spouse to pick you up from the hospital on the way home.	③ Yamada is not in the office.

BUSY新聞

さいふの旅行

Have you ever had the experience of something that you'd lost and completely forgotten about appearing out of the blue? This is the true story of a wallet that was lost in Australia and found one month later in Japan.

A君は*オーストラリアの*ハンターバレーという*地方に住んでいる高校生だ。八月の*ある日、映画を見に行こうと思ってバスに乗ったが、さいふがないのに*気がついた。いつ、どこでなくしたか全然覚えていなかった。誰か拾った人がいたかどうか警察に問い合わせたが、さいふは届いていなかった。

それから*一ヶ月後、このさいふは日本の工場で見つかった。工場で*作業中の人が*石炭の中から見つけたのだ。さいふの中にはオーストラリアのお金が五〇ドルと*運転免許証が入っていた。それで、このさいふがA君のものだとわかったのだ。石炭はハンターバレーの山から日本に運んだものだが、どうしてこのさいふが石炭といっしょに九〇〇〇キロの長い旅行をしたのかだれにもわからなかった。石炭を*輸入した会社の人が十月にオーストラリアに出張したが、そのときこのさいふをA君にわたした。A君は「信じられない！皆さんによろしくお伝えください」と言って*感激していたそうだ。

オーストラリア	*Australia*	作業中	*while at work*
ハンターバレー	*Hunter Valley*	石炭	*coal*
地方	*region, area*	運転免許証	*driver's license*
ある日	*one day*	輸入する	*import*
気がつく	*notice*	感激する	*be deeply moved, be thrilled*
1ヶ月後	*one month later*		

QUESTIONS

1. 日本の工場で見つかったさいふが、どうしてA君のものだとわかったのですか。

2. あなたにも落とし物についての忘れられない話がありますか。

BUSY NEWS

A Wallet's Journey

A is a high-school student who lives in the Hunter Valley area of Australia. One day in August he hopped on a bus to go and see a movie, only to notice that he had lost his wallet. He had absolutely no recollection of when or where he had lost it. He went to the police to inquire if anyone had found it and handed it in, but no such luck.

One month later, his wallet turned up in a factory in Japan, where someone found it in a pile of coal while he was working. In the wallet were fifty Australian dollars and a driver's license—which is how they knew that it belonged to A. The coal had been imported from the mountains of Hunter Valley to Japan, but why the wallet should have accompanied the coal on its 9,000-kilometer (5,600-mile) journey is anybody's guess! In October, someone from the firm which imported the coal went on a business trip to Australia and returned the wallet to A in person. A, who was thrilled, could hardly believe what had happened, and asked him to say thank you to everyone.

L E S S O N

4 Wow, That Looks Delicious!

SENTENCE PATTERN 1

～そうです

A：わあ、おいしそう！	Wow, that looks delicious!
B：作(つく)り方(かた)もかんたんそうですね。	And it looks easy to make too.

This should be a piece of cake!

Bookstores are full of highly illustrated cookbooks with mouthwatering color photographs and appetizing recipies. Japanese food may look difficult, but actually many tasty dishes are simple to make.

PRACTICE

I

1. Study the photographs and then read the captions.

①

②

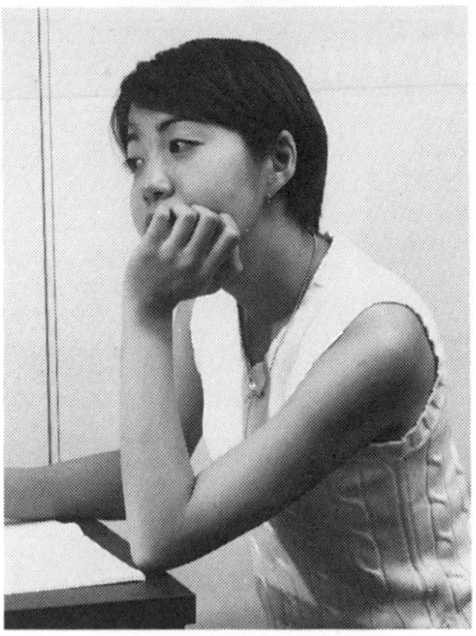

③

④

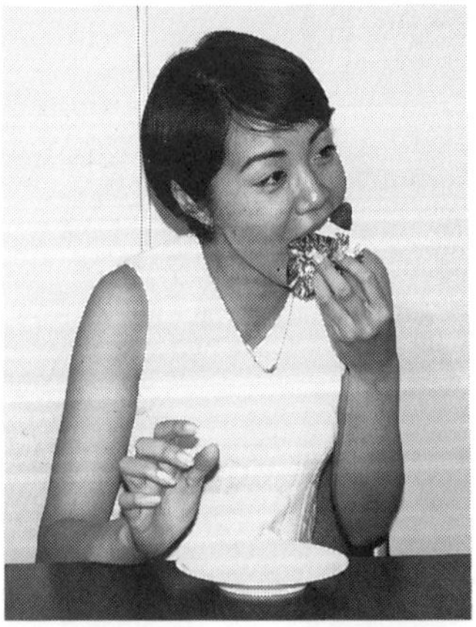

① うれしそうですね。

② ひまそうですね。

③ あたまのよさそうな犬(いぬ)ですね。

④ おいしそうに食(た)べていますね。

PRACTICE

II

1. Listen to the tape while following the pictures below. Write the missing parts the spaces provided.

2. Practice the dialogue while listening to the tape. Take special care with your pronunciation and speak at the same speed as the tape.

BAGGAGE INSPECTION

Bijii-san and Mr. Sato are waiting to have their luggage inspected by the customs. A lot of people are traveling today, so Bijii-san and Mr. Sato discuss which line will be quicker.

ビジー：　どちらの*れつが早いでしょうか。右のれつのほうが①______ですね。

佐藤：　いいえ、左のれつのほうが②______ですよ。並んでいる人の荷物が少ないですから。

ビジー：　でも左の係りの人は、ちょっと③______ですよ。*おこっているように見えます。右の係りの人は④______です。

佐藤：　でも、左に並んでいる人はツアーのようだから、あまり時間がかからないと思いますよ。それに右のれつの人は荷物がとても多いです。

ビジー：　そうですね。右のれつのほうが時間が⑤______ですね。左に並びましょう。

れつ　*line, queue*
おこる　*angry, cross*

PRACTICE

III

もしもし、けいさつですか。車(くるま)が海(うみ)におちそうなんです。すぐに来てください。

Hello, is that the police? A car's about to fall into the sea. Please come quickly.

1. Study each picture and then read its caption.

①

②

③

④

⑤

① あぶない！切(き)れそうです。

② あ！火(ひ)がきえそうです。

③ 雨(あめ)がふりそうです。

④ あと2、3日(にち)で読(よ)み終(お)わりそうです。

⑤ もうすぐさくらがさきそうです。

2. Fill in the blanks with a word chosen from the list below as shown in the example.

ex. 雨がふりそうです。駅も遠いし、かさもないし、今のうちに帰ったほうがいいかもしれません。

① 家の近くのさくらがもうすぐ＿＿＿＿＿＿そうなので、今週の週末に花見パーティーをするつもりです。

② 今、書いている*レポートはあと2、3日で＿＿＿＿＿＿そうです。書き終わったら、どこかにあそびに行きたいと思います。

③ ねだんの＿＿＿＿＿＿そうな*かぶがあったら、買いたいと思って、経済新聞を毎日読んでいます。何かいい*じょうほうがあったら教えてください。

④ 来月、ニューヨーク支店へ転勤します。ニューヨーク支店に行ったら、仕事が＿＿＿＿＿＿＿＿＿そうなので、行きたくないんですが、つまはニューヨークに行くのを楽しみにしています。

ex. ふる	あがる	終わる	さく	いそがしくなる

レポート *report*
かぶ *stock, share, equity*
じょうほう *information*

PRACTICE

IV

1. Read the following passages.

がまんしました
Grin and bear it

① 会社(かいしゃ)のパーティーに行(い)ったときの話(はなし)なんですが、社長(しゃちょう)のスピーチが長(なが)くて、つまらなかったので、ねむくなりました。社長のスピーチを聞(き)いているときに、*あくびが出(で)そうで困(こま)りました。

② 友(とも)だちと*クラシックのコンサートに行ったときの話なんですが、*あいにくひどいかぜをひいていたんです。コンサート中(ちゅう)、*くしゃみが出そうで、困りました。

あくびが出る	*yawn*	あいにく	*unfortunately*
クラシック	*classical (music)*	くしゃみ	*sneeze*

2. Using the pictures as a guide, retell the stories that you have just read.

① 会社のパーティーに行ったときの話なんですが

② 友だちとクラシックのコンサートに行ったときの話なんですが

TALKING

3. Have you ever experienced difficulty in suppressing a sneeze or a yawn or something? Listen to another person's experience on the tape. Choose a topic from the list below and talk freely about it. Finally summarize your story as shown in the table.

＿＿＿＿＿＿ときの話なんですが、＿＿＿＿＿＿EXPLAIN THE CIRCUMSTANCES＿＿＿＿＿＿そうで困りました。

TOPICS

あくびが出る　　*なみだが出る
せきが出る　　*わらい出す

なみだが出る	*burst into tears*
わらい出す	*burst out laughing*

SENTENCE PATTERN 2

ーく／にする
ーく／になる

部屋(へや)がきたないので、きれいにしようと思(おも)って、そうじをしました。そうじが終(お)わったら、きれいになって、気持(きも)ちがよくなりました。

My room was messy, and so deciding to make it tidy, I did some cleaning. After I'd finished cleaning, (my room) had become spick-and-span, and I felt a lot better (for it).

PRACTICE

Fill in the blanks with the correct form of either なる or する.

① 子(こ)どもが生(う)まれていろいろな物(もの)をおいたので、部屋がせまく(a)__________。もう少(すこ)し広(ひろ)く(b)______たいと思って、いろいろな物をすてました。部屋が少し広く(c)_________ので、子どものベッドを買(か)いに行(い)きました。デパートにはいろいろなベッドがありましたが、部屋が小(ちい)さいですから、一番(いちばん)小さいのに(d)__________。デパートからベッドが届(とど)いたら、また部屋がせまく(e)______________。

② かみが長(なが)く(a)______________ので、今日(きょう)初(はじ)めてうちの近(ちか)くの*とこやに行きました。とこやに3センチぐらいみじかく(b)_________ようにたのみました。かみを切(き)っているとき、ずっと本(ほん)を読(よ)んでいました。終わってから、かがみを見(み)たら、とてもみじかく(c)__________ていました。おこった*はりねずみのようでした。とこやは私(わたし)がハンサムに(d)_________と言(い)いましたが、私は気に入(い)りませんでした。

とこや *barber's shop*
はりねずみ *hedgehog*

SENTENCE PATTERN 3

～らしいです

A：田中さんが会社をやめるらしいですよ。
Apparently Ms. Tanaka is going to quit the company.

B：えっ、本当ですか。だれに聞いたんですか。
What? Really? Who did you hear that from?

A：さあ、だれだったか。　Now, who was it …?

PRACTICE

Listen to the tape. A group of people sitting next to you on the train are talking in loud, animated voices. Tell someone what they said as shown in the example.

ex. ちょっと聞いたんですが、ＡＢＣコンピューターは給料がいいらしいですよ。

① ちょっと聞いたんですが、ＭＸ社は新しいスポーツカーを＿＿＿＿＿＿らしいですよ。

② ちょっと聞いたんですが、「知らない人」っていう映画は＿＿＿＿＿＿らしいですよ。

③ ちょっと聞いたんですが、今度ＡＢ社の社長が＿＿＿＿＿＿らしいですよ。

Communication

1. Read the following passage and then listen to the tape.

> ビジーさんと小林さんは出張でアメリカに行くので、今成田空港に来ています。飛行機を待っている間、何か話しています。

① Choose the most appropriate word from alternatives given in parentheses.

(a) 空港はとても（込んでいる／すいている）。

(b) ビジーさんと小林さんは今（映画／ブラジル／サッカー）について話している。

(c) 最近（子ども／外国人／女性）の間で、サッカーは人気があるらしい。

(d) 日本には女性のチームが（ある／ない）。

(e) ビジーさんはサッカーを（おもしろそうだ／むずかしそうだ）と思っている。

② Answer the following questions.

(a) 小林さんは*ゲートの前で待っている人たちをどんな人たちだと思っていましたか。

(b) 小林さんは空港のアナウンスを聞いてどんなことがわかりましたか。

ゲート　*gate*

2. Discuss the following in a group or with a partner.

① あなたの国で人気のあるスポーツは何ですか。

② ビジーさんはサッカーは男性のスポーツだと思っていました。あなたの国では*女性むきのスポーツと*男性むきのスポーツという考え方がありますか。

女性むき　*women's, for women*
男性むき　*men's, for men*

READING

BUSY新聞

お父さんたちのピアノレッスン

Do you play a musical instrument? This is a story about a middle-aged businessman who has started learning the piano.

「*今までピアノを弾いたことはありませんでした。でも、いつか娘といっしょにピアノを弾きたいと思って習い始めたんです」と、銀行員の田中さんは*照れくさそうに言った。田中さんは三ヶ月前から会社の帰りにこの*ピアノ教室に来て練習している。レッスンは午後七時からの一時間。四、五人のグループレッスンだ。最初は*ヘッドホンを使って一人で右手、それから左手の練習をする。次にみんなでいっしょに弾く。どの人もほんとうに楽しそうだ。*最後に自分の好きな*曲を練習する。田中さんは、映画「*タイタニック」の音楽をうれしそうに弾いていた。

このごろ会社の部長とか課長とか、忙しいサラリーマンの間でピアノを習う人が増えている。*中年サラリーマンの楽しみはゴルフが多いだろうと思っていたが、そうではないらしい。出張などでレッスンに出られないときはどうするのかピアノの先生に聞いたら「休む人はそんなに多くないですよ」と言っていた。

今まで	*until that time*	最後に	*ultimately*
照れくさそうに	*self-consciously*	曲	*(piece of) music*
ピアノ教室	*piano lessons*	タイタニック	*Titanic*
ヘッドホン	*headphones*	中年	*middle-aged*

QUESTIONS

1. 田中さんはどうしてピアノを習い始めたのですか。

2. あなたの国の中年サラリーマンの楽しみはどんなことですか。

Piano Lessons for Dads

"I'd never played the piano before, but I thought how nice it would be to play with my daughter, and that's why I started," says Mr. Tanaka, a bank employee, a little self-consciously. Three months ago Mr. Tanaka took up piano lessons at this school on his way home from work. Class begins at 7:00 PM and lasts for one hour. It is a group lesson made up of four or five students. They start off with individual practice, playing with the right hand and then the left while listening through headphones. Next, everyone plays together, and they all look like they're really enjoying themselves. Ultimately you get to practice music of your own choice, and Mr. Tanaka was looking ecstatic as he played the theme from *Titanic*.

These days more and more busy corporate section and sub-section chiefs are taking up the piano. It's assumed that most middle-aged businessmen love golf, but that doesn't seem to be the whole truth. When asked if students skipped lessons because of commitments like business trips, the teacher said that there weren't that many absentees.

CHECK 1

1. Choose the correct expression from the two alternatives provided in parentheses.

このごろ若い人の（間／中）で*おんせんのあるスキー場が人気があります。ビジーさんも山の中の旅館に泊まりに行きました。

ビジー： こんにちは！（先日／前日）電話で部屋の予約をしたビジーですが。

受付係： ビジー様ですね。いらっしゃいませ。お待ちしていました。そうそう、（先に／さっき）佐藤様という方からお電話が（ありました／かけました）。

ビジー： そうですか。佐藤さんも今日いっしょに泊まるんです。でも、かれは今日の昼ごろ東京を車で出発したので、もうこちらに着いている（はず／つもり）ですが、まだ来ていないんですか。

受付係： はい、雪で道が込んでいるそうですから、ご到着は９時ごろになりそうですね。テレビのニュース（によって／によると）新幹線も（おくれている／おそい）そうですよ。

ビジー： そうですか。私がのった新幹線はだいじょうぶだったけど。（そういえば／とにかく）、スキーの道具を４、５日前に送りましたが（届きましたか／もらいましたか）。

受付係： はい、預かっています。こちらですね。

ビジー： ええ、これです。あれっ、これはつりの道具！（かならず／たしかに）スキーの道具を送ったと思いましたが、どうして？

受付係： さあ、どうしてでしょう……。

2. Choose the correct expression from the two alternatives provided in parentheses.

①

佐藤： おや、ビジーさん、今日はずいぶん（うれしいよう／うれしそう）ですね。どうしたんですか。

ビジー： 子どもが生まれたんですよ。かおが長くて、ちょっとうまの（ように／そうに）見えるけど。

*おんせん　*hot spring, spa*
プラン　*plan*

佐藤：　えっ、ビジーさんはどくしんだと思っていましたが。最近はどくしんの映画スターもお母さんに（なるそう／なりそう）ですから。とにかく、おめでとうございます。

ビジー：　？？？犬のメアリーの話ですよ。

②

スミス：　あの大きい花びんを見せてくれませんか。

店の人：　あの青いのですか。いい色でしょう？ああいう海の（ような／ように）青いいろはなかなかないんですよ。

スミス：　でも、ちょっと（重いよう／重そう）ですね。

店の人：　今、ここへ運びます。はい、どうぞ。

スミス：　あっ、これは重い。一人では持てませんね。

店の人：　お客さん、下のテーブルもいっしょに持っていますよ。

③

大山：　林さんから聞きましたよ。札幌のプロジェクトは大せいこうだった（よう／そう）ですね。

小川：　ええ、おかげさまで。実は、社内ではあまりひょうばんがよくなかったので、担当者は（あきらめていたよう／あきらめそう）なんですが、いいけっかで本当によかったです。

大山：　ところで、横浜の方のプロジェクトはどうなったんですか。

小川：　最初は（よいそう／よさそう）だったんですが、いろいろ問題がありまして中止になりました。残念でしたけど。

5 I Went and Put It In the Drier

SENTENCE PATTERN 1-A

～てしまいます

A：そのふく、どうしたんですか。 What happened to your dress?

B：*かんそうきに入れてしまったんです。 I went and put the thing into the drier.

Do you think anyone will notice?

Nowadays most clothes have a special label sewn inside that gives cleaning instructions in symbols. Remember to always check the label, as not all clothes can be put into the drier.

かんそうき *drier*

PRACTICE

I

1. Study the pictures and fill in the blanks with an appropriate form of the verb.

どうしたんですか。
What's the matter?

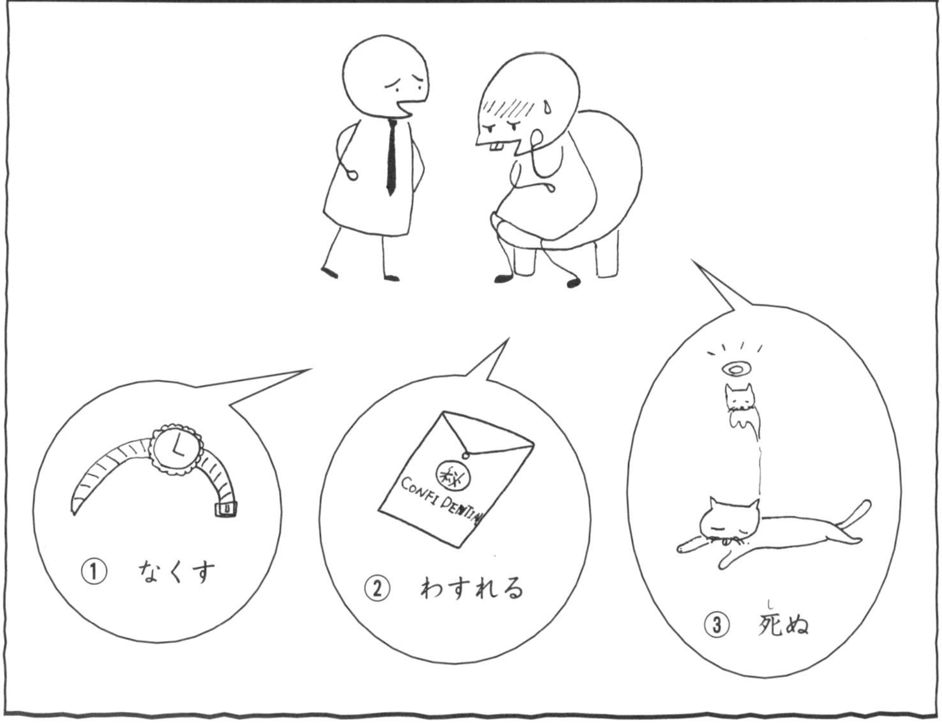

① A：どうしたんですか。

B：時計(とけい)を＿＿＿＿＿＿しまったんです。

母(はは)にもらった大事(だいじ)な時計だったんです。

② A：どうしたんですか。

B：電車(でんしゃ)に大事な書類(しょるい)を＿＿＿＿＿＿しまったんです。

駅(えき)に問(と)い合(あ)わせましたが、わかりませんでした。

③ A：どうしたんですか。

B：飼(か)っていたねこが＿＿＿＿＿＿しまったんです。

家族(かぞく)のように大切(たいせつ)なねこでした。

PRACTICE

II

1. Listen to the tape while following the pictures below. Write the missing parts ①, ②, ③, ④, and ⑤ in the spaces provided.

2. Practice the dialogue while listening to the tape. Take special care with your pronunciation and speak at the same speed as the tape.

ビジーさんは日曜日に小林さんといっしょに富士山にドライブに行きました。今ビジーさんは佐藤さんに日曜日のドライブについて話しています。

佐藤：　ビジーさん、小林さんとドライブに行ったそうですね。

ビジー：　ええ、でも、大変だったんです。

佐藤：　何かあったんですか。

ビジー：　富士山に行ったんですが、雪がふっていたんですよ。

佐藤：　え、雪だったんですか。

ビジー：　ええ、雪の中で車が ①＿＿＿＿＿＿＿＿＿＿＿＿。
直すのに１時間も ②＿＿＿＿＿＿＿＿＿＿＿＿。

佐藤：　それは大変でしたね。

ビジー：　ええ、帰りの道もじゅうたいしていたので、帰るのが
③＿＿＿＿＿＿＿＿。小林さんは ④＿＿＿＿＿＿＿＿＿＿し、
私はさむくて⑤＿＿＿＿＿＿＿＿＿＿し、本当に大変でした。

PRACTICE

III

1. Read the following passages.

私のしっぱい
My Mistake

① じつは*このあいだ、タクシーと*パトカーを*間違えてしまったんです。くらくてよく見えなかったので、タクシーだと思って止めたら、パトカーだったんです。おまわりさんが車から出てきたときは、本当におどろきました。

---

② じつはこのあいだ、電車を間違えて、約束の時間に1時間も遅れてしまったんです。駅のホームに着いたら電車が来ていたので、急いでのったら、*はんたい方向へ行く電車だったんです。待ち合わせの場所は外だったので、友だちは1時間も立って待っていました。とても申しわけなかったです。

このあいだ　*the other day, recently*
パトカー　*police car*
間違える　*mistake for*
はんたい方向　*opposite direction*

2. Using the pictures as a guide, retell the stories that you have just read.

① じつはこのあいだ、

くらくてよく見えなかったので、

本当におどろきました。

② じつはこのあいだ、

駅のホームに着いたら電車が来ていたので、

とても申しわけなかったです。

TALKING

3. Have you ever made a mistake like that? Listen to another person's experience on the tape. Tell your story in your own words and then summarize as shown in the table.

じつはこのあいだ、＿＿＿＿＿＿＿＿＿＿＿＿＿＿＿＿です。 ＿＿＿＿＿＿ADD INFORMATION＿＿＿＿＿＿。 ＿＿＿＿＿＿DESCRIBE HOW YOU FELT＿＿＿＿＿＿。

SENTENCE PATTERN 1-B

～てしまいます

今日は6時からパーティーですから、早く仕事をすませてしまいましょう。
Today there is a party starting at six o'clock, so let's finish work early.

PRACTICE

Fill in the blanks with a verb chosen from the list below.

①

佐藤：　ビジーさん、もう出かけませんか。

ビジー：ちょっと待ってください。出る前に、大阪支社にファックスを__________しまいたいんです。

②

佐藤：　ビジーさん、よかったら、このざっしを読みませんか。私はもう________しまったんです。なかなかおもしろいですよ。

ビジー：じゃ、借りてもいいですか。

③

佐藤：　このコーヒー、なかなかおいしいですよ。

ビジー：そうですか。じゃ、今うちにあるのを________しまったら、買います。

飲む	しらべる	読む	買う	送る	食べる

SENTENCE PATTERN 2

～てみます

A：おいしそうですが、どんな味(あじ)でしょうか。
　That looks good. I wonder how it tastes?

B：さあ、わかりません。ちょっと食(た)べてみましょう。
　I don't know. Why not try a bit?

PRACTICE

I

Fill in the blanks with a verb chosen from the list below.

ex.

A：まだ銀座(ぎんざ)ホールで*生(い)け花展(ばなてん)をやっているでしょうか。

B：さあ、電話(でんわ)で<u>問(と)い合(あ)わせて</u>みましょう。

→ ホールに<u>問い合わせて</u>みたら、生け花展はもう終(お)わっていました。

①

A：新(あたら)しい*モデルですね。

B：ええ、どうぞ(a)＿＿＿＿＿＿＿＿みてください。

→ (b)＿＿＿＿＿＿＿＿みたら、*エンジンの音(おと)が静(しず)かで、よかったです。

②

A：新しいいすですね。ちょっと(a)＿＿＿＿＿＿＿＿みてもいいですか。

B：はい、どうぞ。

→ いすに(b)＿＿＿＿＿＿＿＿みたら、こわれてしまいました。

すわる	運転(うんてん)する	問い合わせる	運動(うんどう)する

生け花展　*ikebana exhibition*
モデル　*model*
エンジン　*engine*

PRACTICE

II

1. Read the following passages.

けっかはどうでしたか
How did it turn out?

① 春になったので、新しいくつがほしいと思っていました。このあいだくつ屋の前を歩いていたら、歩きやすそうなくつがあったんです。デザインもよかったので、はいてみたら、あしに*ぴったりでした。今はいているのがそのとき買ったくつです。

② 最近少しひまになったので、何か勉強を始めたいと思っていました。このあいだ新聞を読んでいたら、*やくにたちそうなけいざい*セミナーの*広告があったんです。セミナーの*こうしも有名な人だったので、行ってみたら、つまらなくてねてしまいました。

ぴったり *a perfect fit*	広告 *advertisement*
やくにたつ *useful*	こうし *lecturer*
セミナー *seminar, course*	

2. Using the pictures as a guide, retell the stories that you have just read.

① 春になったので、新しいくつがほしいと思っていました

このあいだくつ屋の前を歩いていたら

デザインもよかったので

② 最近(さいきん)少(すこ)しひまになったので、何(なに)か勉強(べんきょう)を始(はじ)めたいと思(おも)っていました。

このあいだ新聞(しんぶん)を読(よ)んでいたら、

セミナーのこうしも有名(ゆうめい)だったので

TALKING

3. Have you had a similar experience? Perhaps you tried something that was just right, or maybe you were quite unprepared for what you found. Listen to another person's experience on the tape. Choose a topic from the list below and talk freely about it. Finally summarize your own story as shown in the table.

このあいだ＿＿＿＿＿＿＿＿＿＿たら、＿＿＿＿＿＿＿＿あったんです。
＿＿＿＿＿＿＿てみたら、＿＿＿＿THE RESULT＿＿＿＿＿＿＿。

TOPICS

バーゲンセールに行(い)ったら
道(みち)を歩(ある)いていたら
本屋(ほんや)に行ったら
*インターネットをしらべていたら
デパートやスーパーに行ったら

Communication

Have you ever wanted to do something but didn't know how to go about it? Or maybe you were faced with a tricky problem that you couldn't solve by yourself. At such times a little bit of advice from a friend can be very helpful.

Below you will read about two people's problems and the advice that they have been given. But what do you think they should do? Add your own advice, too.

そうだん ①

このあいだテレビを見ていたら*和だいこをしょうかいしていました。えんそうがとてもすばらしかったし、楽しそうだったので、私もやってみたいと思いました。さっそくれんらくしたいと思って、えんそうしていたグループの名前をメモしましたが、そのメモをなくしてしまったんです。*テレビきょくの名前もわすれてしまったので、そのグループにれんらくできません。どうしたらいいでしょう。

アドバイスa

私があなただったら、テレビを見た日の新聞をさがします。新聞にはテレビの*番組らんがあるので、それを見てテレビきょくに電話してみます。新聞は図書館で見ればいいと思います。

アドバイスb

私があなただったら、インターネットで和だいこのグループをさがしてみます。もしさがしているグループが見つからなかったら、ほかのグループにれんらくして、ほかにどんなグループがあるか聞いてみます。とにかくインターネットで、知っていそうな人をさがせばいいと思います。

和だいこ *Japanese drums*
テレビきょく *broadcasting company*
番組らん *TV listings*

私があなただったら、＿＿＿＿＿＿＿＿＿＿＿＿＿＿＿＿＿＿＿＿

＿＿＿＿＿＿＿＿＿＿＿＿＿＿＿＿＿＿＿＿＿＿＿＿＿＿＿＿＿＿

＿＿＿＿＿＿＿＿＿＿＿＿＿＿＿＿＿＿＿＿＿＿＿＿＿＿＿＿＿＿

そうだん ②

私の知り合いでつりの好きな人がいて、つりに行くと、いつも*つった魚をくれるんです。初めて魚をもらったとき、家族全員が好きだと言ってしまったからなんですが、それから毎週、魚をたくさんくれるんです。最初はよろこんで食べていた家族も、今はあまり食べたがらなくなりました。申しわけないと思いますが、すててしまうこともあります。どうしたらいいでしょう。

アドバイスa

つったばかりの魚はおいしいし、魚は体にもいいですから、いらないと言うのはざんねんですね。私があなただったら、料理が好きな友だちにいろいろな料理の仕方を聞いてみます。料理の*レパートリーを*ふやせば、いいと思います。きっと家族のみんなもよろこんで食べるはずです。

アドバイスb

私があなただったら、魚の好きな友だちにあげます。魚をすててしまうのは*もったいないです。つったばかりのおいしい魚はなかなか*手に入らないので、もらった人はきっとよろこぶはずです。

つる　*go fishing*
レパートリー　*repertoire*
ふやす　*increase*
もったいない　*wasteful*
手に入る　*get hold of*

私があなただったら、______________________________

____

____

READING

BUSY新聞

*カモ猟を見に行きました

In the old days ducks were an important source of protein for the inhabitants of farming villages and they were hunted in various ways in different parts of Japan. But recently, the pace of regional development has caused the number of ducks to drop sharply, and duck hunting has also become subject to restrictions for ecological reasons. I went to witness a duck hunt using nets, a tradition that survives to this day in a small town overlooking the Sea of Japan.

「今晩、よかったらカモ猟を見に来ませんか」と夕方、*知り合いの山田さんから電話があった。今、この伝統的なカモ猟をする人は七五歳の山田さんなど六人になってしまって、なかなか見ることができない。前からカモ猟に興味があった私は、さっそくカメラを持って出かけた。

カモは*ゴルフ場の*池のそばで休んでいた。月が出るころになると、カモは近くの*水田に食べる物をさがしに行くので、それまで四五m×一〇mの*網をセットしてカモが飛ぶの待った。私もちょっと網を持ってみたが、とても重かった。風が強いと、網の音でカモが*逃げてしまう。だからカモの飛ぶコースや高さ、風の強さをよく考えて網をセットしなければならない。うっかりしているとカモの方が頭がよくて、人が*走る前に逃げていなくなってしまうそうだ。カモは急に高くは飛べないので、飛び始めたときに人々は走りながら網を上げたり下げたりして*捕まえるのだ。

実は今、カモ猟はゴルフ場の中でする。十年前にこの辺の*土地を持っていた人が土地をゴルフ場に売ってしまったのだ。木があるのはこのゴルフ場の池のまわりだけになってしまった。飛んで来るカモも少なくなったし、この伝統的なカモ猟も何年かしたらなくなってしまうのかもしれない。

カモ猟 *duck hunt*	網をセットする *set a net*
知り合い *friend*	逃げる *fly away*
ゴルフ場 *golf course*	走る *run*
池 *pond*	捕まえる *catch*
水田 *rice paddy*	土地 *land*

QUESTIONS

1. カモ猟をするとき、どんなことを考えて網をセットしますか。
2. あなたの国でも伝統的な猟がありますか。それはどうやってするのですか。

Watching the Duck Hunters

I got a phone call from my friend Mr. Yamada in the early evening asking me if I would like to come and see a duck hunt that night. Since there are only six people—including the 75-year-old Mr. Yamada—who still engage in this traditional form of duck hunting, one seldom gets an opportunity to see it. I was already curious, so I picked up my camera and out I went.

The ducks were resting near a pond on the golf course, so we set a net of 45 by 10 meters (148 by 32 feet), waiting for them to fly up to look for food in the nearby rice paddies—something they would do when the moon came out. I had a go at lifting the net, but it was extremely heavy. When the wind is strong, the net makes such a noise that the ducks get alarmed and fly away. That's why when you set the net you have to be careful to take into account the height the ducks fly at and the strength of the wind. If you don't concentrate, the ducks will outsmart you and all vanish before the hunters start running. Since ducks do not climb suddenly to great heights, the way you catch them is to run towards them, raising and lowering the net, at the very instant they get off the ground.

The duck hunting here now takes place on the golf course, because ten years ago the owner of this piece of land sold it for development. As a result, the only place where there are any trees left at all is around the pond, and the number of ducks who come here has decreased. I suppose that in a few years this traditional duck hunt will have died out entirely.

LESSON

6 I Took the Pills *Before* I Got on the Boat

SENTENCE PATTERN 1

〜ておきます

A：元気ですね。

You're looking good.

B：ええ。ふねに乗る前に、薬を飲んでおきましたから。

Yes, that's because I took some pills *before* I got on the boat.

There are those who always seem well prepared in what they do and then there are others who act as if they haven't gotten anything ready before they start doing something. Which type are you?

PRACTICE

I

1. Read the following list and check the things that you would do.

How do you get ready for a trip overseas?

❑ ホテルを全部(ぜんぶ)予約(よやく)しておきます。

❑ 旅行中(りょこうちゅう)どこを見物(けんぶつ)するか決(き)めておきます。

❑ *トラベラーズチェックを作(つく)っておきます。

❑ 自分(じぶん)の国(くに)のお金(かね)を旅行する国のお金にかえておきます。

❑ 旅行する国の言葉(ことば)を勉強(べんきょう)しておきます。

❑ *ガイドブックを見(み)て、旅行する国の特別(とくべつ)な料理(りょうり)や*みやげものを調(しら)べておきます。

❑ 旅行する国に知(し)り合(あ)いがいたら、れんらくしておきます。

❑ *ツアーガイドをたのんでおきます。

❑ 旅行する国のれきしについてよく読(よ)んでおきます。

2. A friend is nervous about a first trip abroad. Use the sentences above to offer your friend advice as shown in the example.

A：今度(こんど)初(はじ)めて一人(ひとり)で外国(がいこく)に行(い)くので、心配(しんぱい)なんですが。

B：<u>ホテルを全部予約しておくといいですよ／便利(べんり)ですよ。</u>

トラベラーズチェック　*traveler's checks*
ガイドブック　*guidebook*
みやげもの　*souvenirs*
ツアーガイド　*tour guide*

PRACTICE

II

1. Read the following passages.

あなたはどちらのタイプ
Which type are you?

① 新しい*服を買うとき、店に行く前にだいたいどんな服を買うか考えておく人と、店に行ってから考える人がいます。私はたいてい店に行く前にどんな服を買うか考えておきます。

② けっこんしきなどでスピーチをするとき、前の日までにスピーチの*げんこうを書いておく人と、当日会場に着いてから考える人がいます。私は何を話すか書いておかないと、前の晩なかなかねられません。

服 *clothes*
げんこう *draft*

2. Using the pictures as a guide, retell the stories that you have just read.

① 新しい服を買うとき

② けっこんしきなどでスピーチをするとき

TALKING

3. Prepared or not prepared? Which type are you? Listen to another person on the tape. Choose a topic from the list and talk freely about it. Summarize your own story as shown in the table below.

__________とき、*前もって__________ておく人と__________てから__________人がいます。私は EXPLAIN WHICH TYPE YOU ARE 。

TOPICS

初めての場所に行くとき　　デートのとき
日本語のクラスに出るとき　　旅行をするとき

前もって *beforehand*

PRACTICE

III

1. Listen to the tape while following the pictures below. Write the missing parts in the spaces provided.

2. Practice the dialogue while listening to the tape. Take special care with your pronunciation and speak at the same speed as the tape.

1

2

1

ビールがない！ ① 晩(ばん)ご飯(はん)のときに飲もうと思って、２時間(じかん)ぐらい前(まえ)に＿＿＿＿＿＿＿＿＿＿が。

2

メモがない！① 友(とも)だちの電話番号(でんわばんごう)を＿＿＿＿＿＿＿＿＿＿が。

② いいんです。これからは＿＿＿＿＿＿＿＿＿＿から。

SENTENCE PATTERN 2

～てあります

映画館で

A：Bさん。あの席にすわりましょう。　B-san, let's sit in those seats over there.

B：ええ。あ、でも*プログラムが置いてありますよ。
OK. But, look, a program has been put there.

A：本当ですね。だれか来るようですね。
You're right. Someone must be coming.

プログラム　*program*

PRACTICE

I

Using the above dialogue as a guide, fill in the blanks with the correct form of the verb given in parentheses.

① 受付で

ビジー：　受付で*ネームカードをもらいましょう。

田中：　ええ。ネームカードが*あいうえおじゅんに＿＿＿＿＿＿ありますね。

ビジー：　これなら見つけやすいですね。　(並べる)

BACKGROUND INFO
The roman alphabet is very useful when it comes to ordering things like names in an address book or books in a library. In Japanese it is customary to arrange such things in the order of the hiragana syllabary. Appropriately, this is called "あいうえおじゅん" or "a-i-u-e-o order."

② 空港で

ビジー：　今日は人が多いですね。

田中：　赤いカーペットが＿＿＿＿＿＿ありますから、*VIPが来るようですね。　(*しく)

ネームカード　*name tag*
あいうえおじゅん　*(see BACKGROUND INFO)*
しく　*lay out*
VIP　*VIP*

PRACTICE

II

Read the following passage and answer the questions.

　私はこのあいだ、初めてスーパーで売っている「*すきやきなべパック」を買ってみました。パックを開けると、すきやきを食べるときに必要なものが全部*アルミホイルの*なべの中にそろえてありました。おいしそうな牛肉がきれいに並べてありました。いろいろな野菜やとうふが切ってありました。*だしも用意してありましたから、自分で何もしなくてもよかったです。
　なべを*コンロの上に置くと、とてもかんたんにおいしいすきやきを作ることができました。かぜで、料理をしたくなかったので、とても*たすかりました。

BACKGROUND INFO
Sukiyaki is a popular dish of thinly sliced beef, vegetables, and tofu cooked in an iron pot on a tabletop cooking stove. Some supermarkets now sell special "instant" sukiyaki sets that include all the necessary ingredients and stock in an aluminum foil pot. TV dinner, Japanese-style?

すきやきなべパック	*sukiyaki-in-the-pot set*	だし	*stock*
アルミホイル	*aluminum foil*	コンロ	*gas cooking stove*
なべ	*pot*	たすかる	*to be a help*

① あなたも「すきやきパック」を買ってみたいと思いますか。
それはどうしてですか。

② Look at the picture below and explain what a "sukiyaki-in-the-pot set" is.

PRACTICE

III

1. Read the following passage and answer the questions.

先日、大阪に出張したときの話です。帰りの新幹線が雪で2時間も遅れました。東京駅に着いたら、12時でした。つかれてうちに帰ったら、主人はもうねていました。静かに居間に入ると居間があたためてありました。台所には*シチューとサラダが作ってありました。その日はとてもさむい日でした。おなかもすいていたので、あたたかい部屋でシチューが食べられて、とてもしあわせになりました。

①この人は夜遅く帰ったとき、何に気がつきましたか。

②あなたが家に帰ったとき、何がしてあったらうれしいですか。

シチュー *stew*

2. Using the pictures as a guide, retell the story that you have just read.

つかれてうちに帰ったら

Communication

1. Read the following passage and answer the questions.

田中さんのうちのクリスマス

　*クリスマスイブです。田中さんとおくさんは子どもたちがねてから、静かにそうだんを始めました。「どこにプレゼントを置いておきましょうか。」「子どもの部屋の大きいくつしたの中に入れておいたら？」「やっぱり、*クリスマスツリーの下に置いておきましょう。」

　クリスマスの朝になりました。田中さんの子どもたち、たろうとゆう子は起きるとすぐ一階の居間にはしって行きました。クリスマスツリーの下には赤い箱と青い箱が置いてありました。

　「あ！プレゼントが置いてある。*サンタクロースが来たんだ！」たろうが青い箱を手にとると“たろうくんへ”と書いてありました。箱を開けるとたろうがほしかった*バットが*出てきました。ゆう子も“ゆう子ちゃんへ”と書いてある赤い箱を開けました。中から*ねこの*ししゅうがしてある*クッションが出てきました。ゆう子はそのクッションが本当はお父さんとお母さんからのプレゼントだと知っていました。ゆう子はこのあいだ、そのクッションがお母さんのベッドの下にしまってあるのを見てしまったのです。でも、ゆう子はそのことをたろうには言いませんでした。

クリスマスイブ	*Christmas Eve*	出てくる	*appear, come out*
クリスマスツリー	*Christmas Tree*	ねこ	*cat*
サンタクロース	*Santa Claus*	ししゅう	*embroidery*
バット	*baseball bat*	クッション	*cushion*

① 田中さんとおくさんは子どもたちへのプレゼントをどこに置いておきましか。

② プレゼントを用意しておいたのはサンタクロースですか。

③ クリスマスの朝、ゆう子とたろうが居間に行くとツリーの下に何が置いてありましたか。

④ たろうはどうして青い箱がたろうへのプレゼントだとわかりましたか。

2. Fill in the blanks in the summary below.

田中さんとおくさんはクリスマスイブに＿＿＿＿＿＿＿＿＿＿をクリスマスツリーの下に＿＿＿＿＿ておきました。 クリスマスの朝、たろうとゆう子が居間に行くと、箱がふたつ＿＿＿＿＿＿てありました。青い箱には"たろうくんへ"と＿＿＿＿＿＿＿てありました。 赤い箱には＿＿＿＿＿＿＿＿＿＿てありました。ゆう子のもらったプレゼントは＿＿＿＿＿＿＿＿＿＿てあるクッションでした。

3. Now it's your turn to talk. What kind of special preparations do you make for Christmas or other festivities in your country?

BACKGROUND INFO

Christmas in Japan may not be celebrated as a religious festival as in other countries, but that does not mean that the Yuletide spirit is lacking. Children mimic their North American and European counterparts by putting up Christmas stockings in expectation of a visit from Santa Claus, even if very few Japanese homes have a chimney. And as Christmas is just another ordinary working day, parents hurry home early to enjoy roast chicken, strawberry Christmas cake, and sparkling wine. For couples in love, Christmas is equally important—restaurant and hotel bookings must be made well in advance to guarantee that special place for the most romantic date in the lovers' calendar.

R E A D I N G

BUSY新聞

海外旅行みやげ

Japanese tourists ignoring the local sights and getting in a shopping-frenzy used to be a common sight at overseas holiday destinations. Recently, however, a new service has changed all of that.

最近、旅行に行ったときの日本人のみやげものの買い方が変わったようだ。今までは、日本人が海外旅行に行くと世界各地で山のようにたくさんみやげものを買うので有名だった。四〇〇年前に*ポルトガル人が書いた本にも日本人はみやげものを買うのが好きだと書いてあるので、むかしからの習慣なのだろう。

*ところが、最近は大きなみやげものを持って飛行機から降りて来る人を空港であまり見なくなった。海外旅行がめずらしくなくなったことや経済などの*影響もあるが、みやげものの予約サービスができたことも関係があるようだ。これは旅行に行く前にカタログを見てみやげものを予約しておくと、旅行が終わって日本に帰るころに選んでおいたみやげものが自宅に届いているというサービスだ。出発する前に買ってあれば、旅行中忙しいスケジュールの中でわざわざ買い物をする必要もないし、重い荷物を運ばなくてもよいので人気があるらしい。日本人がカタログを見てよく買うみやげものはチョコレートやウィスキー、ワインなどだ。会社の人、親戚、友達などかなりの人数分を買う。全部で三万円ぐらい買う人が多いと聞いた。でも、旅行に行く前にみやげものを買っておくのはやっぱり変ではないか？

ポルトガル人　*a Portuguese*
ところが　*however*
影響　*influence*

QUESTIONS

1. 最近、大きなみやげものを持って飛行機から降りて来る日本人が少なくなったのはどうしてですか。

2. あなたはこのみやげものの予約サービスについてどう思いますか。

Presents from Abroad

Lately the gift-buying habits of Japanese people on trips have changed. Until now, Japanese people were famous for buying mountains of gifts whenever and wherever they went abroad. Indeed, it is said in a book, written by a Portuguese author some 400 years ago, that the Japanese were enthusiastic about buying souvenirs, so it's certainly a custom with quite a history!

Recently, however, one seldom sees people getting off the plane carrying hefty-sized presents. Of course, overseas travel is no longer the rarity it once was, and there is the influence of the economy and so on, but this appears to have something to do with the establishment of a souvenir-gift reservation service. With this service you can order presents before you even go away, and then when your trip is over and you're back in Japan, the items that you selected are delivered to your house. Apparently the service is popular because, if you buy the presents before you even set out, you don't then have to go out of your way to do any shopping in the midst of your busy schedule, nor do you have to carry any heavy luggage. The gifts most popular with Japanese readers of the catalogue are things like chocolate, wine, and whisky, and they buy enough for several sets of people—colleagues, family, and friends. I hear that most people order goods with a total value of about thirty thousand yen. But isn't it just a little odd to buy souvenirs *before* going on vacation?

L E S S O N

7 Well, I'm Going Even If It Pours Down

SENTENCE PATTERN 1

～ても

A：明日は雨がふるそうですよ。ゴルフ、どうしましょうか。
I see it's supposed to rain tomorrow. What shall we do about the golf then?

B：雨がふったら、やめましょう。　Let's call it off if it rains.

C：え～。雨がふっても行きましょうよ。楽しみにしているんですから。
Come on, let's go even if it does rain. I've been looking forward to this.

Golf is a very popular game in Japan. So many people want to play it that it's very difficult to get a round when you want it. In fact, few people would cancel a round of golf just because of bad weather.

PRACTICE

I

1. A, B, and C, are chatting about a get-together that they are planning for the weekend as they make the circular for the party. Fill in the blanks with appropriate phrases.

JBPコンピューター*しんぼく会

日時：9月15日（日曜日）　12時から6時まで
場所：山中こうえん　*現地集合

12時30分から野球の試合
その後でバーベキュー

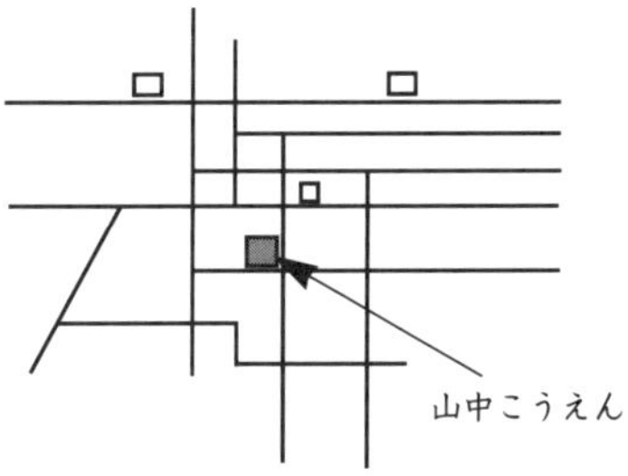

しんぼく会　*get-together*
現地集合　*meet on the spot, make your own way there*

①
A：日曜日、雨だったら、バーベキューはどうしましょう。
B：(a)____________________、やめましょうよ。
C：(b)____________________、しましょうよ。できると思いますよ。

②
A：野球をする人が少なかったら、どうしましょうか。
B：(a)____________________、できませんね。
C：(b)____________________、しましょうよ。きっと楽しいですよ。

③
A：この地図はわかりにくいですね。道に*まよう人が多いかもしれません。
B：道に(a)____________、困りますね。けいたい電話の番号を、みんなに教えておきましょう。
C：道に(b)____________、大丈夫ですよ。山中こうえんは有名ですし、道を聞くところはたくさんありますから。

まよう　*get lost*

PRACTICE

II

1. A, B, and C, are discussing a heliport construction plan. Read about their opinions below.

> *ヘリポートの*建設計画
>
> 2×××年○○町にヘリポートをつくります。
> このヘリポートができれば、日本で3番目に大きいヘリポートになります。

ヘリポート *heliport*
建設 *construction*

Aさん：　私はぜったい*はんたいです。ヘリポートの近くはとてもうるさくてねられないそうです。みどりが多くて、静かな町だから、ここに住んでいるんです。うるさくなったら、ここには住めないと思います。

Bさん：　私は*さんせいです。ヘリポートができたら、とても便利になりますよ。*重い病気の人やけがをした人を、すぐ大きい病院に運べると思います。うるさくなっても、ヘリポートができたほうがいいと思います。

Cさん：　私はこの町にヘリポートをつくるのは、はんたいです。新しくヘリポートをつくるなら、海の上につくったほうがいいと思います。海の上なら木を切らなくてもつくれるので、自然もなくならないでしょう。

はんたい *disagree, be against something*
さんせい *agree, be for something*
重い *serious*

2. Who do you agree with? Explain why you agree. If you have a different opinion, explain how you feel about the heliport.

SENTENCE PATTERN 2

～てほしいです

A：税金(ぜいきん)が高(たか)くて困(こま)りますね。

Taxes are so high that I just don't know what to do.

B：ええ、安(やす)くしてほしいですね。　Yes, I wish they'd bring them down.

PRACTICE

I

Read the following and check the statements with which you agree.

日本人(にほんじん)や日本社会(しゃかい)に言(い)いたいこと

Have your say about the Japanese

- ❏ みどりが少(すく)ないので、さびしい。こうえんをふやしてほしい。
- ❏ 駅(えき)やレストランでたばこをすわないでほしい。
- ❏「日本語(ご)がお上手(じょうず)ですね」と言わないでほしい。
- ❏ 日本の道(みち)はせますぎるので、もっと広(ひろ)くしてほしい。
- ❏ 朝(あさ)のラッシュは、*がまんできない。電車(でんしゃ)の数(かず)をふやしてほしい。
- ❏ 電車やレストランの中(なか)でけいたい電話を使(つか)わないでほしい。
- ❏ まわりの日本人がみんな英語(えいご)を話(はな)すので、日本語が上手にならない。私(わたし)にはできるだけ、日本語で話してほしい。

がまんできない　*cannot stand*

PRACTICE

II

1. Read the following passages.

ちょっと言(い)いたいことがあるんです
There's something I want to say ...

① じつは、会社(かいしゃ)にちょっと言いたいことがあります。休(やす)みも少(すく)なすぎるし、給料(きゅうりょう)も安(やす)いんです。休みはもっと多(おお)くしてほしいし、給料も*あげてほしいんです。

② じつは、となりの家(いえ)の人(ひと)にちょっと言いたいことがあります。よく夜(よる)遅(おそ)くまでパーティーをしているので、うるさくてねられないんです。きのうは朝(あさ)まで*さわいでいました。夜遅くまでパーティーをするのはやめてほしいんです。

③ じつは、主人(しゅじん)にちょっと言いたいことがあります。主人は子(こ)どものころからの本(ほん)やおもちゃをまだたくさん持(も)っているんです。ぜったいにすてません。部屋(へや)がせまいので、できればすててほしいんです。

2. Study the pictures and check that you fully understand what you have just read.

① じつは会社に　② じつはとなりの家の人に　③ じつは主人に

あげる *raise, put up*
さわぐ *make a lot of noise*

TALKING

3. Do you have something that you want to say to someone or some organization? Listen to another person's opinion on the tape. Choose a topic from the list below and have your say. Summarize your opinions in the table below.

じつは、____________________に、ちょっと言(い)いたいことがあります。EXPLAIN THE CIRCUMSTANCES____________________。
____________________________________てほしいんです。

TOPICS

- あなたの会社(かいしゃ)・学校(がっこう)
- ご主人(しゅじん)・おくさん
- 近所(きんじょ)の人(ひと)
- 友(とも)だち

SENTENCE PATTERN 3

～てもらいます

A：*「ありときりぎりす」の話を知っていますか。

Do you know the story of *The Ant and the Grasshopper*?

B：ええ。子どものころ、よく母に読んでもらいました。

Yes, my mother often used to read it to me when I was a child.

「ありときりぎりす」　The Ant and the Grasshopper *(Aesop's Fables)*

PRACTICE

I

Fill in the blanks as shown in the example.

ex. 写真を見せる

A　　私

① 道を教える

けいかん　　私

② かみを切る

私　　とこや

③ しょうかいする

B　　A　　私

ex. 私はAさんに<u>写真を見せてもらった</u>。

① 私はけいかんに____________________。

② 私はとこやに____________________。

③ 私はAさんにBさんを____________________。

PRACTICE

II

1. Read the following passages carefully.

おかげさまで
With all my thanks

① 私は、日本に来たばかりのころ、友だちにすもうにつれて行ってもらいました。すもうのれきしや*ルールを教えてもらったので、とても楽しく見ることができました。そのときからすもうが始まると、かならずテレビで見ています。

---

② 私は、*歯がいたくて困っていたとき、友だちにとてもいい*歯医者さんをしょうかいしてもらいました。その歯医者さんは親切だし、英語も話せるので、本当に安心でした。そのときから歯がいたくなったら、かならずその歯医者さんに行っています。

ルール　*rules, regulations*
歯　*tooth*
歯医者　*dentist*

2. Using the pictures as a guide, retell the stories that you have just read.

①

日本に来たばかりのころ　　すもうのれきしやルール　　すもうが始まると

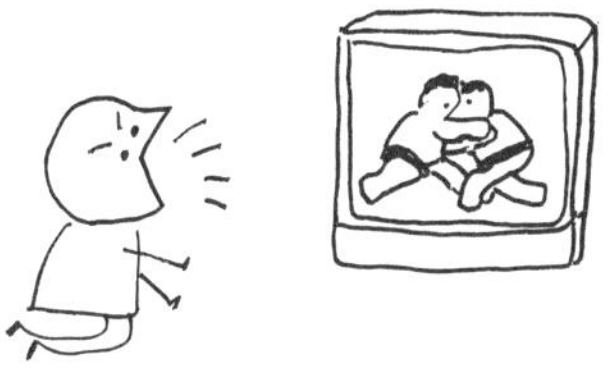

②

歯がいたくて困っていたとき　　親切　英語も話せる　　歯がいたくなったら

TALKING

3. Has someone ever gone to the trouble of helping you like that? Listen to another person's experience on the tape. Talk freely about your experience and summarize as shown in the table below.

＿＿＿＿＿＿＿＿のころ／とき、＿＿＿＿＿＿＿＿＿＿＿＿＿＿
＿＿＿＿＿てもらいました。＿＿ADD INFORMATION＿＿＿＿＿＿＿＿
＿＿＿＿＿＿＿＿＿＿。＿＿DESCRIBE HOW YOU FELT＿＿＿＿＿＿＿。

SENTENCE PATTERN 4

～ていきます／きます

世界(せかい)の人口(じんこう)はだんだんふえてきました。これからもふえていくでしょう。

The world population has risen steadily. This increase will probably continue into the future, too.

PRACTICE

I

1. Study the graph below and describe the trends from the perspective of 1998 as shown in the example.

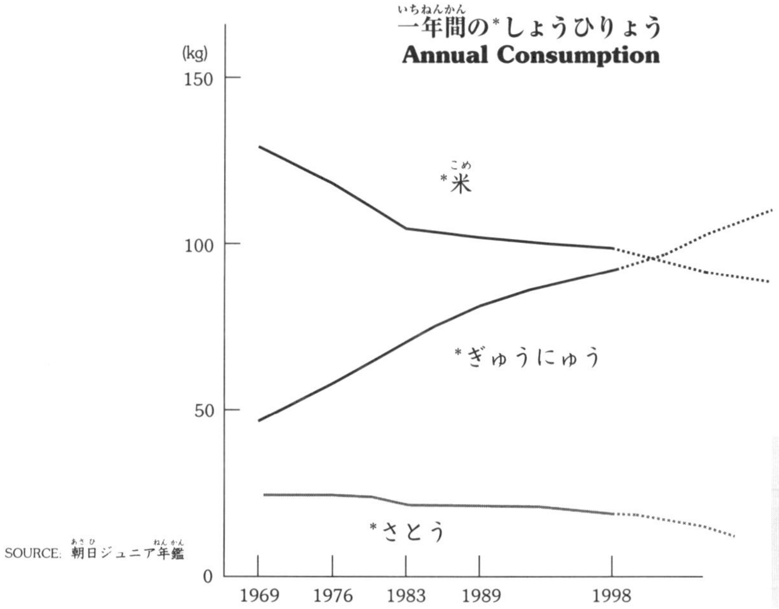

しょうひりょう	*consumption*
米	*rice*
ぎゅうにゅう	*milk*
さとう	*sugar*

ex. 日本人(にほんじん)の一年間の米のしょうひりょうは、だんだんへってきました。
これからもへっていくだろうと思(おも)います。

① 一年間のさとうのしょうひりょうは、1976年からだんだん (a)____________。
これからも (b)____________________と思います。

② 一年間のぎゅうにゅうのしょうひりょうは、だんだん (a)____________。
これからも (b)____________________と思います。

PRACTICE

II

Read the following passage and answer the questions.

日本人の*食生活
The Japanese Diet

むかしは朝ご飯に*ほとんどの人がご飯を食べていました。*けれども、だんだんパンを食べる人がふえてきて、米のしょうひりょうは少しずつへってきました。しかし、最近は*ダイエットをする人たちの間でご飯の人気がでてきました。これからは米のしょうひりょうがまた、ふえていくでしょう。

食生活　*diet*
ほとんどの人　*most people*
けれども　*but*
ダイエット　*diet (for weight reduction)*

① どうして米のしょうひりょうがへってきましたか。

② 米のしょうひりょうはこれからふえていくだろうと言っていますか、へっていくだろうと言っていますか。

③ それはどうしてですか。

④ あなたの国の食生活はどうかわってきましたか。またどうかわっていくと思いますか。

Communication

1. Read the following passage and listen to the Ume Yamada interview on the tape.

> 「私の町の＊お年より」という＊テレビ番組があります。これは町の元気なお年よりに、町がどうかわったか、町に何をしてほしいか、＊インタビューする番組です。今日はA町に80年住んでいる山田うめさんへのインタビューです。

お年より　*senior citizens*
テレビ番組　*TV program*
インタビュー　*interview*

① Under the relevant headings make notes of the things that have changed and the things Ume Yamada wants to be changed in the town.

町がどうかわってきたか

(a)

(b)

(c)

町に何をしてほしいか

(d)

(e)

② Report the results of the interview to a partner.

2. Now it's your turn to talk.

① あなたの住んでいる／住んでいた町は、どのようにかわりましたか。

② あなたの住んでいる／住んでいた町は、これからどのようにかわっていくと思いますか。

R E A D I N G

BUSY新聞

テーブルの上は外国野菜がいっぱい

Recently various novel vegetables and fruits have begun to appear on the Japanese dining table. But this is not limited to new types of vegetables. Even traditional Japanese foods are now being grown abroad and imported into Japan.

テレビの料理番組を見ていたら、*長ネギのような*リーキという名前の野菜を紹介していた。ビタミンがたくさん入っていてスープに入れるとおいしいと言っていたので、さっそくスーパーに買いに行った。店にはリーキのほかにも外国から*輸入しためずらしい野菜や果物がたくさんならんでいた。店の人は「これからも外国の野菜を使った料理のつくり方を紹介していくので、ぜひ食べてみてほしい」と宣伝していた。

じつは、外国から輸入している野菜はこれらの新しいものだけではない。日本の伝統的な*漬物もよく見ると*生産地を*示す*ラベルには外国の名前が書いてあった。二十年前、野菜はほとんどが日本で生産したものだったが、だんだん外国からの輸入が増えてきた。*大豆のように九八%が輸入というものもある。野菜の輸入が増えてきた一番大きい*理由はその安さだ。*新鮮な野菜を運ぶ*技術と*情報システムの開発によって、いろいろな費用が前よりずっと安くなったのだ。日本で生産した野菜の半分ぐらいの値段のものもある。また安くておいしいものが安心して食べられるなら、生産地はどこでもいいと考える人も多くなった。魚や肉、そばなども輸入したものが増えている。私たちの毎日の食事は*ますます「国際的」になっていきそうだ。

長ネギ	*green onion*	示す	*indicate*	新鮮な	*fresh*
リーキ	*leek*	ラベル	*label*	技術	*technology*
漬物	*pickles*	大豆	*soy bean*	情報システム	*information system*
生産地	*country of origin*	理由	*reason*	ますます	*more and more*

QUESTIONS

1. 輸入野菜が安くなった理由は何ですか。

2. あなたの食事のテーブルにも外国から輸入したものがありますか。

BUSY NEWS

Imported Vegetables Galore on Japanese Tables

I was watching a cooking program on TV in which a vegetable called a leek—which looks something like a green onion—was featured. Since the presenter claimed that it was full of vitamins and made a delicious addition to soups, I immediately went out to the supermarket to buy one. In the shop, there were many other exotic imported vegetables and fruits on display, as well as leeks. The sales clerk was enthusiastically promoting them, saying that they were going to show us how to make dishes using these foreign vegetables and that they wanted us to try them out.

In fact it is not just "new" vegetables like these that are imported from abroad. Looking carefully at traditional Japanese pickles, I saw that the country of origin indicated on the label was a foreign one. Twenty years ago, most vegetables were produced in Japan, but imports have gradually increased. There are even certain vegetables like soy beans of which 98% are imported! The single biggest reason for this growth in vegetable imports is their comparative cheapness. As a result of developments in freight technology and information systems, costs have fallen dramatically. There are even vegetables which cost as little as half of their Japanese equivalents. And most Japanese people now think that provided something is cheap and tastes good, one can eat it quite happily regardless of its country of origin. Imports of fish, meat, and buckwheat noodles are growing, too, with the result that our everyday fare is getting more and more "international" all the time.

L E S S O N

8 The Birdman Contest Is Held Every July

SENTENCE PATTERN

passive forms

*鳥人間コンテストは毎年７月末に*琵琶湖で開かれます。

The Birdman Contest is held at Lake Biwako every year at the end of July.

鳥人間コンテスト　Birdman Contest
琵琶湖　Lake Biwako

The annual "Birdman Contest" was set up in 1977 by Yomiuri Television, a Japanese broadcaster and program maker. Entrants compete in homemade planes to see who can fly the furthest. There are two sections open to competitors: human-powered propeller planes and non-assisted gliders that rely totally on the wind.

PRACTICE

I

Write the passive form of each verb as shown in the examples.

	active	passive
RI	**ex.** 言(い)う	言われる
	① 行(おこな)う	
	② 使(つか)う	
	③ わらう	
	④ 開(ひら)く (会議(かいぎ)を)	
	⑤ おす	
	⑥ こわす	
	⑦ 作(つく)る	
	⑧ 死(し)ぬ	
	⑨ たのむ	
	⑩ よぶ	
	⑪ ふる (雨(あめ)が)	
	⑫ とる (さいふを)	
	⑬ しかる	
	⑭ なぐる	
RII	**ex.** うったえる	うったえられる
	⑮ 集(あつ)める	
	⑯ ほめる	
	⑰ たてる	
	⑱ 調(しら)べる	
Irr.	**ex.** する	される
	ex. 来(く)る	来(こ)られる
	⑲ 輸入(ゆにゅう)する	
	⑳ 持(も)ってくる	

PRACTICE

II

1. Study the examples in the box and then make sentences to describe what is happening in the pictures using the verb provided in parentheses.

> 1. 部長(ぶちょう)はビジーさんをよんだ。
> →ビジーさんは部長によばれた。
> *Bijii-san was called over by his boss.*
>
> 2. 部長はビジーさんに通訳(つうやく)をたのんだ。
> →ビジーさんは部長に通訳をたのまれた。
> *Bijii-san was asked to interpret by his boss.*

①

②

③

④

① 部長は(a)____________________ました。(ほめる)
ビジーさんは(b)____________________ました。

② 部長は(a)____________________ました。(さそう)
ビジーさんは(b)____________________ました。

③ 部長は(a)____________________ました。(わらう)
ビジーさんは(b)____________________ました。

④ 部長は(a)____________________ました。(*注意(ちゅうい)する)
ビジーさんは(b)____________________ました。

注意する *caution, warn*

2. Read the following passages and answer the questions below.

Aさん

私は*高校のとき、英語のクラスがあまり好きではありませんでした。英語の先生によく間違いを直されたからです。もっとがんばるようにいつも言われて、楽しくなかったんです。私はクラスで先生にほめられるほうが好きなんです。

Bさん

私は高校のとき、スペイン語のクラスが好きでした。スペイン語の先生によく間違いを直されたからです。間違いを直されたので、スペイン語が上手になったと思います。

① Aさんはどうして英語のクラスがあまり好きではありませんでしたか。

② Bさんはどうしてスペイン語が上手になったと思っていますか。

高校　*high school*

3. Read the following statements. Check those with which you agree. Practice Ⅳ on page 95 may help you.

How do you like to be taught?

- ❏ クラスで話しているとき、先生に自分の間違いを直されるのはいやだった。
- ❏ クラスで先生に間違いを直されたので、上手になったと思う。
- ❏ *クラスメートに自分の間違いを直されるのはいやだった。
- ❏ クラスで先生にほめられるのはうれしかった。
- ❏ クラスで先生にほめられたので、上手になったと思う。

クラスメート　*classmate*

PRACTICE

III

1. Study the examples in the box and then fill in the blanks with the correct form of the verb in parentheses.

1. (人が) 会議を　毎週月曜日に　開く。
→会議は　毎週月曜日に　開かれる。
The meeting is held every Monday.
2. *シェークスピアが　*「ハムレット」を　書いた。
→ハムレットは　シェークスピアによって　書かれた。
Hamlet *was written by William Shakespeare.*

シェークスピア　*Shakespeare*
「ハムレット」　Hamlet

① *国会議事堂は1936年に(a)__________ました。ここで日本の*国会が(b)________ます。　(たてる　開く)

② *浅草寺の今のたてものは1958年に(a)__________ました。毎年5月になると、*三社まつりが(b)________ます。　(たてる　開く)

③ *東京タワーは1958年に(a)__________ました。東京の*シンボルとして(b)________ています。　(たてる　*したしむ)

④ *レインボーブリッジは1993年に(a)__________ました。よるはたくさんの*ライトで(b)________ます。　(つくる　*かざる)

⑤ *東京ドームは1988年に(a)__________ました。日本の初めての*ドームスタジアムです。野球のほかにいろいろなイベントに(b)________ます。「ビッグエッグ」と(c)________ています。　(つくる　利用する　よぶ)

国会議事堂　*the Diet Building*
国会　*the Diet*
浅草寺　*the Sensoji Temple*
三社まつり　*"Sanja" Festival*
東京タワー　*Tokyo Tower*
シンボル　*symbol*
したしむ　*love*
レインボーブリッジ　*Rainbow Bridge*
ライト　*lights*
かざる　*decorate*
東京ドーム　*Tokyo Dome*
ドームスタジアム　*domed stadium*

2. This map of Tokyo shows some of the city's most famous buildings. Explain when each building was built and what it is used for. Talk about a famous building in the town where you live or used to live.

東京タワー
1958年 東京のシンボル

レインボーリッジ
1993年 ライト

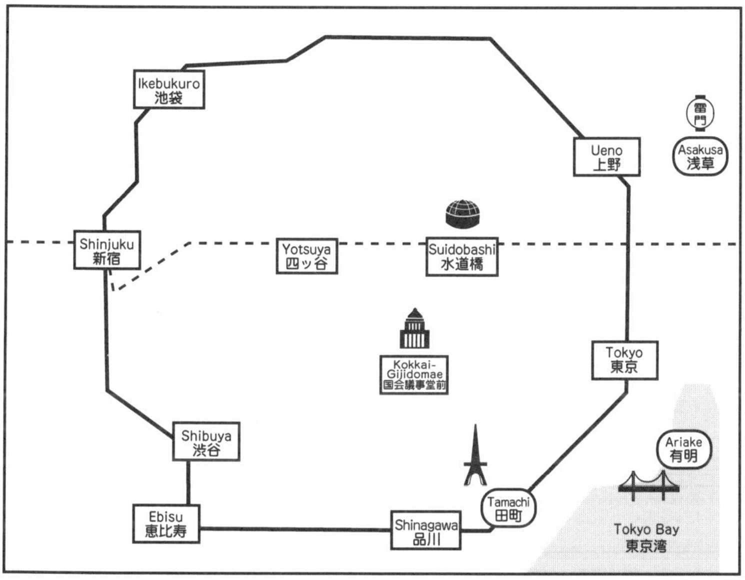

浅草寺
1958年 毎年5月まつり

国会議事堂
1936年 日本の国会

東京ドーム
1988年 野球やイベント
「ビッグエッグ」

3. Fill in the blanks with the correct form of the verbs listed below. (The same verb may be used more than once.)

① おさけは米(こめ)から(a)____________ていて、日本(にほん)ではむかしから(b)________________ています。飲(の)みすぎなければ、体(からだ)にいいと(c)__________ています。最近(さいきん)では外国(がいこく)にもよく(d)__________ているようです。

② とうふは*大豆(だいず)から(a)__________ていて、日本ではむかしからよく(b)_______________ています。今(いま)では大豆のほとんどがアメリカから(c)__________ているそうです。

大豆　*soy beans*

輸入(ゆにゅう)する・飲む・言(い)う・作(つく)る・輸出(ゆしゅつ)する・食(た)べる

③ 野球(やきゅう)は1873年(ねん)に*ホラス・ウィルソンというアメリカ人(じん)の教授(きょうじゅ)によって日本に(a)________________ました。今では日本人が一番好(いちばんす)きなスポーツだと(b)_________ています。

④ *「源氏物語(げんじものがたり)」は1000年以上前(いじょうまえ)に*紫式部(むらさきしきぶ)という女性(じょせい)によって(a)_______________ました。たくさんの*作家(さっか)によって今の言葉(ことば)に(b)_______________て、多(おお)くの人(ひと)に(c)__________ています。

ホラス・ウィルソン　*Horace Wilson*
「源氏物語」　The Tale of Genji
紫式部　*Murasaki Shikibu*
作家　*writer, author*

書(か)く・しょうかいする・言う・読(よ)む・書き直(なお)す

4. Now talk about things—e.g., popular songs, novels, sports, paintings, etc.—from your country in the same way.

PRACTICE

IV

1. Study the examples in the boxes and change the sentences to describe the pictures.

> 男の人は　私の足を　ふんだ。
> →私は　男の人に　足を　ふまれた。
> *My foot was stepped on by a man (and it hurt).*

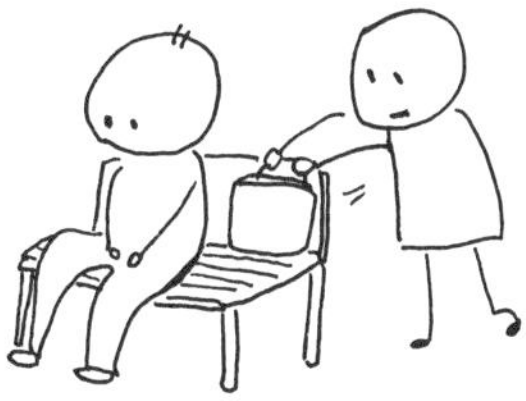

① 若い男は私のバックをとりました。

私は＿＿＿＿＿＿＿＿＿＿＿＿＿＿＿＿。

② つまは私のブランデーを飲みました。

私は＿＿＿＿＿＿＿＿＿＿＿＿＿＿＿＿。

③ 後ろの人は電車の中で私の背中をおしました。

私は＿＿＿＿＿＿＿＿＿＿＿＿＿＿＿＿。

> 雨がふった。
> →私は雨にふられた。
> *I was rained upon.*

④ となりの人が朝早く来ました。

私は＿＿＿＿＿＿＿＿＿＿＿＿＿＿＿＿＿＿＿＿。

⑤ 秘書がやめました。

私は＿＿＿＿＿＿＿＿＿＿＿＿＿＿＿＿＿＿＿＿。

2. Have you experienced any of the following? Check for a "yes" answer. Then ask them as questions to a partner.

❏ 込んでいる電車で、足をふまれたことがある。
❏ どろぼうに入られたことがある。
❏ 家族に大切なものをすてられて、おこったことがある。
❏ 海外旅行に行って、パスポートをとられたことがある。
❏ 友だちに日本語をほめられたことがある。
❏ セールスマンにうちに来られて、困ったことがある。
❏ 小さい子どもに*話しかけて、その子どもになかれたことがある。
❏ かさをもっていないときに雨にふられて、*ずぶぬれになったことがある。

話しかける *speak (to a person)*
ずぶぬれ *soaked through to the bone*

Communication

1. Read the following passage and answer the questions.

鳥人間コンテスト

空を飛んでみたいと思ったことはありませんか。「鳥人間コンテスト」は空を飛びたいと思っている人ならだれでも*参加できるコンテストです。第一回コンテストは、1977年に京都の近くの琵琶湖で開かれました。*それ以来、毎年7月末に琵琶湖で行われています。参加するチームは大学や会社のチームが多いそうです。

飛行機のデザインは何か月もかけて、チームのメンバーによって考えられます。お金のないチームは、飛行機の*部品を集めるのが大変だそうです。

コンテストの*じゅんいは飛行機のデザインと飛んだ*きょりによって決められます。第一回大会のときは82メートルでしたが、1998年の第22回大会では、23,688メートルというしんじられない*きろくが生まれました。

チームのみんなの力を集めて作られた飛行機が大空を飛ぶ様子は*感動的です。毎年参加している人は「空が好きだからやめられない」と言っていました。
興味がある人は7月末に琵琶湖に行けば、楽しい空のコンテストを見ることができるでしょう。

参加する	*enter (a competition)*	きょり	*distance*
それ以来	*since then*	きろく	*record*
部品	*component*	感動的	*thrilling*
じゅんい	*position, place*		

① 受身形（PASSIVE）にアンダーラインを書いてください。
② 第一回鳥人間コンテストはいつ開かれましたか。
③ 鳥人間コンテストは毎年何月に開かれますか。
④ コンテストのじゅんいはどうやって決められますか。
⑤ コンテストはどんな人が参加できますか。

2. Now it's your turn to talk.

① あなたも鳥人間コンテストに参加してみたいと思いますか。
② あなたが知っているおもしろいコンテストについて話してください。

R E A D I N G

BUSY新聞

*サッカーボールをよく見ると……

I am sure that when you were a child, you—like everybody else—played ball games, kicking or throwing a ball around on vacant ground and in town squares. Soccer is now popular all over the world, and I investigated the history of the soccer ball.

今、世界で一番人気のあるスポーツはサッカーだと言われている。*ワールドカップのような大きい試合は世界中に放送されて、*延べ三億人以上がテレビで見るそうだ。サッカーは十一世紀ごろイギリスで戦争のとき*頭蓋骨を*けって遊んだ（?）のが最初だと伝えられている。その後、十九世紀の末に*ルールが決められて今のようなサッカーになった。ルールがあるのはゲームのやり方だけではない。ボールについても形、まわりの長さ、重さ、かたさなどが決められている。むかしは革のボールだったが、このごろは*ポリウレタンが多く使われている。そして、よく見ると*正五角形十二枚と*正六角形二〇枚の*パネルで作られている。これも最初は十二枚だったが、だんだん増えて三二枚になった。一枚のパネルの大きさが少し変わるだけで、ボールの強さや見やすさが全然違ってくるそうだ。色は長い間*茶色が多かったが、テレビでもよく見えて分かりやすい白に変わった。今のようなボールが使われ始めたのは一九七〇年のワールドカップ・メキシコ大会からだ。サッカーボールはほとんどが*アジアの国で一つ一つ手で作られている。

サッカーボール *soccer ball*
ワールドカップ *World Cup (soccer)*
延べ3億人 *three hundred million people in total*
頭蓋骨 *skull*
ける *kick*
ルール *rule*
ポリウレタン *polyurethane*
正五角形 *pentagon*
正六角形 *hexagon*
パネル *panel*
茶色 *brown*
アジア *Asia*

QUESTIONS

1. サッカーボールをよく見るとどうなっているのですか。
2. あなたの国で一番人気のあるスポーツは何ですか。それはどんな道具を使いますか。

If You Look Carefully At a Soccer Ball

It is claimed that soccer is the world's most popular sport, and that when big games such as those of the World Cup are broadcast worldwide, over three hundred million people in total watch the games on TV. The story goes that soccer has its origins in a game that involved kicking skulls around in an English war of the eleventh century. Considerably later, at the end of the nineteenth century, proper rules were established, and soccer became the kind of game we know today.

Rules are not restricted to how the game has to be played. There are also regulations about the shape, the circumference, the weight, and the hardness of the ball itself. In the old days the ball was made of leather, but now many soccer balls are made of polyurethane. If you look closely at the ball, you can see that it is made of 12 pentagonal panels and 20 hexagonal panels. Originally there were 12 panels, but they were gradually increased to the current 32. Apparently if the size of a single panel is changed, the strength and the visibility of the ball change dramatically. For a long time the ball was brown, but was changed to white—a color which is far easier to see on television. Soccer balls of the type in use now were first introduced at the 1970 Mexico World Cup. Soccer balls are generally individually handmade in Asia.

9 What Would You Make Your Robot Do?

SENTENCE PATTERN

causative forms

もし、家(いえ)に*ロボットがいたら、あなたは何(なに)をさせますか。

If you had a robot at home, what would you make it do?

ロボット *robot*

Recent progress in robot technology is quite astounding. Today, many factories use robots to make things all over the world. Unfortunately, more time is needed before consumer robots become available at an affordable price. But if you could buy one, what would *you* make your robot do?

PRACTICE

I

1. Write the causative form of each verb as shown in the examples.

	active	causative
RI	ex. 書(か)く	書かせる
	① 作(つく)る	
	② 行(い)く	
	③ あそぶ	
	④ 急(いそ)ぐ	
	⑤ 待(ま)つ	
RII	ex. しらべる	しらべさせる
	⑥ たしかめる	
	⑦ やめる	
	⑧ 届(とど)ける	
Irr.	ex. する	させる
	ex. 来(く)る	来(こ)させる
	⑨ 早退(そうたい)する	
	⑩ 出勤(しゅっきん)する	
	⑪ むかえに来る	

2. Have another look at the picture on the previous page. Ms. Hayashi is enjoying a well earned rest with a hot cup of tea and a magazine. But what has she made her robot do for her? Study the box and then complete the sentences as shown in the example.

> 1. 林(はやし)さんはロボットを（に）買(か)い物(もの)に行かせる。
> *Ms. Hayashi makes her robot do the shopping.*
> 2. 林さんはロボットに手紙(てがみ)を書かせる。
> *Ms. Hayashi makes her robot write a letter.*

ex. 林さんはロボットを（に）　買い物に行かせます。　（買い物に行く）

① 林さんは＿＿＿＿＿＿＿＿＿＿＿＿＿＿＿＿＿。（むかえに来る）

② 林さんは＿＿＿＿＿＿＿＿＿＿＿＿＿＿＿＿＿。（手紙を書く）

③ 林さんは＿＿＿＿＿＿＿＿＿＿＿＿＿＿＿＿＿。（*アイロンをかける）

④ 林さんは＿＿＿＿＿＿＿＿＿＿＿＿＿＿＿＿＿。（車を洗う）

⑤ 林さんは＿＿＿＿＿＿＿＿＿＿＿＿＿＿＿＿＿。（*まどをふく）

⑥ 林さんは＿＿＿＿＿＿＿＿＿＿＿＿＿＿＿＿＿。（料理を作る）

⑦ 林さんは＿＿＿＿＿＿＿＿＿＿＿＿＿＿＿＿＿。（そうじをする）

アイロンをかける　*do the ironing*　　まどをふく　*clean windows*

3. Now it's your turn to talk. What would you make an office or home robot do for you?

PRACTICE

II

1. Here is a list of activities for new company recruits. Read them from the perspective of the company's president and mark those ideas that have your full approval with a ○, those ideas that have your conditional agreement with a △, and those ideas that you strongly oppose with a ×. Next to the ★ add your own idea.

2. Ask others what they think.

(　) 新入社員に毎日レポートを書かせる。

(　) 新入社員にあいさつの仕方を練習させる。

(　) 新入社員に取引先の名前をおぼえさせる。

(　) 新入社員に*ざぜんをさせる。

(　) 新入社員に*電話の受け方を練習させる。

(　) 新入社員にオフィスのそうじをさせる。

(　) 新入社員に野球などの*チームプレーのスポーツをさせる。

(　) 新入社員に課長といっしょに取引先にあいさつに行かせる。

★＿＿＿＿＿＿＿＿＿＿＿＿＿＿＿＿＿＿＿＿＿＿＿＿＿＿＿＿

ざぜん　*Zen meditation*

電話の受け方　*telephone manner*

チームプレー　*team work*

PRACTICE

III

1. Study the graph and read the text.

How do you want to bring up your kids?

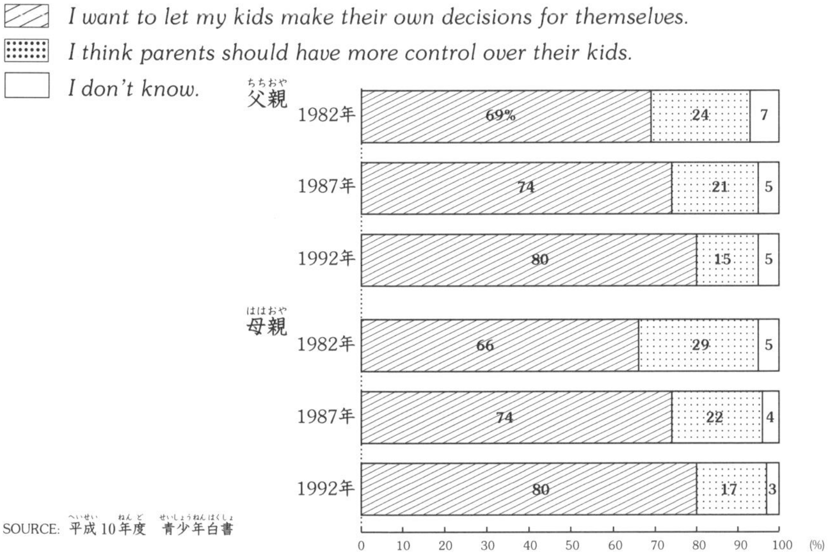

最近、中学生や高校生の子どもを持つ親の考え方がかわってきました。上の*グラフを見ると、「なるべく子どもに*はんだんさせたい」と考えている親がふえています。あなたはどう思いますか。

グラフ　*graph*
はんだんする　*judge, decide*

2. A and B are the parents of teenage children. We asked them both what they would do if their children said that they wanted to travel alone for a month. Read what they told us and then answer the questions.

中学生の子どもがひとりで旅行をしたいと言ったら
If your child in junior high said he wanted to travel alone for a month....

Aさん：　私は子どもが一人で1ヵ月、旅行に行きたいと言ったら、行かせます。子どもにいろいろなことを*けいけんさせたいからです。中学生のころからいろいろなことをけいけんさせれば、自分ではんだんができる大人になるはずです。子どものころから、自分ではんだんさせることが一番大切だと思います。

けいけん　*experience*

Bさん：　私は子どもが一人で１ヵ月旅行に行きたいと言っても、行かせません。中学生の子どもが一人で１ヵ月も旅行に行くのは早すぎます。中学生の子どもには、何があぶないか、はんだんすることはできません。子どものころは、あぶないことをさせないことが一番大切だと思います。

① Aさんは子どもが一人で旅行に行きたいと言ったら行かせますか。

② Aさんは何が一番大切だと思っていますか。

③ Bさんは子どもを一人で旅行に行かせますか。

④ Bさんは何が一番大切だと思っていますか。

3. If you were the parent of a thirteen-year-old child, what would you let and not let them do? How would you feel about the following situations, and what would your reasons be for letting or not letting your child do something? Discuss with a partner.

① 子どもが夜、*ピザ屋でアルバイトしたいと言ったら、どうしますか。

② 子どもが外国に*留学したいと言ったら、どうしますか。

③ 子どもが一人で国内を自転車でまわりたいと言ったら、どうしますか。

④ 子どもが*なんみんキャンプで*ボランティアをしたいので、夏休みに行きたいと言ったら、どうしますか。

ピザ屋　*pizzeria*
留学　*study overseas*
なんみんキャンプ　*refugee camp*
ボランティア　*volunteer work*

PRACTICE

IV

A：体の調子がよくないので、明日休ませてください。

Will you let me take tomorrow off? I don't feel very well.

B：いいですよ。ゆっくり休んでください。

That's fine. Have a good rest.

1. Listen to the tape while following the pictures below. Not all the dialogue has been reproduced. Write the missing parts ①, ②, and ③ in the spaces provided on the next page.

2. Practice the dialogue while listening to the tape. Take special care with your pronunciation and speak at the same speed as the tape.

① ______________________________

② ______________________________

③ ______________________________

3. Ask your boss for permission to do the following things as shown in the example.

あなた： 新(あたら)しいプロジェクトにぜひ、参加(さんか)させてください。ずっと前(まえ)から興味(きょうみ)があったんです。

上司(じょうし)　： わかりました。がんばってください。*期待(きたい)していますよ。

ex. 前から興味のあった新しいプロジェクトに参加したい。

① 日本語(にほんご)でビジネスをしたいので、日本語のレッスンを受(う)けたい。

② これからの仕事(しごと)に大切(たいせつ)なセミナーなので、来月(らいげつ)、*沖縄(おきなわ)で開(ひら)かれるセミナーに出席(しゅっせき)したい。

③ ビジネススクールに行(い)って勉強(べんきょう)しなおしたいので、週(しゅう)に２日(か)は５時(じ)に帰(かえ)りたい。

期待する　here: *I hope you won't let me down*
沖縄　*Okinawa*

Communication

1. Read the following passage and then answer the questions.

*もうどう犬のトレーニング
Guide Dog Training

あたまのよさそうな犬。やさしそうな犬、静かな犬。人によってもうどう犬の*いんしょうはいろいろだと思いますが、もうどう犬になるには*きびしいトレーニングがあります。*トレーナーは*トレーニング中のもうどう犬にどんなことをさせているのでしょうか。

① もうどう犬があそびたがっても、もうどう犬をあそばせない。
② もうどう犬がほかの人から食べ物をもらっても、食べさせない。
③ 歩くときは、トレーナーの左側を歩かせる。
④ 交差点の手前でかならずもうどう犬を止まらせる。
⑤ 交差点を渡ってもいいかどうか、もうどう犬にはんだんさせる。

交差点を渡ってもいいかどうか、はんだんさせるのはたいへんです。トレーナーが「go!」の*サインを出しても、*車が走って来たら、もうどう犬は交差点を渡ってはいけません。それに犬は信号のいろがわからないので、いつ渡ったらいいか、はんだんすることができないのです。

ではどうやってこのむずかしいトレーニングをさせているのでしょうか。トレーナーはもうどう犬に近くの人をよく*かんさつさせるのだそうです。そして近くの人が歩いたら歩かせて、待っていたら待たせるのだそうです。
ですから、もし交差点で信号を待っているもうどう犬がいたら、赤のとき渡らないでください。もうどう犬があなたをかんさつしています。

もうどう犬 *guide dog, seeing-eye dog*	トレーニング中 *in training*
いんしょう *image, impression*	サインを出す *give a sign*
きびしい *strict*	車が走って来る *a car comes*
トレーナー *trainer*	かんさつする *observe*

① 使役形（CAUSATIVE）にアンダーラインを書いてください。全部で11あります。

② いろいろなトレーニングの中で一番むずかしいトレーニングは何ですか。

③ トレーナーはもうどう犬に交差点を渡ってもいいかどうか、どうやってはんだんさせますか。

④ *そのほかにトレーナーはもうどう犬にどんなトレーニングをさせますか。

そのほかに　*what else*

2. Now it's your turn to talk.

あなたはもうどう犬をしあわせだと思いますか。

R E A D I N G

BUSY新聞

*チェスの*チャンピオンはコンピューター？

Do you play chess? Chess is a game that demands considerable brainpower. If a celebrated chess-player and a computer were to play a match, who do you think would win?

一九九七年五月、アメリカでチェスの世界チャンピオン、*カスパロフさんとＩＢＭ社のコンピューター「*ディープブルー」が*対戦した。じつは、カスパロフさんとコンピューターの対戦は一九九六年二月にも行われた。そのときはカスパロフさんが*勝った。チェスは頭を使うゲームだ。人々はコンピューターが*どんなに*進歩しても、*人間に勝てるはずがないと信じていた。だから、二回目の対戦でディープブルーが勝ったというニュースは人々をとてもおどろかせた。

ディープブルーをつくったのはＩＢＭ社の*技術者、Ｓさんだ。Ｓさんはディープブルーをつくった後、ディープブルーにチェスの勉強をさせた。毎日チェスのチャンピオンと対戦させて、ゲームのいろいろな進め方を覚えさせた。今では、ディープブルーは一*秒間に*四億通りの*シナリオが考えられるそうだ。

しかし、コンピューターはほんとうに人間に勝ったのだろうか。これについてＳさんは次のように話している。「コンピューターは道具です。コンピューターが自分で考えるのではありません。人間が考えて、コンピューターにやらせているだけなのです。」

チェス *chess*	進歩する *improve*
チャンピオン *champion*	人間 *human being, man*
カスパロフ *Garry Kasparov*	技術者 *technical expert*
ディープブルー *Deep Blue*	秒 *second*
対戦する *play a tournament*	4億通り *400 million (ways)*
勝つ *win*	シナリオ *scenario*
どんなに *however much*	

QUESTIONS

1. ＩＢＭ社の技術者、Ｓさんはディープブルーにどんな勉強をさせてチェスのチャンピオンにしたのですか。
2. あなたの国にチェスのようなゲームがありますか。そのゲームをコンピューターに覚えさせたら人間より強くなると思いますか。

BUSY NEWS

The Chess Champion... A Computer?

In the United States in May 1997 Garry Kasparov, the chess world-champion, and IBM's Deep Blue computer played a tournament against one another. In fact they had played once before in February 1996, but Kasparov had won that match. Chess is a game that requires intelligence, and people generally believed that however much computer technology improved, a computer would never be able to beat a man. Consequently, Deep Blue's victory in the second tournament caused a big sensation.

Deep Blue was made by Mr. S, an IBM technical expert. After making the machine itself, he then made it learn how to play chess. Every day Deep Blue had to play against the champions and memorize different plays and moves. At present, Deep Blue is able to review 400 million scenarios in a single second!

Did, however, the computer really outwit its human opponent? Mr. S had the following to say: "A computer is a tool and cannot think by itself. A human being first thinks, and only then gets the computer to act."

LESSON

10 Now You Can Get There in Thirty Minutes

SENTENCE PATTERN A

～ようになります

ふじみのに新しく東武東上線の駅ができました。
前は東京に行くのに1時間かかりましたが、今は30分ぐらいで行けるようになりました。東上線が通るようになって、とても便利になりました。

A new Tobu Line station has been built at Fujimino. Before it used to take an hour to get to Tokyo, but now you can go in about thirty minutes. Since the Tobu Line has started running there, it's become very convenient.

Before

Now

Time changes everything. More amenities can make a town more convenient and sometimes make it possible to do things that couldn't be done before. On the other hand, it is sometimes no longer possible to do all of the things that could be done in the past. How has your town changed?

PRACTICE

I

1. The town where Ms. Hayashi lives has changed dramatically with recent development. Fill in the blanks to explain the things that are now possible and the things that are no longer possible. Two examples have been done for you.

	前 →	今
ex.	(a)あまり店がなかったので、町でいろいろなものが買えませんでした。	大きいデパートができました。
ex.	(b)川がきれいだったので、およげました。	川がよごれてしまいました。
①	駅の近くの店は夜７時には閉まっていたので、会社の帰りに買い物ができませんでした。	新しくできたスーパーは夜10時まで開いています。
②	映画館がなかったので、町で映画が見られませんでした。	新しく映画館ができました。
③	駅前にはいつでも車がとめられました。	駅前は駐車禁止になりました。

ex. (a) 大きいデパートができて、何でも買えるようになりました。

ex. (b) 川がよごれてしまって、およげなくなりました。

① 新しくできたスーパーは夜10時まで開いているので、________________なりました。

② 新しく映画館ができて、________________なりました。

③ 駅前が駐車禁止になって、________________なりました。

2. Talk about your town. What things can't you do now that you could do before and what things can you do now that you couldn't do before?

JAPANESE FOR BUSY PEOPLE

THE VIDEO

Revised Edition

Educational Advisor : Association for Japanese-Language Teaching (AJALT)

改訂版 コミュニケーションのための日本語／ビデオ

社団法人国際日本語普及協会（AJALT）監修

A new and exciting video course based on the best-selling textbook series

- 58-part drama series in three volumes—authentic Japanese presented in real-life business and social contexts
- Educational studio talks—essential expressions explained in plain English
- Computer graphic animations—extra usage examples in the form of short, funny cartoons
- Cultural Background—unique insights into life in Japan in every episode
- 32-page booklet—useful tips for self-study and using the videos in the classroom

大好評の日本語教材がビデオになって新登場！

- 全3巻を通したストーリー仕立て
  生きた日本語を、会社や家庭の日常的な58のエピソードで構成
- 学習に役立つスタジオトーク
  基本表現を平易な英語で説明
- 楽しいCGアニメ
  豊富な用例をアニメで愉快に紹介
- 日本の文化紹介
  ドラマを通して日本の文化や生活習慣の理解が可能
- 32ページの小冊子
  自習にも教室での使用にも最適

After watching *Japanese For Busy People: The Video*, you will be able to do all of the following and more in natural and fluent Japanese:

Volume I 21 episodes

- Go shopping at a famous department store—and buy exactly what you want at a price you are prepared to pay
- Ride a taxi—and tell the cabby exactly how to get there
- Phone for a pizza—and get what you want to eat delivered to your door

Volume II 18 episodes

- Report lost or stolen property—and recover your belongings
- Make an appointment at the dentist—and tell the dentist which tooth aches
- Sing at a karaoke party—and decide for yourself which songs you want to sing

Volume III 19 episodes

- Book into a hotel—and effectively complain when you're not happy with the service
- Talk about what you've seen on TV—and make your conversations more interesting
- Direct a full-scale sales presentation—and impress important clients

Each Title: 50 min x 2 video tapes VHS Stereo in NTSC or PAL format

Volume I
ISBN 4-7700-2188-7(NTSC)
ISBN 4-7700-2396-0(PAL)

Volume II
ISBN 4-7700-2189-5(NTSC)
ISBN 4-7700-2397-9(PAL)

Volume III
ISBN 4-7700-2190-9(NTSC)
ISBN 4-7700-2398-7(PAL)

「ビデオ版 コミュニケーションのための日本語」を使って勉強すれば、つぎのような場面で流暢かつ自然な日本語が話せるようになります。

第1巻 21のエピソード

有名デパートで買い物する………そして値段を確認して商品を手に入れる
タクシーに乗る………そして運転手に行き先を正確に告げる
電話でピザの注文をする……そして注文と住所を正しく伝えて届けさせる、等々

第2巻 18のエピソード

落とし物を届ける………そして所持品が戻る
歯医者の予約をする………そしてどこが痛いかを正確に伝える
カラオケに行く……そして歌いたい歌を自分で選ぶ、等々

第3巻 19のエピソード

ホテルを予約する………そしてホテルのサービスで不満な点はきちんと抗議する
テレビで見たことを人に話す………そして会話を盛り上げる
仕事で本格的なプレゼンテーションをする……そして大事な顧客の信頼を得る、等々

各巻：50分×2本

講談社インターナショナル 〒112-8652 東京都文京区音羽 1-17-14 Tel. 03-3944-6492 Fax. 03-3944-6323

Japan
KODANSHA INTERNATIONAL
1-17-14 Otowa, Bunkyo-ku, Tokyo 112-8652
Tel. 03-3944-6492 Fax. 03-3944-6323

North America
KODANSHA AMERICA
575 Lexington Ave, New York, NY 10022
Tel. 917-322-6200 Fax. 212-935-6929

U.K.&Europe
KODANSHA EUROPE
95 Aldwych, London WC2B 4JF U. K.
Tel. 0171-304-4095 Fax. 0171-304-4096

Australia&New Zealand
BOOKWISE INTERNATIONAL
54 Crittenden Road, Findon 5023 South Australia
Tel. 08-8268-8222 Fax. 08-8268-8704

South-East Asia
KINOKUNIYA BOOKSTORES
Marketing Department
205 Henderson Road #08-02 Henderson Industrial Park, Singapore 159549
Tel. 276-5558 Fax. 276-5570

Printed in Japan 9904

PRACTICE

II

1. Read the following passages.

できるようになりました
Now I can do it

① この町に引越して来てから、2ヵ月*すぎました。はじめは町のどこに何があるかわかりませんでしたが、最近は町の様子がわかるようになりました。近所に友だちもふえたので、いろいろそうだんできるようになりました。

② 会社に入ってから3ヵ月すぎました。はじめは仕事のやり方がわからなくて、何でもまわりの人に聞いていましたが、最近は聞かなくてもできるようになりました。*通勤にもなれたので、あまりつかれなくなりました。

③ スキーを始めてから、3年すぎました。初めはスキーをはくと、まっすぐ立っていることもできませんでしたが、最近は上手にスピードを*コントロールできるようになりました。どんな*スロープでも*自由にまがれるようになったので、スキーが楽しめるようになりました。

すぎる *pass*	スロープ *slope*
通勤 *commute*	自由に *freely*
コントロール *control*	

2. Using the pictures as a guide, retell the stories that you have just read.

① この町に引越して来てから

初めは

最近は

友だち

② 会社に入ってから

初めは

最近は

通勤

③ スキーを始めてから

初めは

最近は

TALKING

3. Most of us know the feeling of gradually becoming able to do something that we couldn't do to start with. Listen to another person's experience on the tape. Choose a topic from the list below and talk freely about it. Finally summarize your story as shown in the table.

__________ てから、__________ すぎました。初(はじ)めは __________ が、最近(さいきん)は __________ ようになりました。 HOW YOU FEEL NOW 。

TOPICS

- 新(あたら)しい会社(かいしゃ)に入(はい)ってから
- けっこんしてから
- 日本(にほん)に来(き)てから
- 日本語(ご)の勉強(べんきょう)を始(はじ)めてから
- インターネットを始めてから
- 新しい車(くるま)を買(か)ってから

SENTENCE PATTERN B

～ようになります

A社では去年まで各支店から本社に人が集まって会議をしていましたが、今年からテレビ電話を使って会議をするようになりました。

Until last year people from all the branch offices used to assemble for meetings at the head office of A, Inc., but this year they are now able to use video telephones for their conferences.

PRACTICE

1. Read the following sentences and number them according to their most logical order. An example has been done for you.

ex.

（1）日本ではむかしは働くときも休むときも着物を着ていました。

（3）今では着物を着る人が本当に少なくなりました。

（2）しかし洋服のほうが動きやすいので、ほとんどの人がいつも洋服を着るようになりました。

①

(　) 最近では女性の*管理職もふえてきました。

(　) しかし*家事が*きかいかされ、時間がかからなくなったので、女性も社会に出ていろいろな仕事をするようになりました。

(　) むかしは家の仕事と子どもの世話が女性の*主な仕事でした。

②

(　) しかし町に*ゆうえんちができると、*かんこう客が大勢来るようになりました。

(　) 最近では新しい仕事がふえて、若い人が町にもどって来るようになりました。

(　) むかしは若い人は学校を卒業すると町を出て*都会に働きに行ってしまいました。

(　) 町には*みりょくのある仕事がなかったからです。

管理職　*management*
家事　*housework*
きかいか　*mechanization*
主な　*main*
ゆうえんち　*theme park*
かんこう客　*tourist*
都会　*city*
みりょく　*attraction*

2. Time and changing social environments inevitably lead to different lifestyles. Talk about the changes in your lifestyle.

READING

BUSY新聞

はる子さんの*挑戦

In a triathlon, athletes actually do three sports—swimming, cycling, and long-distance running—trying to complete the elements in the shortest possible time. Said to be the most punishing of all sports, the triathlon is also called the "Iron Man Race" in Japanese.

はる子さんは五年前に交通事故で右足を*失ったが、今はパソコンのインストラクターとして元気に仕事をしている。はる子さんがスポーツを始めたのはテレビで*パラリンピックを見てからだ。それまでパラリンピックは体に*障害がある人のスポーツ大会だと思っていたが、スポーツ*選手として*記録に挑戦している人達を見てはる子さんはとても*感動した。そして自分も何かスポーツをやってみたいと思った。

子どものとき水泳をしていたので仕事が終わってから近くのプールに行ってみた。はじめは二五メートル泳ぐのも大変だったが、半年で五〇〇メートル泳げるようになった。はる子さんは大いに*自信をもち、次にジョギングと自転車に挑戦した。いっしょに泳いだり走ったりする友達も増えた。以前は休日はうちで静かに本を読んだり音楽を聞いたりしていたが、このごろはよく友達と海や山に出かけるようになった。今年初めて*トライアスロンに挑戦した。水泳は人が多くて*おぼれそうになった。走っているとき、何度も苦しくなりあきらめようかと思った。*だから、自転車で二〇キロを走り終えたときは、うれしくて*泣いてしまった。今、はる子さんは障害があっても挑戦する*勇気をもっていれば何でもできるようになると信じている。

挑戦　*challenge*
失う　*lose*
パラリンピック　*Paralympic Games*
障害　*handicap*
選手　*athletes*
記録　*record*
感動する　*be thrilled*
自信　*(self-) confidence*
トライアスロン　*triathlon*
おぼれる　*drown*
だから　*therefore*
泣く　*cry*
勇気　*courage*

QUESTIONS

1. スポーツを始める前と後で、はる子さんの休日はどう変わりましたか。

2. 今、あなたが一番いっしょうけんめいしていることは何ですか。

BUSY NEWS

Haruko Has A Go

Haruko lost her right leg in an automobile accident five years ago and is now working happily as a computer instructor. She took up sports after watching the Paralympic Games on television. Until that point she had assumed that the Paralympics was a sportsmeet for people with physical handicaps, but was thrilled to see that in fact it involved people competing for records as professional athletes. It was then that she decided she wanted to try her hand at some kind of sport.

Since she had swum as a child, she first went to the local pool on her way back from work. At first even to swim 25 meters (27 yards) was a terrible ordeal for her, but after six months she was able to swim 500 meters (547 yards). This served as a great confidence booster, so she decided to give jogging and cycling a go. She made many friends among her fellow swimmers and cyclists. Previously she had spent her days off quietly at home, reading books or listening to music, but now she frequently went to the sea and the mountains with her friends. This year for the first time she tried to do a triathlon. When she was swimming, there were so many people she was nearly drowned. In the running part, she was in such pain that she repeatedly thought about giving up. When she had finally finished the 20-kilometer cycle ride she burst into tears of joy. Haruko now believes that even with a handicap, provided you have courage, you can do absolutely anything.

CHECK 2

1. Put the verb in parentheses in an appropriate **-te-form** sentence pattern as shown in the example. The same pattern can be used more than once.

～ている、～てしまう、～てみる、～ておく、～てある ～ていく、～てくる、～てもらう、～てほしい

（デパートの*ドレス売り場です）

店員：　お客様のものをおさがしですか。

客：　いえ、ちょっと**ex.** <u>（見る→見ている）</u>だけです。

店員：　こちらのドレス、いかがですか。今年の夏とても人気があるんですよ。お客様によく似合うと思いますが、よかったら ①（着る）ませんか。

客：　あら、しゃれた色ね。サイズは15なんですが、ありますか。

店員：　15ですか。さっき、あちらのたなの上に ②（おく）のを見ました。今、③（見る）からちょっとここでお待ちください。

ございました。では、こちらでごゆっくりどうぞ。

客：　あら、ちょっと小さいかしら。15で入るはずなんだけど。④（気をつける）んだけど、最近だんだん ⑤（ふとる）ようで……。入るかしら。*ファスナーが　うーん！上がらない！

店員：　どうかしましたか。

客：　すみません。ちょっと着るのを ⑥（手伝う）たいんですが。

店員：　はい。あ、ちょっと小さいようですね。

客：　大きいサイズはありますか。

店員：　この色の大きいサイズは全部 ⑦（売り切れる）たんですが、どうしましょうか。

客：　じゃあ、このドレス、サイズを直して自宅に ⑧（送る）んですが。

店員：　かしこまりました。1週間ぐらいでお届けできると思います。

ドレス売り場　*dress floor*
ファスナー　*zipper*

2. Read the following passages taking particular care over the underlined passive and causative parts and the underlined ～してもらう／てくれる phrases.

①

(a) 大事なデータをパソコンに入れておいたのですが、だれかに消されてしまいました。困りました。

(b) 会社を出るとき、コンピューターのスイッチを消すのをわすれて家に帰ってしまいました。電話をしたら、同僚の山田さんが残業していたので、かれにたのんで消してもらいました。たすかりました。

(c) *敬語の勉強を始めたとき、使い方がわからなくて教室でよく先生に直されました。でも、会社で話しているとき日本人の友達がいつも直してくれたので最近はだいぶ上手に使えるようになりました。

②

(a) A：工場の中を見ることができますか。

B：はい、では担当者に案内させますのでちょっとお待ちください。

(b) スポーツクラブを見に行きました。クラブの人が親切に案内してくれたので、よくわかりました。

(c) 年末は正月のじゅんびで大変です。いつも主人に手伝ってもらっていますが、来年からは子どもたちにも手伝わせるつもりです。

③ 私は子どものときから写真をとられるのがきらいでした。*はずかしかったのです。ですから、いつもだれにもとらせなかったのですが、先日友達のけっこんしきで*プロのカメラマンが*ぐうぜんとってくれた写真はすごくきれいにとれていてとても気に入りました。10さいぐらい若く見えるし、この私が映画スターのようでした。じつは、あのカメラマンにもう一度とってもらいたいと思ってかれの名刺をさがしているんです。

敬語　*honorific language*

はずかしい　*shy, embarrassed*

プロ　*professional*

ぐうぜん　*by chance, coincidentally*

3. Circle the most appropriate expression from the alternatives given in parentheses.

①

取引先：　先週、お願いした見積書がまだ届いていないんですが。

加藤：　えっ、それは申しわけございません。では、さっそく担当の者に（届けさせます／届けてもらいます）。

②

田中：　ご病気だと聞きましたが、お元気そうですね。

大山：　おかげさまでよくなりました。林さんにいいお医者さんをしょうかい（させて／されて／してもらって）たすかりました。

田中：　そうだったんですか。よかったですね。

③

母親A：　うちの子ども、にんじんがきらいでぜったいに食べないんですよ。どうしたらいいんでしょう。

母親B：　うちの子どももきらいなんですけど、小さく切って*カレーライスに入れて（食べさせて／食べてもらって）いるんです。

④

小林：　英語の手紙を書いたんだけど、これでいいかしら。

佐藤：　手紙を出す前にビジーさんに（見させたら／見られたら／見てもらったら）どうでしょう。

小林：　そうねえ、お願いしてみるわ。

⑤

吉田：　新しくできた空港はどうでしたか。

スミス：　*税関で荷物を全部（開けさせて／開けられて／開けてもらって）空港を出るのに１時間もかかってしまいました。

吉田：　それは大変でしたね。

カレーライス　*curry with rice*
税関　*customs*

LESSON

11 Thank You for Asking Me to Come

SENTENCE PATTERN

〜てくれます　　　〜ていただきます／てくださいます

A：今日はお招きいただいて、ありがとうございました。いろいろ教えてくださったので、よくわかりました。

Thank you for inviting me over today.

I've learned a lot because you have been kind enough to teach me many things.

B：こちらこそ、来ていただいてありがとう。　And thank you for coming.

How do you usually express your gratitude to someone who has been kind to you and shown you support?

PRACTICE

I

わからないと言ったら、友だちが（私に）地図を書いてくれました。
When I said that I didn't understand, my friend drew me a map.

困っていたら、部長が（私に）説明してくださいました。
When I was mixed up about something, my boss explained it all for me.

1. Study the box and then fill in the blanks as shown in the example.

2. Practice the dialogue while listening to the tape.

AさんとBさんが会社で話しています。Bさんは最近まで入院していました。

A：もうすっかりよくなりましたか。
B：ええ、おかげさまで、すっかり元気になりました。**ex.**友だちがスープやくだものを何度も持ってきてくれたり、①________________たりして、うれしかったです。社長が②________________たり、取引先の部長が③____________________て、申しわけなかったです。
A：みんなBさんに早く元気になってもらいたかったんですよ。

PRACTICE

II

道がわからないので、(友だちに)地図を書いてもらいました。
As I didn't know the way, I got my friend to draw me a map.

部長にたのんで、(部長に)げんこうを書いていただきました。
I asked my boss to write the draft for me.

1. Fill in the blanks with verbs given below as shown in the example.

2. Listen to the tape carefully and practice the underlined parts of the dialogue.

吉田夫人：ビジーさん、よくすもうを見に行くそうですね。

ビジー：ええ、日本に来る前はすもうについて何も知らなかったんですよ。でも吉田部長にすもうを見に（**ex.** つれて行っていただいて）から、とても好きになりました。

吉田夫人：今は主人よりずっとくわしいと聞きましたよ。

ビジー：部長にルールや力士の名前を（①＿＿＿＿＿＿＿＿）ので、今ではだいたいわかるようになりました。

吉田夫人：すもうのチケットはなかなか買えないんでしょう。

ビジー：じつは、最近すもうの*ファンクラブの人と友だちになったんです。それでたのんでチケットを（②＿＿＿＿＿＿＿＿）ことができるようになりました。

吉田夫人：それはいいですね。

ビジー：この間は*すもう部屋に（③＿＿＿＿＿＿＿＿）て、*よこづなにサインを（④＿＿＿＿＿＿＿＿）んです。

吉田夫人：へー。サインを。

ex. つれて行く　① 教える　② 買う　③ つれて行く　④ する

ファンクラブ　*fan club*　　よこづな　*Grand Champion*
すもう部屋　*sumo stable*

PRACTICE

III

Write a thank-you letter for each journal entry as shown in the example.

Diary

ex. ◯月◯日

今日吉田部長にお茶会につれて行ってもらった。お茶の*作法を知らなかったので部長にいろいろ教えてもらった。お茶の先生にもしょうかいしてもらった。お茶のレッスンもおもしろそうだと思った。部長に*お礼状を書いてからねよう。

今日はお茶会につれて行っていただいて、ありがとうございました。とても楽しかったです。お茶の作法も教えていただき、とても*感謝しています。おかげさまで日本の文化を少し知ることができました。本当にありがとうございました。

*とり急ぎお礼まで。

吉田様

ビジー

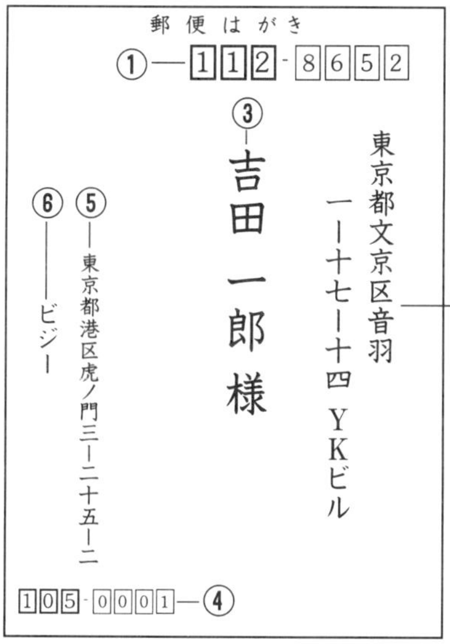

KEY

① Addressee's zip code
② Addressee's address
③ Addressee's name

④ Sender's zip code
⑤ Sender's address
⑥ Sender's name

BACKGROUND INFO

The diagram shows the correct way to address a postcard in Japanese. The key on the left explains all the parts.

作法 *manners (in tea ceremony)*

礼状 *thank-you letter*

感謝する *appreciate, be grateful*

とり急ぎお礼まで *(letter ending; lit.: "Greetings in haste")*

Diary

○月○日

① 日曜日大林社長のうちに招いてもらった。おくさんに日本料理をたくさん作ってもらった。家族が集まってとてもにぎやかだったので、アメリカの家に帰ったような*気がした。

(a)________________様

日曜日は(b)________________て、ありがとうございました。

(c)________________て、とても感謝しています。ご家族のみなさんとにぎやかに楽しい時間がすごせました。おかげさまで、アメリカの家に帰ったような気がしました。本当にありがとうございました。

とり急ぎお礼まで。

★月☆日

○○○○（あなたの名前）

気がする　*feel like*

Communication

1. Mr. Yamada and Mr. Kato are talking about visiting New York for their winter vacation. Listen to the tape and circle the correct statements.

① ニューヨーク支店長(してんちょう)は　1　加藤(かとう)さんの同僚(どうりょう)です。
　　　　　　　　　　　　　2　加藤さんの上司(じょうし)です。

② 山田(やまだ)さんは　1　加藤さんの同僚です。
　　　　　　　　2　加藤さんの上司です。

③ 山田さんがニューヨークで泊(と)まるところはどこですか。

1　友(とも)だちのうち

2　ホテル

3　支店長のうち

④ 加藤さんがニューヨークで　泊まるところはどこですか。

1　友だちのうち

2　ホテル

3　支店長のうち

2. After coming back from New York, Mr. Kato decides to write a thank-you letter to Mr. Hayashi, the New York branch manager. Read Mr. Kato's journal entry and complete his thank-you letter.

かとうさんの日記(にっき)

○月○日

ニューヨークで支店長(してんちょう)の林(はやし)さんにとてもお世話(せわ)になった。いろいろなところへつれて行(い)ってもらったり、いろいろな人(ひと)にしょうかいしてもらったりした。

一人(ひとり)だったら、ニューヨークのクリスマスを楽(たの)しむことはできなかったと思(おも)う。

(a)____________様(さま)

先日(せんじつ)はたいへん(b)____________
て、ありがとうございました。
いろいろなところへ
(c)________________たり、
(d)________________たりし
て、感謝(かんしゃ)しています。おかげさまで
(e)________________
ことができました。本当(ほんとう)にありがと
うございました。
またゆっくり手紙(てがみ)を書(か)きますが、
取(と)り急(いそ)ぎ(f)____________。

1月(がつ)10日　加藤(かとう)ゆうじ

3. In this lesson you learned how to write a simple thank-you letter to someone who has been specially kind to you. You can use these examples whenever you need to say thank you in Japanese.

BUSYお知らせ

*ペットボトルの*リサイクルにご*協力をお願いします

Increasing levels of garbage created by our modern convenient lifestyles are posing a problem for society at large. PET bottles have recently been in the spotlight as a re-usable resource, but people are ill-informed about how the bottles are collected and re-used.

リサイクル運動グループ　*吉田よう子

毎日の生活の中でペットボトルはジュース、水、*しょうゆなどの*容器として使われています。これらは捨ててしまえばゴミにしかなりませんが、リサイクルすればまた新しい*製品になります。たとえば、ペットボトル10本で工場で働く人の制服を*1着つくることができます。ほかに、シャツ、靴下、*スキーウェア、*文房具などもつくられています。

日本でも1997年に*法律ができてから、ペットボトルはずいぶんリサイクルされるようになりました。私たちはゴミを少なくして、美しい地球を守っていきたいと考えてペットボトルをリサイクルする運動をしています。

リサイクルはまず皆さまにペットボトルを出していただくことから始まります。残念なことですが、時々ペットボトルの中にゴミやタバコが入っていることもあります。きれいに中を洗ってから出してくださると助かります。それからもう一つ、大事なお願いがあります。リサイクルしてできた製品をぜひ皆さまに買っていただきたいのです。なるべく多くの方が使ってくださるとうれしいと思います。皆さまのご協力をお願いいたします。

ペットボトル	*PET (polyethylene terephthalate) bottle*	製品	*product*
リサイクル	*recycling*	1着	*(set of clothes)*
協力	*cooperation, help*	スキーウェア	*skiwear*
吉田よう子	*Yoshida Yoko (female name)*	文房具	*stationery*
しょうゆ	*soy sauce*	法律	*law*
容器	*container*		

QUESTIONS

1. ペットボトルを出すときどんなことに注意をするようにと言っていますか。

2. あなたの国のゴミのリサイクル運動について話してください。

Please Help with the Recycling of PET Bottles

PET bottles are a part of our everyday life, used as containers for things like fruit juice, water, or soy sauce. If you just throw them out, they end up as trash—pure and simple—but if you recycle them, they can become entirely new and different products. Ten PET bottles, for example, can be used to make one pair of overalls for a factory worker. Products such as shirts, socks, skiwear, and stationery can also be made this way.

In Japan, since the passing of a law in 1997, PET bottles have been recycled in considerable quantities, and we set up a group to encourage recycling because we want to reduce garbage levels and to preserve the beauty of the planet for the future.

The recycling process begins with all of you being kind enough to put out your PET bottles. Unfortunately, bottles sometimes contain trash or cigarette ends: It really helps us if you can wash inside the bottles for us before putting them out. Next, we have one more important favor to ask all of you. Please buy recycled products. We hope that as many people as possible will support us and use recycled products. Please work with us on this one!

Yoko Yoshida of the Movement for Recycling

LESSON 12 When Flying I Try Not to Eat Anything ....

SENTENCE PATTERN 1

～ようにします

A：食べないんですか。Aren't you going to eat it?

B：ええ、飛行機にのったら、何も食べないで、すぐねるようにしているんです。*時差ボケになりませんよ。

No, when I'm on an airplane, I try not to eat anything and go to sleep quickly. Then I don't suffer from jet-lag.

Long-haul air travel can be tough on passengers flying to foreign destinations for either business or pleasure. What things do you try and do to make your flight more comfortable?

時差ボケ　*jet-lag*

PRACTICE

1. Mr. X has drawn up a list of all the things that he makes a point of doing to keep fit and in good health. Read his list and check all the health tips that you think are effective.

Mr. X's Keep Fit & Healthly Top Ten Tips

- ❑ 毎朝、ジョギングをするようにしている。
- ❑ 週に3回プールでおよぐようにしている。
- ❑ 会社まで歩くようにしている。
- ❑ 夜は12時までにねるようにしている。
- ❑ 週末はみどりの多いところに行くようにしている。
- ❑ 野菜をたくさん食べてビタミンをとるようにしている。
- ❑ 毎晩ねる前に*ストレッチを30分するようにしている。
- ❑ 週末は仕事のことを考えないようにしている。
- ❑ エレベーターやエスカレーターを使わないようにしている。
- ❑ コーヒーやおさけを飲みすぎないようにしている。

2. Talk about the tips that you have checked as shown in the following dialogue.

A：Bさんは何か体にいいことをしていますか。

B：ええ。毎朝、ジョギングをするようにしています。

A：それはいいですね。でも、続けるのはたいへんでしょう。

B：ええ、でも、なるべく、するようにしているんです。

A：それでいつも元気そうなんですね。

ストレッチ　*stretching exercises*

SENTENCE PATTERN 2

～なくて

友だちに会えなくて、ざんねんでした。

It was a pity that I couldn't see my friend.

PRACTICE

1. Make sentences by matching the statements on the left with those on the right as shown in the example.

ex. 前、飼っていた犬がわすれられなくて	(a) さびしい。
① 飛行機のきっぷがとれなくて	(b) 新しいペットが飼えない。
② *最終電車に間に合わなくて	(c) よかった。
③ 引越したばかりなので友だちがいなくて	(d) 新幹線で行くことになった。
④ *せっかく作った料理をだれも食べてくれなくて	(e) 歩いて帰らなければならなかった。
⑤ 雨にふられなくて	(f) がっかりした。

(ex. → (b))

2. Complete the following sentences by adding what you think is the most appropriate phrase.

①会議がなかなか終わらなくて、約束の時間に____________________。

②辞書がなくて、____________________。

③家族に*れんらくがとれなくて、____________________。

最終電車 *the last train*
せっかく *(I took all the trouble to ...)*
れんらくをとる *make contact, reach*

SENTENCE PATTERN 3

～ないで

テキストを見ないで、ショートダイアログの練習をしてください。
Practice the Short Dialogues without looking at the text.

PRACTICE

I

What do you do when you study Japanese? First check the things that you do, and then ask other members of your class.

What do you do when you study Japanese?

- ❑ 漢字を何回も書いて、おぼえる。
- ❑ 読むときは声を出さないで、静かに読む。
- ❑ わからないことばがあっても、辞書で調べないで最後まで読む。
- ❑ クラスではできるだけ英語を使わないで、勉強している。
- ❑ できるだけテキストの会話を覚えてから、クラスに出席する
- ❑ テキストを見ないで、ダイアログが言えるようになるまで練習する。

PRACTICE

II

1. Read the following passages.

どうやって決めますか
How do you decide?

① 私は今の仕事をえらぶとき、いろいろな人にそうだんして、決めました。ほかの人の意見を聞けば、いろいろなことがよくわかるようになるからです。仕事をえらぶときは、なるべくいろいろな人とそうだんして、決めるのがいいと思います。

② 私は今の仕事をえらぶとき、だれにもそうだんしないで、決めました。人によって、考え方も*かちかんもちがうからです。仕事をえらぶときは、できるだけ自分で考えて、一人で決めるのがいいと思います。

*かちかん values

2. Using the pictures as a guide, retell the accounts that you have just read.

①

私は今の仕事をえらぶとき

②

TALKING

3. What do you do to make an important decision? Listen to another person's experience on the tape. Choose a topic from the list below and talk freely about it. Finally summarize your account in the table below.

私は__________とき、__________て（ないで）決めました。__________からです。__________ときは、__________て（ないで）決めるのがいいと思います。

TOPICS

- 大学をえらぶとき
- 車を買うとき
- 新しいプロジェクトを決めるとき
- けっこんの相手を決めるとき
- 旅行に持って行く本をえらぶとき
- 両親の誕生日プレゼントをえらぶとき

Communication

1. Top executives were asked about what they had learned in their twenties and thirties. What was the secret of their success? Read on to find out.

What did you try and do when you were in your twenties and thirties?

① 仕事に集中することが大切でしょう。でも、仕事だけではだめです。私の場合は週末はできるだけ仕事のことを考えずに、あそんだり本を読んだりするようにしていました。仕事と*ゆとりのバランスが一番大切だと思います。

② 若いころから、いつも今の自分に何ができるか、そして何ができないか考えるようにしていました。自分のできることとできないことがはっきりわかれば、自分の*能力をうまく使うことができて、人生はせいこうするでしょう。

③ つまらなくても、ひとつの仕事を続けるようにすることが大切です。つまらないからという理由で仕事をやめたら、仕事の*基本をおぼえることはできません。私が入社したとき、初めてもらった仕事は本当におもしろくありませんでした。でもそこでがんばったので、仕事の基本がおぼえられたのだと思います。

ゆとり *relaxation*
能力 *abilities, skills*
基本 *the basics*

④ 私がいつも気をつけていたことは２つです。できるだけ大きいことを考えるようにすること、長い*視野で考えるようにすることです。この２つをわすれないで、仕事をしていれば必ずせいこうするはずです。

⑤ 仕事で一番大切なのは人間関係です。私は*先輩や*後輩とよくコミュニケーションをとるようにしていました。そして*説得しなければならないときは、２回で説得するようにしました。１回であきらめるのは早すぎます。でも３回も説得したら、*しつこいと思われるからです。

視野 *field of vision*
先輩 *(colleague who joined the firm before you)*
後輩 *(colleague who joined the firm after you)*
説得 *persuade*
しつこい *overbearing, stubborn*

2. Fill in the blanks in the summaries below.

① ________________が大切でしょう。でも、週末は________________________

________________していました。

② 若いころから、____________________________か、__________________か

________________していました。

③ ____ことが大切です。

④ __________________________________ことと、________________________

________________ことに気をつけていました。

⑤ 仕事で一番大切なのは______________ので______________________________

_______していました。そして説得するときは___________________しました。

3. Discuss the following.

① あなたは今読んだ意見についてどう思いますか。

② あなたがせいこうするため (to succeed) にいつも気をつけていることは何ですか。

R E A D I N G

BUSY新聞

*ダイレクトメール（DM）の *あて名は猫の「*ミミ」

Do you get a lot of junk mail and telephone sales calls to your house? What kinds of things are they peddling? How do you think they found out your address, your name, and your telephone number?

それは、一年前のことでした。近所を散歩していたとき、*売り出し中のマンションがあったのでちょっと中に入ってみました。コーヒーをごちそうになりながら、親切そうな担当者の説明を聞きました。帰るとき*アンケートに答えるように言われました。どうしてもことわれなくて住所や名前、電話番号、家族の人数などを書きました。

その一週間後から、毎日たくさんのダイレクトメールやセールスの電話がかかって来るようになりました。旅行、バーゲンセール、スポーツクラブの案内などいろいろありました。私の住所や電話番号がそのときのアンケートから*もれたのはまちがいありません。あて名がうちの猫の名前「ミミ」になっていたからです。じつは、私は自分の名前を書きたくなかったので猫の名前を書いたのです。担当者は「ミミ」が猫の名前だとは知らないで、私が書いた住所と名前のリストを別の会社にわたしたのでしょう。私は届いたダイレクトメールを集めてマンションの担当者に送り、名前のリストがもれていると注意しましたが、担当者からは何の返事もありません。これからは、よく知らない会社のアンケートには答えないようにしようと思います。今でも、ダイヤモンドの会社やダンス教室から猫の「ミミ」に*毎日のようにダイレクトメールやセールスの電話が来ています。

ダイレクトメール	*direct mail (DM)*	アンケート	*questionnaire*
あて名	*addressee, addressed to*	もれる	*leak*
ミミ	(cat's name)	毎日のように	*almost every day*
売り出し中	*up for sale, on the market*		

QUESTIONS

1. 猫の「ミミ」にDMやセールスの電話が来るようになった理由は何ですか。
2. あなたはセールスの電話やDMになやまされた (to be vexed) ことがありますか。

Direct Mail Addressed To Mimi the Cat

This is something that happened one year ago. When I was walking in my neighborhood, I happened to notice a condominium that had just been put on the market, so I went in to have a quick look. As I drank the complimentary cup of coffee, I listened to the pitch of the helpful-looking salesman. On leaving I was asked to fill out a questionnaire. I couldn't see any way to wriggle out of it, so I dutifully wrote down my address, name, phone number, and the number of people in my family.

Then from about a week later, loads of direct mail and sales calls started to pour in every day. Vacations, store sales, sports club brochures, you name it! There was no question about it. My address and phone number had been "leaked" from that questionnaire. I knew because all the mail was addressed to Mimi, the name of our pet cat. I had written down the cat's name because I didn't want to give my own name. Unaware that Mimi was a cat's moniker, the salesman had evidently sent my address and phone number on to another company. I gathered up all the direct mail that had been sent to me and redirected it to the condominium salesman, warning him that names from his list were being passed around, but I never got even a word in reply. After that I decided on a policy of never responding to questionnaires of companies that I am not familiar with. Even now, we get direct mail and telephone calls almost every day pushing everything from diamonds to dancing lessons for Mimi the cat!

L E S S O N

13 I Will Bring You the Chopsticks Right Away

SENTENCE PATTERN

お／ご～になります　お／ご～します

A：おはしをお使(つか)いになりますか。Would you like to use chopsticks?

B：ええ、お願(ねが)いします。Yes, please.

A：すぐ、お持(も)ちします。I'll bring them right away.

Proper and correct usage of honorific expressions in Japanese makes for smoother and better human relationships. Do you know when and to whom Japanese people use the different levels of honorific speech?

PRACTICE

I

1. Study the following chart and write in the missing words.

Respect	Neutral	Humble
いらっしゃいます	行(い)きます	まいります
いらっしゃいます	来(き)ます	①
②	います	おります
③	言(い)います	申(もう)します
④	します	⑤
⑥	食(た)べます	いただきます
ごらんになります	見(み)ます	⑦

2. Fill in the blanks with the correct honorific form of each verb given in parentheses as shown in the example.

Mr. Rajan and Mr. Nakata are meeting for the first time at a party.

中田(なかた)： 初(はじ)めまして。中田と**ex.**<u>申します</u>。(言います)

ラジャン： 初めまして、ラジャンと①________。(言います)

中田： ラジャンさんは、いつ日本(にほん)に②__________。(来ましたか)

ラジャン： 4年前(ねんまえ)に③__________________。 (来ました)

中田： そうですか。今(いま)、どちらに④______________。(住(す)んでいますか)

ラジャン： 目黒(めぐろ)に⑤__________________。(住んでいます)

中田： 日本の食べ物(もの)は何(なん)でも⑥________________。(食べられますか)

ラジャン： ええ、ほとんど。でもときどきインドのカレーが食べたくなります。

中田： じゃ、ご自分で⑦______________________。(料理(りょうり)しますか)

ラジャン： いいえ、私(わたし)は料理はぜんぜん⑧______________。(しません)

PRACTICE

II

Study the table below, and then fill in the blanks with the correct honorific form of each verb given in parentheses as shown in the example.

neutral		respect
待ちます	→	お待ちになります
出発します	→	ご出発になります

A professor and student are talking.

ex.

学生：　シンガポールの会議からいつ<u>お帰りになり</u>ますか。（帰る）

教授：　来週の月曜日に帰ります。

①

学生：　先生、これから研究室に＿＿＿＿＿＿＿＿＿＿ますか。（よる）

教授：　いいえ、まっすぐ家に帰ります。

②

学生：　「サイエンス」に発表された論文をもう＿＿＿＿＿＿＿＿ましたか。（読む）

教授：　ええ、もう読みましたよ。

③

学生：　今日何時に＿＿＿＿＿＿＿＿＿＿か。（出かける）

教授：　10時半に出かける予定です。

④

学生：　この*OHPはまだ＿＿＿＿＿＿＿＿＿＿か。（使う）

教授：　ええ、つぎの授業で使いますから、出しておいてください。

OHP　*overhead projector*

PRACTICE

III

Study the table below, and then fill in the blanks with the correct honorific form of each verb given in parentheses as shown in the example.

neutral		humble
送ります	→	お送りします
ほうこくします	→	ごほうこくします

Bijii-san is talking to Ms. Yamanaka, a client who has come all the way from Osaka to attend a conference at JBP.

ex.

ビジー：　会議室は303号室です。すぐ<u>ご案内します</u>。(案内する)

山中：　ありがとうございます。

①

ビジー：　あ、お荷物はどうぞそこにお置きください。よろしければ ______________ので。(あずかる)

山中：　じゃ、お願いします。

②

山中：　すみません。今晩大阪へ帰らなければなりません。新幹線の切符をとりたいんですが。

ビジー：　はい、すぐ電話して、 ______________。(とる)

③

山中：　すみません、東京駅までタクシーで行こうと思うんですが、予約しておいたほうがいいでしょうか。

ビジー：　いいえ、私が東京駅まで ______________から、大丈夫です。(送る)

山中：　いろいろと、申しわけありません。

④

山中：　ところで、会議室でOHPを使えますか。

ビジー：　はい、301の部屋に置いてありますので、すぐ ______________。(持つ)

PRACTICE

IV

1. Listen to the tape while following the pictures below. Write the missing parts in the spaces provided.

2. Practice the dialogue while listening to the tape. Take special care with your pronunciation and speak at the same speed as the tape.

1

① ______________________________

② ______________________________

③ ______________________________

④ ______________________________

⑤ ______________________________

⑥ ______________________________

2

① ______________________________

② ______________________________

③ ______________________________

④ ______________________________

⑤ ______________________________

Communication 1

1. Mr. Smith has recently changed jobs. This evening he made a speech at his welcome party. Listen to the tape and answer the questions.

① スミスさんはどこで日本語を勉強しましたか。

② スミスさんはどうしてよろこんでいますか。

2. Listen to the tape again and fill in the blanks.

(a)＿＿＿＿＿＿＿＿＿＿ジョン・スミスです。
大学で経済と日本語を勉強いたしました。ずっと日本で仕事をしてみたいと思っておりましたので、この会社に入れて、大変うれしく思っております。
(b)＿＿＿＿＿＿＿＿＿＿ので、(c)＿＿＿＿＿＿＿＿＿＿と思います。どうぞよろしくお願いいたします。

3. Use the table below to help you make a speech to introduce yourself.

(a)＿(HOME COUNTRY)＿＿＿＿＿＿＿＿＿＿(NAME)＿です。

(b)＿＿＿＿＿＿＿＿＿＿＿＿＿＿＿＿＿＿＿(TALK ABOUT YOURSELF)

＿＿＿＿＿＿＿＿＿＿＿＿＿＿＿＿＿＿＿＿＿＿＿＿＿＿＿＿

＿＿＿＿＿＿＿＿＿＿＿＿＿＿＿＿＿＿＿＿＿＿＿＿＿＿＿＿

＿＿＿＿＿＿＿＿＿＿＿＿＿＿＿＿。

(c)＿(GREETING TO SUM UP)＿＿＿＿＿ので、(d)＿＿＿＿＿＿＿＿＿＿と思います。どうぞよろしくお願いいたします。

Communication 2

1. The wedding guests have been invited to make their speeches. Listen to the tape and answer the questions.

① 話している人は何という人ですか。

② このパーティーはどんなパーティーですか。

③ よし子さんとたろうさんは会社に入ってから知り合いましたか。

2. Listen to the tape again and fill in the blanks.

*司会：　それでは山田様においわいのスピーチをお願いいたします。

山田：　(a)______________________________山田 (b)________________。

よし子さん、たろうさん、(c)__________________________。

本日はすばらしいけっこんしきに (d)__________________________。

よし子さんとたろうさんは大学を卒業なさる前から、けっこんの約束をなさっていたそうです。お二人ともスポーツがとてもお上手で、よくテニスやスキーにいらっしゃっていました。これからはお二人で、明るく元気な家庭をおつくりになると思います。

(e)________________________________。

司会　*master of ceremonies, host*

3. If you were invited to make a speech at a friend's wedding, what would you say? Make a wedding speech in Japanese.

R E A D I N G

先生はメガネ屋のご主人

Schools are increasingly resorting to non-teachers with specific skills and knowledge in an effort to make education relevant to modern lifestyles and to respond to the diversification of studies. There are lessons for things like tea ceremony, pottery, local cooking and swimming. This is a thank-you letter from the teacher-in-charge at a school to the proprietor of an optician's who had worked as a part-time teacher.

---

*中田英様

*この度は私どもの小学校の特別授業「パソコンで遊ぼう」にご*協力いただきましてありがとうございました。

中田様が三年前までパソコン*ソフトの会社でお仕事をなさっていたと*うかがって、ぜひ子どもたちに教えてくださるようお願いをいたしました。あれから一年間、授業の進め方やソフトの準備などについても相談させていただき、たいへんお世話になりました。メガネ屋さんのお仕事もお忙しいとうかがっておりましたが、貴重なお時間を毎週いただいてしまい、ご迷惑をおかけしたのではないかと心配しております。おかげさまで、ご*指導くださいました小さい子どもたちの「誕生日カードを作ろう」、大きい子どもたちの「*インターネットで調べよう世界の*動物」などのクラスは、子どもたちの間でとても人気がありました。機会がございましたらまた教えていただきたいと申しております。これからもよろしくお願いいたします。簡単ですが*まずは、お礼まで。

三月二十四日　*藤原さやか

中田英	*Nakata Hide (male name)*	指導する	*give advice*
この度	*recently*	インターネット	*Internet*
協力	*cooperation, hard work*	動物	*animals*
ソフト	*software*	まずは、お礼まで	*(Anyway,) thank you*
うかがう	*hear (humble form)*	藤原さやか	*Fujiwara Sayaka (female name)*

QUESTIONS

1. メガネ屋の主人の中田さんが、どうして小学校で特別授業をしたのですか。
2. あなたの国でもこのような特別授業がありますか。

Teacher is the Proprietor of an Optician's Shop

March 24th

Dear Mr. Hide Nakata

Thank you very much indeed for all your hard work in setting up the recent "Let's Have Fun with PCs" course at our elementary school.

I asked you if you could teach the children because I had heard that three years ago you were working in a computer software company. Since then, over the course of this year, your advice on how the courses should be structured and the preparation of the software has really been invaluable. I know that you must already be extremely busy in your role as an optician and am therefore concerned that I may have inconvenienced you by making weekly demands on your precious time.

Thanks to your sterling efforts, however, both the "Making a Birthday Card" course for the young children and the "Investigating the Animals of the World on the Internet" for the older children were wildly popular. If another opportunity should arise, we would be delighted if you could teach here again.

With very best wishes for the future and my thanks.

Sayaka Fujiwara

CHECK 3

1. Choose the correct expression from the two alternatives provided in parentheses.

(*和だいこの練習)

佐藤：　ビジーさん、和だいこの練習を①（始まった／始めた）って本当ですか。

ビジー：　ええ、そうなんです。毎週、日曜日にうちの近くの小学校に10人ぐらいグループの人が②（集まって／集めて）練習しているんです。

佐藤：　練習はどうやってするんですか。

ビジー：　まず最初に、先生③（が／に）やって見せてくださるんです。それから3時間ぐらいみんなで練習するんですが、いい運動になりますよ。*楽譜のようなものもありますが、ほとんど④（見なくて／見ないで）やります。

佐藤：　これが練習しているときの写真ですね。*かっこいいですねえ。これ、ビジーさんですか。信じられないですね。

ビジー：　どういう意味ですか。時間が⑤（なくて／ないで）練習に行けないこともありますが、なるべく休まないように⑥（なって／して）います。

佐藤：　そうですか。⑦（今度／今後）聞かせて⑧（もらえませんか／あげませんか）。

ビジー：　いいですよ。じゃあ、今週の日曜日に練習を見に来ませんか。

佐藤：　今週の日曜日ですか。うかがいたいんですが、あいにく⑨（その／あの）日は用事があってだめなんですよ。来週はどうですか。

ビジー：　だいじょうぶですよ。

佐藤：　ありがとう。私、たいこが大好きなんです。では、来週の日曜日、とても⑩（よろこんでいます／楽しみにしています）。

和だいこ *Japanese drum*
楽譜 *(musical) score*
かっこいい *nice, cool*

2. Read the following passages taking particular care over the underlined parts.

グリーンさんは先月できたばかりの新しいマンションに住んでいます。建物に入るときグリーンさんはかぎを使いません。入り口の*プレートを手で*さわります。するとドアが静かに開きます。*センサーが*しもんを*チェックするので、ほかの人がさわっても開きません。エレベーターにのったとき、ボタンをおさなくても「15階」と言えば、15階でちゃんと止まります。部屋のドアは、人が入ると*自動的に閉まり、カギがかかります。トイレや台所の電気は、人が入ると自動的について、人が出るとまた自動的に消えます。テレビのチャンネルは、テレビに向かって番号を言うと、チャンネルがかわります。何でも自動的にできてとても便利ですが、コンピューターのシステムがこしょうしたらどうするのでしょう。グリーンさんの話によると、これも自動的になおるシステムになっているそうです。

私は40年前に建てられた古いアパートに住んでいます。建物の玄関のドアはふつうのドアですから、いつでも、だれでも開けることができます。エレベーターはありませんから4階まで階段をのぼります。部屋のドアは自分でかぎを使って開けなければなりません。部屋に入るときは自分で電気をつけ、部屋を出るときは自分で消さなければなりません。テレビのチャンネルはボタンをおしてかえるのですが、最近調子が悪くて困っています。今度、電器屋さんになおしてもらうつもりです。便利なアパートではありませんが、ふんいきがいいので気に入っています。

プレート *plate*	しもん *fingerprint*
さわる *touch*	チェックする *check*
センサー *sensor*	自動的に *automatically*

3. Choose the most appropriate verb from the two alternatives given in parentheses and write it in its correct form in the spaces provided, as shown in the example.

ex. （入(はい)る／入(い)れる）

A：このコーヒー、ちっともあまくないけどさとうは<u>入っています</u>か。

B：あれ、あまくないですか？ちゃんと二(ふた)つ<u>入れた</u>と思(おも)ったけど　。

① （集(あつ)まる／集める）

A：*バザーの品物(しなもの)はたくさん________ましたか。

B：ちょっとたりませんね。もう少(すこ)しがんばって________たほうがいいと思いますけど。

② （落(お)ちる／落とす）

A：階段(かいだん)から________てけがをしたと聞(き)きましたが、だいじょうぶですか。

B：ええ、階段で書類(しょるい)を________てしまったんです。それをひろおうと思ったら、体(からだ)の*バランスがくずれてあたまから________てしまいました。

③ （決(き)まる／決める）

A：転勤(てんきん)だそうですね。ご出発(しゅっぱつ)の日(ひ)はもう______ているんですか。

B：早(はや)く______たいんですが、いろいろと事情(じじょう)がありまして……。

④ （こわれる／こわす）

A：ちょっと、この時計(とけい)、だれが________たの？

B：知(し)らないよ。ぼくが来(き)たときは、もう________ていたよ。

⑤ （下(さ)がる／下げる）

A：病院(びょういん)でもらった薬(くすり)を飲(の)んでいるんですが、*けつあつがちっとも________ないんですよ。薬をかえたほうがいいんでしょうか。

B：けつあつを急(きゅう)に________とよくないらしいですよ。

バザー *bazaar*
バランスがくずれる *lose balance*
けつあつ *blood pressure*

4. Write the expressions in their correct forms in the spaces provided as shown in the example.

ex. （片付いている／片付けておく）

母：　はる子さんと、今駅に着いたのであと10分ぐらいしたら帰るけど居間は片付いている？

子ども：　弟のおもちゃがたくさん出ているけど。

母：　じゃ、早く片付けておいて。

① （書いてある／書いておく）

A：お花見に行くのは来週の火曜日ですね。わすれる人がいるかもしれないから、*けいじばんに日にちと時間を________________ください。

B：いいですよ。あら、もう________________。だれが書いたんでしょう。

② （入れてある／入れておく）

おっと：　加藤さんたち、6時ごろ来ると言っていたね。れいぞうこにビールは________________かな？

つま：　だいじょうぶ。さっき、私がちゃんと______________わ。

③ （開いている／開けておく）

A：まどが________さむいね。閉めてもいいかな？

B：ええ、どうぞ。さっきここでたばこをすっていたので、____________んです。もう閉めましょう。

けいじばん　*message board*

L E S S O N

14 Despite Queuing for Hours, I Still Couldn't Get the Tickets

SENTENCE PATTERN 1

〜のに

A：コンサートの切符(きっぷ)は買(か)えたんですか。

Did you manage to buy tickets for the concert?

B：３時間(じかん)も並(なら)んだのに、買えなかったんです。

No, I couldn't get any. Even though I stood in line for three hours.

Whether it's a visiting opera star, the latest hit rock band, or the newest and trendiest computer game, it can be quite an ordeal trying to get one's hands on something that just about everyone seems to want. It's disappointing, too, to go home empty-handed after queuing in vain for hours.

PRACTICE

I

1. Read the following, paying particular attention to the underlined parts.

① 田中(たなか)さんとビジーさんはテニスを習(なら)っています。

コーチ： テニスは毎日練習(まいにちれんしゅう)すれば、上手(じょうず)になりますよ。

それから2か月後(げつご)

田中： 毎日練習したので、上手になりましたよ。

ビジー： いいですね。私(わたし)は毎日練習したのに、上手になりませんでした。

② 田中さんとビジーさんはロックコンサートの切符(きっぷ)を買(か)いに行(い)きます。

まりこ： *売(う)り出(だ)しの日(ひ)の8時(じ)までにプレイガイドに行って並(なら)べば、買えると思(おも)いますよ。

それから数日後(すうじつご)

田中： 7時半(はん)に*渋谷(しぶや)のプレイガイドに行って並んだので、買えました。

ビジー： いいですね。私は7時に*新宿(しんじゅく)のプレイガイドに行って並んだのに、買えませんでした。

売り出し *go on sale, be put on sale*
渋谷 *Shibuya (place in Tokyo)*
新宿 *Shinjuku (place in Tokyo)*

2. Do you think that you would find the following situations strange?

Odd Situations

- ❏ 空(そら)がはれているのに雨(あめ)がふっているとき
- ❏ 自動(じどう)ドアの前(まえ)に立(た)ったのにドアが開(あ)かないとき
- ❏ 春(はる)なのに木(こ)の*葉(は)が全部(ぜんぶ)おちてしまったとき
- ❏ 午前(ごぜん)1時なのに道(みち)が込(こ)んでいるとき
- ❏ 雨がふっているのにサングラスをかけている人(ひと)を見(み)たとき

葉 *leaf*

PRACTICE

II

1. Listen to the tape while following the pictures below. Write the missing parts ①, ②, and ③ in the spaces provided.

2. Practice the dialogue while listening to the tape. Take special care with your pronunciation and speak at the same speed as the tape.

ビジー：　パソコンの調子が悪いんですか。
小林：　ええ、①________________のに、またこしょうしたようです。

ビジー：　しんじられない。②________________のに、合格したんです。
小林：　おめでとう。

吉田：　ビジーさん、どうしたんですか。元気がありませんね。
ビジー：　③____________________のに、スピーチがうまくできなかったんです。

PRACTICE

III

1. Read the following dialogue and think about how Bijii-san must have felt.

きのうはＪＢＰコンピューターのニューモデルの発表会でした。ビジーさんはいろいろ*宣伝しましたが、お客さんが少ししか来ませんでした。

ビジー：	佐藤さん、聞いてください。 きのうはＪＢＰコンピューターのニューモデルの発表会だったのに、お客さんが20人しか来なかったんです。
佐藤：	宣伝しなかったんですか。
ビジー：	いろいろ宣伝したのにそれしか来なかったんですよ。
佐藤：	ざんねんでしたね。でも、いっしょうけんめいしたんですから、あまり気にしないほうがいいですよ。

宣伝する　*advertise*

2. Pretending that you are Ms. Tanaka, tell Bijii-san about your progress with the piano.

東京電気の田中さんは２年前からピアノを習っていますが、なかなか上手になりません。仕事の後で毎晩うちで練習していますが、上手になりません。

田中：	ビジーさん、聞いてください。
ビジー：	どうしたんですか。
田中：	①＿＿＿＿＿＿＿＿＿＿のに、②＿＿＿＿＿＿＿＿＿＿。
ビジー：	うちでも練習していますか。
田中：	ええ、③＿＿＿＿＿＿＿＿＿＿のに、④＿＿＿＿＿＿＿＿＿＿。
ビジー：	そうですか。でも、練習を続けていれば、きっと上手になると思いますよ。

SENTENCE PATTERN 2

～ようとしたとき

すみません、うちを出(で)ようとしたとき、電話(でんわ)がかかってきたんです。

Sorry, I was just about to leave when the phone rang.

PRACTICE

1. Study the pictures below and then fill in the blanks as shown in the example.

ex. 帰(かえ)る

① ケーキを出(だ)す

② お金(かね)を払(はら)う

ex. <u>帰ろう</u>としたとき、部長(ぶちょう)によばれました。

① ＿＿＿＿＿＿＿＿としたとき、玄関(げんかん)のベルがなりました。

② ＿＿＿＿＿＿＿＿としたとき、さいふがないことに気(き)がつきました。

2. Referring to the pictures on the previous page, fill in the blanks. Practice the dialogues through repeated reading.

タイミングが悪(わる)かったですね
Bad Timing

①

・今日(きょう)は小川(おがわ)さんの息子(むすこ)のじろうくんの誕生日(たんじょうび)です。

小川：　ただいま。

小川夫人(ふじん)：　お帰(かえ)りなさい。今日は早(はや)く帰ると言(い)っていたのに、もう10時(じ)よ。

小川：　[1]それが、**ex.**<u>帰ろうとした</u>とき、部長(ぶちょう)によばれたんだよ。

小川夫人：　[2]それで？

小川：　仕事(しごと)もたのまれて今日中(じゅう)にすませるように部長に言われたんだ。

・小川さん一家(いっか)は食事(しょくじ)をすませました。

じろう：　おかあさん、ケーキは？

小川夫人：　[1]それが、*オーブンから(a)＿＿＿＿＿＿とき、玄関(げんかん)のベルがなって。

小川：　[2]それで？

小川夫人：　いそがしくて、ケーキのことをわすれてしまったの。

・おさらの上(うえ)にこげたケーキがありました。

②

A：Y子(こ)さんとの初(はじ)めてのデートはどうでしたか。

B：[1]それが、(a)＿＿＿＿＿＿＿＿とき、(b)＿＿＿＿＿＿＿＿＿＿＿。

A：[2]それで？

B：Y子さんに払(はら)ってもらいました。

NOTES:

1 Used to explain a reason for something

2 Used to illicit further information

オーブン　*oven*

こげた　*burned*

Communication

1. A has a problem which she discusses with her counsellor. Listen to the tape to find out about her problem and then talk about what you have understood.

2. Read the passages below and answer the following questions.

カウンセリング
Counselling

A子さん

「私は21さいの学生です。*ルームメートのK子さんのことで*なやんでいます。K子さんはそうじがきらいなんです。『台所は使った人が片付けましょう。』と毎日K子さんに言っているのに、K子さんはなかなか片付けてくれないんです。夜は私は早くねたいから、10時*以降は静かにしてほしいと言っているのに、K子さんは12時ごろまで音楽を聞いたり、テレビを見たりしています。それから、週末はゆっくりしたいのに、いつもK子さんの友だちがあそびに来るので困っています。」

カウンセラー

「あなたの気持ちはよくわかります。ルームメートといっしょに住むといろいろむずかしいことがあるだろうと思います。でも、ちょっとK子さんの*立場も考えてみてください。仕事でつかれていると、片付けようと思ってもなかなか片付けられないことがあります。早くねたほうがいいとわかっていてもねる前にテレビを見たり、音楽を聞いたりしてゆっくりしたいのかもしれません。週末にお客さんが多いのは大変ですね。でも、K子さんもことわりたくてもことわれないのかもしれませんよ。

それから、もう一つ、K子さんのほうもあなたに何か言いたいことがあるかもしれません。K子さんともう一度よく話をしたらどうですか。」

ルームメイト　*roommate*
なやむ　*worry about, be concerned about*
以降　*from, after*
立場　*position, perspective*

① A子さんはだれのことでなやんでいますか。

② A子さんはどうしてなやんでいますか。

③ カウンセラーはどうしたらいいと言っていますか。

3. Now put yourself in K's shoes who is bothered by her roommate, A. What do you think she would say about her roommate to the student counsellor?

R E A D I N G

BUSY新聞

*サイレンススズカの*悲劇

On November 1st, 1998, the 118th Emperor's Cup Race was held at the Tokyo Racecourse. Silence Suzuka, a five-year-old stallion, fell just before the fourth corner, broke his left foreleg, was unable to continue, and had to be destroyed after the race.

その日、*東京競馬場には一四万人が集まった。サイレンススズカは一番人気のある馬だった。はじめの一〇〇〇メートルを五七*秒四で走り、*トップになった。そして、*第四コーナーをまわろうとしたとき、悲劇が起きた。急にサイレンススズカが走るのをやめたのだ。*ゴールまで、あと八〇〇メートルだった。後から走って来る馬とは*一〇馬身以上の差があった。らくに*優勝できたはずなのに、いったい何が起きたのか。

サイレンススズカの左脚は*骨折していたのだ。これほどの大きいケガをしてしまうとなおすことはできない。レースの後で関係者はサイレンススズカを*安楽死させた。馬は*眠るときも立っている動物なので、立てない馬は死ぬしかないのだ。それに*手術をしても自分で立っていることができないし、寝かせると体の下側が*くさってしまう。「かわいそうに。なおしてやれないのか」という手紙が日本中からたくさん届けられたが、安楽死はしかたがないことだった。この年、サイレンススズカは*六連勝中だった。次の年には海外でG1レースに出る計画もあったのに、*夢だけで終わってしまった。しかし、馬を*愛する人々の間でサイレンススズカの名前はいつまでも忘れられることはないだろう。

サイレンススズカ *Silence Suzuka (racehorse name)*　悲劇 *tragedy*　東京競馬場 *Tokyo Racecourse*
秒 *second*　トップになる *take the lead*　第4コーナー *fourth corner*　ゴール *finish line*
10馬身 *ten [horse's] lengths*　優勝する *win*　骨折 *fracture*　安楽死 *mercy killing*
眠る *sleep*　手術 *operation*　くさる *develop bedsores*　6連勝 *six consecutive victories*
夢 *dream*　愛する *love*

QUESTIONS

1. レースの後で関係者はどうしてサイレンススズカを安楽死させたのですか。
2. この話を読んであなたはどう思いましたか。

BUSY NEWS

The Tragedy of Silence Suzuka

That day there were 140,000 people at the Tokyo Racecourse, and Silence Suzuka was by far the best-loved horse there. He covered the first thousand meters in 57.4 seconds and had taken the lead. Then, just as he was about to take the fourth corner, the tragedy occurred. Quite suddenly Silence Suzuka stopped running. There were still 800 meters (875 yards) to the finish line, but Silence Suzuka was ten lengths ahead of the nearest horse and should have won the race easily. What on earth had happened?

Silence Suzuka had suffered a comminuted fracture of the left leg. When a horse has suffered so grave an injury, there is no way it can be set right. After the race, the trainer and owner decided to destroy Silence Suzuka. Since a horse is an animal that stands even when asleep, the inability to stand upright is tantamount to death. Even with an operation, the horse cannot stand up unsupported, and if made to lie down develops bedsores on its lower body. Many letters saying that it was just too sad and asking if there was no way in which the injury could be healed flooded in from all over Japan, but a mercy killing was the only viable option. That year, Silence Suzuka had won six consecutive races, and it was planned that he would run in a G1 Race abroad the next year, but this all ended as an unfulfilled dream. Nonetheless, the name Silence Suzuka will always live on unforgotten among people who love horses.

15 After Much Consideration I Have Decided to Retire

SENTENCE PATTERN 1

〜ことにします

いろいろ考(かんが)えましたが、やはりやめることにしました。

After much consideration I have decided to retire after all.

I'm telling ya boss, this is big news!

The world of Sumo is tough and competitive. If a wrestler fails to achieve acceptable results, he must make up his own mind to retire from the sport.

PRACTICE

I

Fill in the blanks using the phrase ～ことにしました as shown in the example.

ex.

ビジー：　このあいだ話していたスポーツクラブに申し込みましたか。

吉田：　ええ、会費が高いんですが、会社から歩いて行けるので、申し込むことにしました。明日申し込みに行きます。

ビジー：　そうですか。

①

ビジー：　このあいだ話していたビジネススクールの試験を受けるんですか。

山本：　はい。むずかしそうなんですが、ぜひもう一度勉強したいので、________________。3か月後に試験があるので、終わるまであそびに行けません。

ビジー：　そうですか。がんばってくださいね。

②

ビジー：　このあいだ話していたマンションを買ったんですか。

林：　いいえ。いろいろ考えましたが、やはり駅から遠いので、________________。ほかのをさがすつもりです。

③

ビジー：　病院でのボランティア活動に参加するかどうか決めましたか。

山本：　ええ、行ってみたら、みんながよろこんでくれたので、________________。

ビジー：　そうですか。ぼくも時間があったらするんですが。

PRACTICE

II

1. Read the following passages and answer the questions.

いろいろ考えましたが……
After much consideration ...

① Aさん：　このあいだ、部長に来月ホンコンに転勤するように言われました。高校生の息子は今の学校がとても気に入っているようですが、一人で東京に置いておくのは心配なので、息子をいっしょにつれて行くかどうかまよいました。けっきょくみんなでいっしょにくらしたいのでホンコンにつれて行くことにしました。来月家族全員でホンコンに引越します。

(a) Aさんは息子をホンコンにつれて行くことにしましたか。
(b) それはどうしてですか。

---

② Bさん：　このあいだ、友だちのうちにあそびに行ったら、かわいい犬がたくさんいました。友だちは私が犬を飼いたければ、1ぴきくれると言いました。私は犬が好きなのですが、犬の世話は大変なので、飼うかどうかまよいました。けっきょく、家にいる時間が少ないので、飼わないことにしました。明日友だちに電話をしてことわります。

(a) Bさんは犬を飼うことにしましたか、飼わないことにしましたか。
(b) それはどうしてですか。

2. What do you have trouble making your mind up about? Listen to a third person's account on the tape and talk about what you have understood. Now talk about your own decisions.

SENTENCE PATTERN 2

～ことになります

すみません。ごみは集める日の朝、出すことになりましたのでよろしくお願いします。

It has been decided that all trash should be put out on the morning of collection. Please understand this and cooperate with us on this one.

PRACTICE

I

Recently there has been a major revision of the rules and regulations for residents at the ABC condominium. The main changes were announced in the following notice that was sent to all residents.

4月5日の*理事会でつぎのことが決まりましたので、ご*協力をお願いします。

新しいきそく

- ごみは集める日の朝に出してください。
- *洗濯物はベランダに*ほさないでください。
- 自転車は*ろうかに置かないでください。
- *びんは*リサイクルに出しますので「*あきびん」と書いてある箱に入れてください。
- 管理人は*届け物をあずかりません。

前のきそく

- ごみは集める前の晩に出してもいい
- 洗濯物はベランダにほしてもいい
- 自転車はろうかに置いてもいい
- びんは「*もえないごみ」と書いてある箱に入れる
- るすの時、管理人に荷物をあずかってもらうことができる

理事会	*(residents') committee*
協力	*support, cooperation*
洗濯物	*laundry*
ベランダ	*veranda, balcony*
ほす	*dry*
ろうか	*corridor*
びん	*bottle, jar, glass container*
リサイクル	*recycling*
あきびん	*empty bottle*
届け物	*a delivery*
もえないごみ	*nonburnable trash*

As the janitor, you are bothered that many of the residents don't seem to have got used to the new rules. It is up to you to remind them of the changes using the expression 〜ことになりました.

Subsitute the underlined parts of the dialogue as shown in the example.

ex. ごみを集める日は明日ですが、Aさんがごみを出しに来ました。

あなた：すみません、ごみは集める日の朝出すことになりましたので、よろしくお願いします。

Aさん：ルールがかわったんですか。

あなた：ええ、エレベーターの前に書いてありますので読んでおいてください。

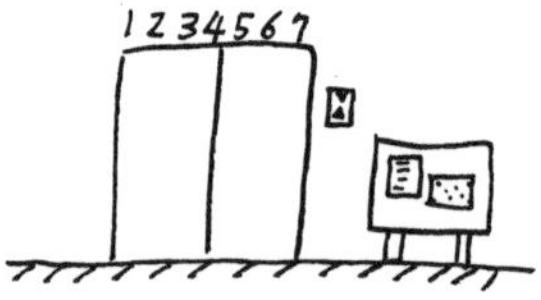

① Bさんのベランダに洗濯物がたくさんほしてあります。

② Cさんの子どもが自転車をろうかに置こうとしています。

③ Dさんがあきびんを「もえないごみ」と書いてある箱に入れました。

④ Eさんにるす中に荷物が届いたらあずかってほしいとたのまれました。

BACKGROUND INFO

Generally garbage must be separated for refuse collection in Japan. Paper, wood, food waste, and the like are put out as burnable rubbish. Plastics and other synthetics are treated as nonburnable trash. Glass, aluminum and steel cans, PET bottles, etc, should be recycled.

PRACTICE

II

1. Practice the following dialogues.

I'd like to change our appointment ...

①

A：江戸美術館に行く日はあさってですよね。

B：ええ、そうですよ。

A：じつは、明日から3日間ホンコンに出張することになってしまったんです。

B：そうですか。じゃあ、来週にかえましょうか。

A：すみません、お願いします。

②

A：お花見に行くのは、木曜日の夕方ですよね。

B：ええ、そうですよ。

A：じつは、部長にたのまれて、木曜日に取引先のパーティーに出席することになってしまったんですが。

B：そうですか。じゃ、金曜日にかえましょうか。

A：ええ、ぜひ、お願いします。

TALKING

2. How do you go about rearranging an appointment? Listen to the dialogue on the tape. Choose a topic from the list below and practice the dialogue as shown in the box.

> A：<u>CONFIRM PREVIOUSLY AGREED TIME/DATE ENGAGEMENT/APPOINTMENT</u> ですよね。
> B：ええ、そうですよ。
> A：じつは<u>REASON FOR CHANGE</u>ことになってしまったんです。
> B：そうですか。じゃあ、<u>SUGGESTED ALTERNATIVE TIME/DATE</u>かえましょうか。
> A：すみません、お願いします。

TOPICS

ピクニック　食事などの約束
映画

Communication

1. Read the article below and study the graph. Answer the questions.

日本では大学や高校を卒業してすぐ会社に就職し、60さいの定年までその会社に勤めるというのが一般的なけいこうでした。ところが、最近*退職金のシステムがかわり、会社によっては定年の60さいより早く退職する人には、退職金を多く支払うようになりました。40代、50代で会社をやめて新しく店を始めたり、自分の会社をつくったりする人もいます。*業績が上がらなくて困っている会社では社員に早めに退職するように*すすめる場合もあるようです。これとはんたいに会社がもっといてほしいと言っても、ほかの仕事を始めたいからと言って、会社をやめてしまう20代の社員もいるそうです。一度会社に入ったら定年までその会社で働くという*終身雇用の制度は*くずれはじめているようです。

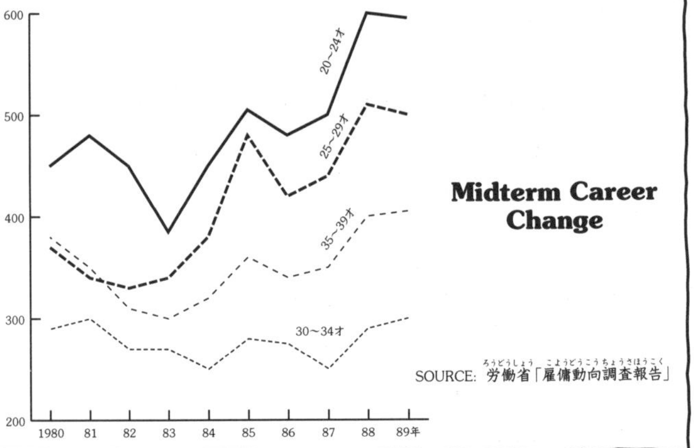

退職金　*severance pay, golden handshake*
業績　*(company) results*
すすめる　*encourage*
終身雇用　*lifetime employment*
くずれはじめる　*begin to collapse*

① 日本では、終身雇用の制度は変わってきていますか。
② 定年の前に会社をやめる人はふえてきていますか、へってきていますか。
③ それは、どうしてだと思いますか。
④ 早めに会社をやめた人は、たとえばどんなことを始めますか。

2. Listen to the tape and answer the questions.
① 大田さんは会社をやめて、何をしようと思っていますか。
② 大田さんの会社の退職金のシステムはどうかわりましたか。

3. Now it's your turn to talk. Discuss the following.
① あなたは大田さんの会社の新しい退職金のシステムをどう思いますか。
② あなたは一つの会社に定年まで勤めたほうがいいと思いますか。今の仕事よりいい仕事が見つかったら、新しい仕事にかえたほうがいいと思いますか。

4. Have you experienced any recent changes with a system or rules?

READING

BUSY新聞

信じられないミス

In a university hospital it actually happened that a nurse mixed up two patients when she brought them to the operating theater and that the doctor—despite thinking something was odd—nonetheless proceeded with the operation as planned. There were any number of stages at which patient-details had to be confirmed, but somehow they all failed.

父は*心臓の具合が悪かったのですが、もう一度元気になりたいと思い*手術を受けることにしました。手術を受ける日の朝、担当の看護婦が父を部屋まで呼びに来ました。父が*ストレッチャーに乗って部屋の外に出ると、もう一台ストレッチャーがありました。別の*患者のKさんが乗っていました。看護婦は一人で父とKさんのストレッチャーを押して*手術室の前まで運んで行きました。病院の*決まりでは、そこで患者と*カルテを確認してから手術室の看護婦に*引きわたすことになっていました。それが、どうしてこういう間違いが起きたのかわからないのですが、父とKさんは手術室に運ばれたとき*入れかわってしまったのです。Kさんも父と同じ時間にとなりの手術室で*肺の手術を受けることになっていました。二人は年齢も同じぐらいで顔も体も*似ていたそうです。

間違った手術室に運ばれた二人の患者に、医者はカルテに書いてある名前を呼びながら*麻酔をかけました。そして手術が始まってから、初めてカルテと病気のようすが違うことに気がつきました。変だと思ったらしいのですが、途中でやめずに最後まで手術を続けました。二人の患者は悪くない心臓と肺を切られて、今*集中治療室に入っています。看護婦も医者も病気は見ても、患者のことは見ていなかったのでしょうか。今でも、信じられません。

心臓	*heart*	引きわたす	*hand over*
手術	*operation*	入れかわる	*be mixed up*
ストレッチャー	*stretcher, trolley*	肺	*lungs*
患者	*patient*	似ている	*be alike*
手術室	*operating theater*	麻酔をかける	*anesthetize*
決まり	*regulation*	集中治療室	*intensive care (unit)*
カルテ	*medical chart*		

QUESTIONS

1. 二人の患者はいつ入れかわってしまったのですか。

2. このような間違いを防ぐにはどうしたらいいと思いますか。

BUSY NEWS

An Unbelievable Mistake

My father had a bad heart, and, in an effort to be cured, decided to have an operation. On the morning he was to have the operation, the nurse in charge came up to my father's room to call him. He was moved onto a trolley and taken out of his room where there was another trolley, on which, it seems, there was another patient, K, lying. The nurse took my father and the other patient to just outside the operating theater by herself. According to hospital regulations she then had to check the patients and their medical charts before handing them over to the operating theater nurse. Given that, I cannot understand how on earth a mistake of this kind occurred, but when my father and the other male patient, K, were brought into the operating theater, they got mixed up. K was due to have a lung operation at the same time as my father in the adjacent operating theater. They were both about the same age and they looked alike, with similar physiques.

As the doctor read out the names of the patients from the medical charts of the two patients who had been brought into the wrong operating theaters, anesthetic was administered. Then, only once the operation had begun, did the doctor notice for the first time that the actual characteristics of the condition and the notes on the chart did not match. The doctor thought it strange, but nonetheless proceeded with the operation until it was complete. Both patients had their healthy heart and lungs respectively cut into and are both now in intensive care. Could it be that the nurses and doctors looked at the disease, but never actually looked at the individual patients? Even now I still can't believe it!

L E S S O N

16 Fast Asleep on the Sofa With His Clothes Still on

SENTENCE PATTERN 1

〜たまま

田中さんはつかれているようです。ソファーで洋服を着たままねています。

Mr. Tanaka must be exhausted. He's fast asleep on the sofa with his clothes still on.

"Tonight's late night at the Lincoln Center Ballet performance will be 'Sleeping Beauty.'"

Have you ever awoken in the morning, surprised to find that you had been so tired the night before as to fall asleep without switching off the lights and TV, or even without getting changed into your pajamas?

PRACTICE

I

Have you ever experienced any of the following? Check the statements that apply to you.

Odd Experiences

- ❑ 車のエンジンをかけたまま、外に出て、ドアを*ロックしたことがある。
- ❑ *パジャマを着たまま、洋服を着たことがある。
- ❑ テレビをつけたまま、朝までねていたことがある。
- ❑ *ネームカードをつけたまま、パーティーから帰ってきたことがある。
- ❑ クリーニング屋の*タグやねだんのタグを洋服につけたまま、出かけたことがある。

- ❑ 雨がやんでいるのに、かさを*さしたまま、あるいていたことがある。

- ❑ *ポケットにお金を入れたまま、洗濯したことがある。
- ❑ 時計をしたまま、おふろに入ったことがある。
- ❑ カメラの*キャップをしたまま、写真をとったことがある。

- ❑ 電車の中で立ったまま、ねたことがある。

ロックする *lock*	かさをさす *open an umbrella*
パジャマ *pajamas*	ポケット *pocket*
ネームカード *name tag*	キャップ *(lens) cover / cap*
タグ *(price) tag*	

PRACTICE

II

1. Listen to the tape while following the pictures below. Write the missing parts ①, ②, and ③ in the spaces provided.

2. Practice the dialogue while listening to the tape. Take special care with your pronunciation and speak at the same speed as the tape.

① ______________________________

② ______________________________

③ ______________________________

SENTENCE PATTERN 2

Plain imperatives

A：火事(かじ)だ！にげろ！　Fire! Fire! Run for your lives!
B：エレベーターは使(つか)うな！　Don't use the elevators!

PRACTICE

I

1. Study the plain imperative forms in the table below.

	PLAIN FORM		AFFIRMATIVE		NEGATIVE
R I	行(い)く	→	行け	・	行くな
R II	食(た)べる	→	食べろ	・	食べるな
Irr	する	→	しろ	・	するな
	来(く)る	→	来(こ)い	・	来るな

2. Choose the most appropriate verb from the list at the bottom of the page and write its correct form in the parentheses.

① (　　　　　)

② (　　　　　)

③ (　　　　　)

④ (　　　　　)

⑤ (　　　　　)

⑥ (　　　　　)

動(うご)く　がんばる　火(ひ)をけす　外(そと)に出(で)る　急(いそ)ぐ　あわてる

PRACTICE

II

You are Mr. Takuya Sato. Recently you have had three conversations with your doctor, your boss, and your father. Listen to the tape and fill in the blanks with a plain imperative expression as shown in the example.

ex. Tell Yoshida what the doctor said.

吉田：	おつかれさまでした。まあ、ビールでもいっぱいどうですか。
佐藤：	すみません。医者にまださけを飲むなと言われているんです。

① Tell Bijii-san what your boss said.

ビジー：	佐藤さん、今度のプロジェクトのたんとう者だそうですね。
佐藤：	ええ、初めてなので、ちょっと心配なんですが、部長に_______ って言われているし、せいこうさせたいです。
ビジー：	がんばってください。

② Tell Bijii-san what your father said.

たくや：	おとといい、父から電話があったんです。
ビジー：	お父さんは何と言っていたんですか。
たくや：	母の具合が悪いので、日曜日に____________と言っていました。
ビジー：	それはいけませんね。

SENTENCE PATTERN 3

～とおりに

9時になりました。まだみなさんそろっていないようですが、予定どおりに始めさせていただきます。

It's nine o'clock now. Although we still seem to be missing a few people, I would like you to let me begin as scheduled.

PRACTICE

Fill in the blanks with the underlined expression and either とおりに or どおりに as shown in the example.

ex.

A：プロジェクトの計画は*うまくすすんでいますか。

B：ええ、計画どおりにすすんでいます。

①

A：見積書をいただいたんですが、もうすこし安くなりませんか。

B：すみません。________________お願いしたいんですが……。

②

A：また、このパソコン動かなくなってしまったんですが。

B：マニュアルに直し方が書いてありますよ。

A：________________やってみたんですが、だめなんです。

③

A：今度のプレゼンテーションがちょっと心配なんです。

B：ずっと練習していたんだから、________________やれば、うまくいきますよ。

うまくすすむ　*make good progress*

Communication

1. Messrs. A and B, junior managers at ABC, Inc., are talking about their underlings. Mr. A seems to be having some problems. Listen to the tape and make notes in the table below. Use your notes to talk about their underlings.

山田	
町田	
木村	
小川	

2. Read the following sentences. Check the statements that describe someone you know. Talk about your experiences.

Do you know somebody like that?

- ❑ 私が仕事中なのに、マニュアルを読まないで、パソコンの使い方を教えろと言う上司
- ❑ 私が飲みたくないのに、おさけを飲めと言う上司
- ❑ お客様と仕事で問題があったらすぐ話せと言っているのに、問題が大きくなってから話す部下
- ❑ お客様を待たせたまま社内の人と話している受付の人
- ❑ 出したらしまえと言っているのに、言われたとおりにしない子ども
- ❑ テレビつけたまま*長電話をしているおっと／つま
- ❑ ぬいだ洋服をそのままにして片付けないおっと／つま
- ❑ 夜ピアノをひくな、静かにしろとうるさく言う管理人

長電話 *on the phone for a long time*

READING

BUSY新聞

*122対0

The National High School Baseball Competition, in which more than 4,000 Japanese high schools take part, has a long history. It is very popular and is broadcast on consecutive days on TV and radio. There is a lot of drama in the games, and this is the story of one such dramatic episode.

野球の試合で*一〇点以上の点が入ることはあまり多くないが、高校生の野球大会で「一二二対〇」という*ワンサイドゲームがあった。三人の*ピッチャーが「いったい、いつになったら終わるんだ。もうこれ以上*打たないでくれ」と思いながら*投げたボールの数は全部で四七五。約四時間もの試合の間、見ていた人達は「がんばれ」「打て」「あきらめるな」と休まずに*応援を続けた。相手チームも、「*気をぬくのは失礼だ」と思い最後までがんばった。もちろん*審判か*負けている方のチームがやめると言えば、もっと早く試合を終わりにすることもできた。しかし「みんなが応援してくれている。最後まで試合を続けたい」と言うピッチャーに*監督はなかなか「やめろ」と言えなかったようだ。

このようなワンサイドゲームになったとき、アメリカでは早めにやめるのがふつうだそうだ。最後まで続けるのは時間がもったいないし、負けている相手の*プライドを大切にするからだと聞いた。選手たちの健康も考えて早めにやめたほうがよいのか、それともワンサイドゲームになっても最後まで続けるほうがよいのか難しい問題だ。

122対0	*122 to 0*	応援	*support*
10点	*10 runs*	気をぬく	*relax*
ワンサイドゲーム	*one-sided game*	審判	*umpire*
ピッチャー	*pitcher*	負ける	*lose*
打つ	*hit*	監督	*coach*
投げたボールの数	*pitch count*	プライド	*self-respect*

QUESTIONS

1. どうして監督は「122対0」のワンサイドゲームになるまで試合を続けたのですか。

2. あなたはこのような場合、どうしたらいいと思いますか。

122 to O

In a baseball game it is unusual for more than ten runs to be scored, but once in the National High School Baseball Competition there was a one-sided game that ended with a score of 122 to zero. As the three pitchers asked themselves when their ordeal would end, and prayed that the batters wouldn't hit any more runs, the total number of pitches hurled reached 475. And in the course of an approximately four-hour match, the spectators kept up their support, urging the team to fight on, to hit the ball, and not to give up. The opposing team also, thinking that to scamp would be disrespectful, kept going till the end. Of course, if the umpire or the losing team decided to pack it in, the game could have ended a great deal earlier. The coach, however, couldn't find it in his heart to tell the pitchers to stop when they told him how enthusiastically everyone was supporting them and how they wanted to continue the game to its end.

When a game has become as one-sided as this, in America it is normal to stop the game early. To continue till the end is merely a waste of time, and there's also the issue of not damaging the self-respect of the losing team. It is a difficult question whether it might be better to finish the game early for the sake of the players' health or if one should continue, even if the game has become hopelessly one-sided.

CHECK 4

1. Choose the correct expression from the alternatives provided in parentheses.

（レストランの困ったお客）

リンダ：　お待たせしてすみません。ちょうどうちを出ようと①（するとき／したとき）電話がかかってきて……。

まり子：　どうしたんだろうって、ちょっと心配したわ。場所はすぐわかった？

リンダ：　このへんは前に一度来たことがあって、道を②（覚えていた／思い出していた）のでまよわなかったわ。

まり子：　そう、よかった。ところで、夏休みはどうするの。

リンダ：　主人ともそうだんして、今年は９月に３週間休みをとる③（ことになった／ことにした）ので東京にいるわ。

まり子：　えっ、何て言ったの？よくわからなかったわ。ちょっと、見て！あそこのテーブルの人、料理が目の前に来ている④（とき／のに）さっきからずっと*けいたい電話で話しているのよ。このごろ、レストランの中でも食事を⑤（したまま／しながら）電話する人がいるのね。

リンダ：　レストランの中で電話をするのはやめてもらいたいわねえ。

まり子：　そうよ。食事の⑥（うちに／途中で）電話をするなんて、マナーの問題として⑦（ぜったいに／必ず）他のお客さんにも失礼よ。こういうことはレストランの人が注意をしてくれなければ困るわ。レストランの人は⑧（いったい／ぜったい）何をしているのかしら。

リンダ：　本当、まり子さんの言う⑨（まま／通り）よ。

まり子：　この店、注文もなかなかとりに来ないし、⑩（さっそく／もう）出ましょう。この近くに知っている店があるので、そっちに行きましょう。

リンダ：　そうね。込んでいる時間だけど、席があるかしら。

まり子：　けいたい電話を持っているわ。聞いてみましょうか。

リンダ：　えっ、？？？

けいたい電話　*mobile phone*

2. Fill in the blanks with the word in parentheses and either のに or ても as shown in the example.

ex. (並ぶ)

A：コンサートの切符を買おうと思って、きのう３時間も並んだのに買えませんでした。明日の朝５時ぐらいから並べば買えるでしょうか。

B：予約でほとんど売り切れているそうですから、５時から並んでも買えないと思いますよ。

① (聞く)

A：田中さんからご自宅の電話番号を＿＿＿＿＿、メモをなくしてしまいました。住所がわからないんですが、電話の*番号案内に聞いたらわかるでしょうか。

B：住所がわからないんでしたら、番号案内に＿＿＿＿＿だめですよ。

② (不便な)

A：私は＿＿＿＿＿、かんきょうがいいところに住みたいな。

B：今でも＿＿＿＿＿、もっと不便なところに住むつもり？

③ (安い)

A：先週のバーゲン、あんなに＿＿＿＿＿何も買わなかったんですか。

B：ええ、＿＿＿＿＿気に入ったものがなければ買いたくないですからね。

④ (日本語の先生)

A：Nさんは＿＿＿＿漢字をときどき間違えるんですよ。

B：*神様ではないんですから、＿＿＿＿うっかり間違えることはあると思いますよ。

番号案内　*information desk*
神様　*God*

17 A Maneki-Neko Is Put by The Door to Attract Business

SENTENCE PATTERN 1

～ように

これは「招きねこ」です。お客さんが来るように、店の入り口に置いてあります。

This is a "maneki-neko." It's placed at a store entrance to bring in customers.

お守り

Available from Shinto shrines and Buddhist temples, a charm or amulet allegedly offers the owner protection from misfortune or danger, and is also believed to bring good health and success.

招きねこ

Displayed at the entrance of a restaurant or bar, a *maneki-neko*—an ornament in the shape of a sitting cat with a raised paw—is believed to attract a lively trade and encourage business success.

千羽鶴

A string of one thousand folded-paper cranes is often made to pray for someone's recovery, success, or victory.

てるてるぼうず

With a spherical head and flared skirt, this paper or cloth doll is hung outside in hope that fine weather will soon grace the skies.

It is impossible, of course, to wield absolute and total control over everything that happens in life. Sometimes people feel the need to put their faith into something special for their prayers, hopes, or wishes to be granted. What superstitions are there in your country?

PRACTICE

I

1. Bijii-san has five effective habits for successful living. Check the things that you also do.

Bijii's Five Effective Habits

- ❏ 朝起きたら、目がさめるように、冬でもつめたいシャワーをあびる。
- ❏ 朝出かける前に、その日の予定を間違えないように、かならず手帳をかくにんする。
- ❏ 電話で伝言をたのまれたときは、わすれないようにメモに書いておく。
- ❏ 自分の仕事のスケジュールが同僚にもわかるように、スケジュールを知らせておく。
- ❏ ねる前に１日のつかれがとれるようにゆっくりおふろに入る。

2. With reference to the previous page, fill in the blanks using ～ように as shown in the example.

ex.

A：何を持っているんですか。

B：「おまもり」です。事故や悪いことに*あわないように持っているんです。

①

A：たくさん*つるを*おっているんですね。

B：ええ、友だちのけがが____________________「せんばづる」をおっているんです。

②

A：何を作っているんですか。

B：「てるてるぼうず」です。明日ハイキングに行くので、______________作っているんです。

(～に) あう *meet with (disaster, accident, etc.)*
つる *Japanese crane*
おる *fold*

PRACTICE

II

1. Read the following passages and answer the questions.

① レストランやお店で「招きねこ」という*置物を見たことがありますか。日本では「招きねこ」には人を*よぶ力があると言われています。いろいろな店でお客さんに大勢来てもらえるように*レジの近くによく置いてあります。最近、外国人の間でも人気があり、国に帰るときおみやげに持って帰る人が多いそうです。

置物 *ornament*
よぶ *invite, attract*
レジ *cash register, till*

(a) 「招きねこ」にはどんな力がありますか。
(b) レストランにはどうして「招きねこ」が置いてあるのですか。

② *「おせち料理」という特別な料理を知っていますか。「おせち料理」は新しくむかえた1年を元気にすごせるように正月の元旦から三日まで食べる料理です。年の初めから食事のじゅんびをしなくてもいいようにおおみそかまでに作っておきます。最近は*以前ほど「おせち料理」を自分で作らなくなって、デパートやレストランで買う人もふえてきたようです。

おせち料理 *special New Year food* (see BACKGROUND INFO)
以前ほど〜ない *... not as much as before*

(a) 「おせち料理」はいつ食べる料理ですか。
(b) どうしておおみそかまでに作っておくのですか。

BACKGROUND INFO
Osechi cooking was originally food which was prepared and offered to the gods as part of the New Year celebrations. The cooking was done on the last days of the passing year and packed into *jubako* (special lacquered boxes which can be stacked on top of each other). The food is cooked in such a way that it keeps for the period of New Year celebrations, so there is no need to do any cooking during the actual celebrations. Recently, it is common to have Western-style *osechi* and hors d'oeuvre style *osechi* in addition to the more traditional recipes. In many families the *osechi* is bought at restaurants and department stores and not cooked at home.

2. Now it's your turn to talk. Talk about any special food or things for special occasions in your country.

SENTENCE PATTERN 2

～ために

インターネットを利用するとき、コンピューター*ウィルスは大きい問題です。新しいウィルスの*ワクチンを開発するために、多くのエンジニアたちが研究を続けています。

Computer viruses on the Internet are a major problem. Many engineers are engaged in ongoing research to develop vaccines for new viruses.

ウィルス *virus*
ワクチン *vaccine*

PRACTICE

I

1. Make sentences by matching the statements on the left with those on the right as shown in the example.

ex. かんきょうほごのために • — • リサイクル運動に協力しています。(c)

① けんこうのために •
② ビザをもらうために •
③ 日本語のうたをおぼえるために •
④ 中国で仕事をするために •
⑤ マラソン大会に出るために •

• 毎日走っています。 (a)
• 中国語の勉強を始めました。(b)
• リサイクル運動に協力しています。 (c)
• 大使館に行かなければなりません。 (d)
• できるだけ体にいいものを食べるようにしています。 (e)
• 毎晩カラオケに行って練習しています。 (f)

2. Fill in the blanks as shown in the example.

ex. 友だちに会うために、日本に来ました。

① ＿＿＿＿＿＿＿＿＿＿＿＿ために、日本に来ました。

② ＿＿＿＿＿＿＿＿＿＿＿＿ために、お金をためました。

③ ＿＿＿＿＿＿＿＿＿＿＿＿ために、＿＿＿＿＿＿＿＿＿＿＿＿。

PRACTICE

II

1. Young people from around the world were asked about their professional objectives. Study the graph and answer the questions.

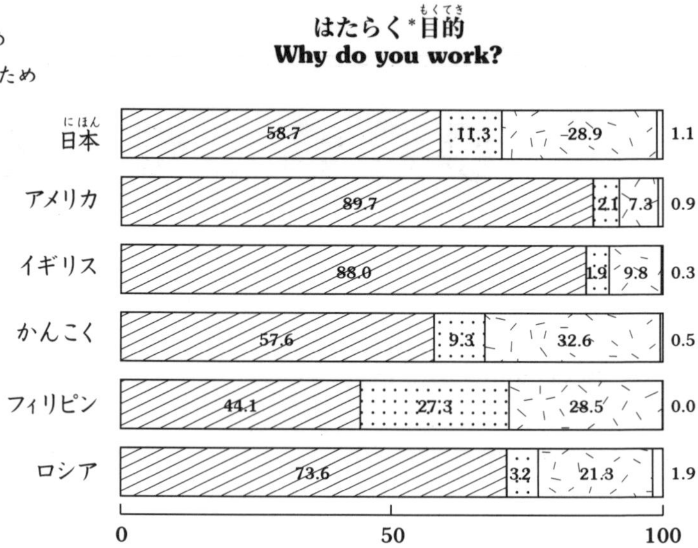

目的　*objective*
収入をえる　*receive a salary*
能力をいかす　*make use of one's skills*

① 六か国全体で、何のために働いている人が一番多いですか。

② いい社会をつくるために働いている人は、どこの国の人が一番多いですか。

2. Read the following. Who do you agree with?

あなたは何のために働いていますか。
Why do you work?

A：私は収入をえるために働いています。お金がなければいいアパートに住めないし、旅行もできないし、友だちとあそびに行くこともできません。

B：私はいい社会をつくるために働いています。大人になったら社会にたいして*せきにんがあると思います。

C：私は自分の能力をいかすために働いています。やりがいのある仕事ができれば毎日楽しいと思います。

3. Now it's your turn to talk. Why do you work?

せきにん　*responsibility*

PRACTICE

III

Fill in the blanks with either ように or ために.

① 旅行中パスポートやお金をとられると大変です。私はパスポートやお金をとられない＿＿＿＿＿、ホテルの金庫に入れておきます。

②
A：*やっと*グライダーの*ライセンスをとることができました。今度はグライダーを買う (a)＿＿＿＿＿＿、お金をためなければなりません。
B：自分でグライダーも買うんですか。
A：借りることもできますが、いつでも好きなときにとべる (b)＿＿＿＿＿、自分のグライダーを買いたいんですよ。

③ 知らない場所で人と会う時は心配です。約束の時間に遅れない＿＿＿＿＿、いつも少し早目に家を出るようにしています。

④
A：また、新しいモデルを出すんですか。３か月前に*モデルチェンジをしたばかりなのに。
B：*しょうひ者に新しいものを買わせる (a)＿＿＿＿＿、どんどん*新製品を出さなければならないんですよ。
A：それはちょっと古い*考えではありませんか。今はみんなかんきょうほごの (b)＿＿＿＿＿＿＿＿、使えるものはなるべく長く使おうという考えになっていると思いますが …… 。

⑤（スーパーで）
A：ええと、何を買うのかわすれてしまいました。
B：わすれない＿＿＿＿＿、メモに書いておくといいですよ。
A：ええ、そう思って書いたんですが、そのメモを持ってくるのをわすれてしまったんですよ。

やっと *at last, finally*
グライダー *glider*
ライセンス *permit, license*
モデルチェンジ *model change*
しょうひ者 *consumer*
新製品 *new product*
考え *way of thinking*

SENTENCE PATTERN 3

～れる～られる（敬語(けいご)）

インタビューアー：　ちょっとうかがいます。1年(ねん)に何日(なんにち)ぐらい休(やす)みをとられますか。

INTERVIEWER:　I'd like to ask you a question. How many days do you take off a year?

通行人(つうこうにん)：　10日(か)ぐらいかな。

PASSERBY:　About ten days, I think.

PRACTICE

I

1. Write the honorific form for each of the verbs below as shown in the examples.

Regular I	
ex. 行(い)く	行かれる
① 買(か)う	
② 読(よ)む	
③ 会(あ)う	
④ 話(はな)す	
⑤ とる	

Regular II	
ex. 出(で)かける	出かけられる
⑥ 出る	
⑦ 決(き)める	
⑧ 続(つづ)ける	
⑨ 集(あつ)める	
⑩ とめる	

Irregular	
ex. する	される
⑪ 説明(せつめい)する	
⑫ 外出(がいしゅつ)する	
⑬ あいさつする	
ex. 来(く)る	来(こ)られる
⑭ 持(も)って来る	

PRACTICE

II

1. What meaning does the ～られる form have in the sentences below? Select A, B, or C as shown in the example.

A　スミスさん、どちらにお車(くるま)をとめられましたか。　(RESPECT)

B　スミスさんは家(いえ)の前(まえ)に車をとめられて、困(こま)っています。　(PASSIVE)

C　スミスさんの家の前に車がとめられます。　(POTENTIAL)

ex.　(A)　この本(ほん)を読(よ)まれたんですか。いかがでしたか。

①　(　)　今朝(けさ)はいつもの時間(じかん)に起(お)きられなくて、会社(かいしゃ)に遅(おく)れてしまいました。

②　(　)　田中部長(たなかぶちょう)はもうすぐ来(こ)られると思(おも)いますから、そろそろ始(はじ)めましょう。

③　(　)　手伝(てつだ)ってもらいたいんですが、あした8時(じ)までに来られますか。

④　(　)　グリーンさんは京都(きょうと)でご家族(かぞく)におみやげを買(か)われました。

⑤　(　)　ほしかったソファーをほかの人(ひと)に買われてしまいました。

⑥　(　)　グリーンさんがご自分(じぶん)でその手紙(てがみ)をすてられたんです。

⑦　(　)　ここにメモを置(お)いておいたのに、だれかにすてられてしまったようです。

⑧　(　)　これは大切(たいせつ)な思(おも)い出(で)の手紙なので、すてられません。

2. Listen to the tape and answer the questions.

①

(a)　インタビューされている人は夏休(なつやす)みをどのようにすごすと言(い)っていますか。

(b)　海外(かいがい)と国内(こくない)とどちらに行(い)くと言っていますか。

②

(a)　インタビューされている人は夏休みをどのようにすごすと言っていますか。

(b)　海外と国内とどちらに行くと言っていますか。

③

(a)　カーターさんはどのぐらい日本(にほん)にいましたか。

(b)　カーターさんは日本でどんなことをしましたか。

Communication

1. Listen to the tape and answer the questions.

① 木村さんはどんなボランティアをしていますか。
② 木村さんはどうしてそのボランティアを始めたんですか。
③ 木村さんの友だちは仕事をしていますか。
④ 木村さんの友だちは英語を教えるとき、どんな努力をしていますか。

2. Read the following dialogue and underline all the honorific expressions.

インタビューアー：木村さん、今日はおいそがしいところお時間をとっていただきまして、ありがとうございました。

木村：いいえ、おやくにたちますかどうか。

インタビューアー：さっそくですが、木村さんはボランティアをされているとお聞きしましたが。

木村：ええ、*点字のボランティアをしております。

インタビューアー：点字といいますと、目の見えない方のために作られた文字のことですね。

木村：はい、そうです。目の見えない方がさわって読むことができるんです。

インタビューアー：どうして点字のボランティアを始めようと思われたんですか。

木村：じつは、友だちが急に目が見えなくなる病気になってしまったんです。目が見えないのに、働くということの大変さを近くで見て、何かできることはないかと考えました。

インタビューアー：そうですか。その方は今、何をされているんですか。

木村：友だちはまだ学校で英語を教えています。授業中困らないように、テキストを全部おぼえていくそうです。それを聞いて、私も友だちのために、何かしたいと思ったんです。

インタビューアー：よくわかります。今日はとてもいいお話しを聞かせていただき、ありがとうございました。

*点字　*braille*

3. Talk about any volunteer work that you have been involved in.

BUSY新聞

「たまに入ろう、大きなお風呂」

From time immemorial the Japanese have been crazy about baths. The *sento*, the public bath at the street corner, was a social meeting place. But because nearly every house now has its own bath, the number of people going to *sentos* has dropped drastically. Facing financial difficulties, bath managers from all over Japan have created an advertising slogan and are vigorously promoting the merits of the public bath.

*銭湯の大きな*湯船に肩まで入って手足を*伸ばすと、とても幸せな気分になります。そんなとき、日本人に生まれて良かったと思われる方も多いでしょう。しかし今はどこのお宅にもお風呂がありますから、銭湯を利用されるお客様は大変少なくなってしまいました。そこで、私たち銭湯の*経営者は銭湯の良さを皆様にもっと知っていただくために「たまに入ろう、大きなお風呂」という*キャッチフレーズを作りました。

銭湯ではいろいろな人といっしょに湯船に入りますから、湯船に水を入れたり体を洗うために*お湯を流したりするとき、必ずまわりの人に「水を入れてもいいですか」とか「流してもいいですか」と*声をかけます。また、みんなで気持ち良く入るためにはお風呂のお湯が汚れないように一人一人が気をつけなければなりません。銭湯はこのような*マナーを子どもたちに教えるいいチャンスです。

自宅の風呂では一人が出るとお湯を捨ててしまうご*家庭もあるようですが、もったいないと思います。銭湯は地球の環境を守るためにもがんばっています。それに、何と言ってもお風呂の中ではみんな*裸ですから平等です。名刺を持って風呂に入られる方はいないでしょう。銭湯ではみんながのんびりできるのです。どうぞ、一人でも多くの方が銭湯に来てくださるようお待ちしています。

お風呂に入る *take a bath*	湯を流す *run hot water*
銭湯 *public bath*	声をかける *say something*
湯船 *bathtub*	マナー *manners*
伸ばす *stretch*	家庭 *family*
経営者 *the management*	裸 *be naked*
キャッチフレーズ *slogan*	

QUESTIONS

1. この銭湯の経営者は、銭湯のよさについてどんなことを言っていますか。
2. あなたの国のお風呂のようすについて話してください。

BUSY NEWS

"Take a Big Bath from Time to Time"

When you get into the big bathtub at the *sento*, right in up to your shoulders, and you stretch your arms and legs, you feel wonderful. In fact, at such moments there must be a lot of people who think to themselves, "I was lucky to be born Japanese!" But now, since every house has its own bath, the number of customers at *sentos* has fallen dramatically. That is why we, the management, have created the slogan "Take a Big Bath from Time to Time" in order to make everyone aware of the merits of the public bath.

Since at the *sento* you get into the tub with other people, when you pour cold water into the hot tub or run the hot water in order to wash yourself, you always say to the people nearest you, "May I add cold water?" or "Is it alright if I run the water?" Also, everyone has to take care not to make the bathwater dirty so that the bath can be enjoyed by everyone. In this way the public bath provides a good opportunity for teaching manners and etiquette to children.

Moreover, while there are families that throw out the bath water after only one person has had a bath, we think this is very wasteful. In this way, public baths are making efforts to be environmentally responsible. In addition, once in the bath, everyone—by virtue of being naked—is completely equal. I don't think anyone climbs into the bath clutching his business card! In the public bath anyone and everyone can really and truly relax. Please come! We are looking forward to even one new customer coming to visit our *sentos*!

LESSON

18 I'm Starving. Let's Grab A Bite to Eat.

SENTENCE PATTERN 1

Speech levels

女(おんな)1：おなかがすいた。何(なに)か食(た)べない？I'm hungry. Shall we eat?

男(おとこ)1：いいね。何食べる？Sounds great. What do you want?

女2：やきとり食べたいな。I'd love some yakitori.

男2：うん、そうしよう。Great. Let's do it.

Do you use different words or expressions when talking to friends in your language?

PRACTICE

I

1. Paying attention to the underlined parts, read the following family conversation.

今日は日曜日です。家族４人で海に行きます。

母：　おはよう。

花子：　おはよう。あ、おべんとう作ってるの？おいしそう。

母：　そうよ。海で食べようと思って。

父：　おはよう。まだか？たろうは。

母：　まだなの。今日は早く出なきゃならないのに。

父：　ああ。食べたらすぐ出られるように、さっき車の中に持って行くもの入れといたよ。

母：　ありがとう。

たろう：　おはよう。

母：　おはよう。遅いわよ。早くご飯食べちゃって。

花子：　そうよ。早く出かけよう。置いて行くわよ。

たろう：　はい。

2. Change the sentences as shown in the example.

ex.　おべんとう作ってるの？　→　おべんとうを作っているんですか。

① 出なきゃならないのに　→　__________

② 入れといたよ　→　__________

③ 早くご飯食べちゃって　→　__________

④ 早く出かけよう　→　__________

PRACTICE

II

Some friends are talking in a coffee shop. Listen to the tape and write a ○ in the parentheses next to the correct statements.

①

(a) (　) 山田さんはレポートをまだ書いていません。

(b) (　) 山田さんは、レポートを書いてしまいました。

②

(a) (　) れい子さんの会社の*ダイエットヨーグルトは今どこの店でも買うことができます。

(b) (　) れい子さんの会社のダイエットヨーグルトは今どこの店にも売っていません。

③

(a) (　) 加藤さんはプレゼンテーションについて心配していたら、同僚から*自信をもってやるように言われました。

(b) (　) 加藤さんはプレゼンテーションする同僚に自信をもってやるように言いました。

④

(a) (　) 林さんがすることにした仕事は子どもの世話です。

(b) (　) 林さんがすることにした仕事は*ペットの世話です。

ダイエットヨーグルト　*diet yogurt*
自信　*(self-) confidence*
ペット　*pet*

SENTENCE PATTERN 2

~たところ

A：コンサートはもう始(はじ)まってしまいましたか。
　Has the concert already started?

B：いいえ、今(いま)始まるところですから、お急(いそ)ぎください。
　No, it's about to start now, so hurry up.

PRACTICE

I

Look at the photographs and read the following.

きょうは*プロのテニスプレーヤーの*サーブの仕方(しかた)をくわしく説明(せつめい)します。

①

②

③

④

⑤

① 今からサーブするところです。

② ボールを上(あ)げるところです。

③ ボールを上げているところです。

④ *ラケットでボールをうつところです。

⑤ ちょうどうったところです。

プロ　*professional*
サーブ　*serve*
ラケット　*racquet*

PRACTICE

II

1. Think up statements with ～ところ to describe the pictures.

①

②

③

④

⑤

2. Fill in the blanks with a verb chosen from the list below.

> 今日*ロックミュージシャンの「*マック・タイガー」が日本に初めて来ます。*レポーターの人が成田空港で話しています。

レポーター：

① マック・タイガーがのっている飛行機がたった今__________ところです。

② あ！今ドアが__________ところです。

③ マック・タイガーが__________ところです。

④ 手をふりながら、*タラップを__________ところです。

⑤ これからインタビューが__________ところです。

出てくる	開く	始まる	おりる	着く	始める	開ける

ロックミュージシャン *rock musician*
マック・タイガー *Mack Tiger*
レポーター *reporter*
タラップ *landing steps*

Communication

1. Listen to the tape. Mark true statements with a "T" and false statements with an "F."

① 木村さんはそうだんしたいことがあって、大学のときの友だちに会うことにしました。

(a) (　) 木村さんは最近給料があがった。

(b) (　) 木村さんは今度ホンコンへ出張する。

(c) (　) 木村さんは先週*ヘッドハンティングの会社から電話をもらった。

② よう子さんはそうだんしたいことがあって、大学のときの友だちに会うことにしました。

(a) (　) よう子さんはこのあいだ仕事が楽しくなってきたところだと言っていた。

(b) (　) よう子さんの子どものころからのゆめは*ジャズボーカリストになることだった。

(c) (　) よう子さんは*ハリウッドにあそびに行きたいと思っている。

ヘッドハンティング *headhunting*
ジャズボーカリスト *jazz vocalist*
ハリウッド *Hollywood*

2. Now it's your turn to talk. Are there different levels of politeness in your language that change according to the situation or to whom you are speaking to? Do men and women speak differently?

READING

BUSY新聞

*携帯電話

Mobile phones are spreading at a phenomenal rate. As the number of young people who walk about literally inseparable from their phones increases, the cityscape itself also changes. What is it that young people really want from their mobile phones?

先日、電車に乗っていたときのことだ。となりに立っていた若い女性が急にまるで友達といっしょにいるみたいに大きい声で笑いだしたのでおどろいた。携帯電話で話をしていたのだ。

このごろの若い人*にとって携帯電話はかっこいい*ファッションであるとともに、生活に絶対必要なもののようだ。話の内容はたいていの場合たいしたことがない。よく「今、電車。えっ、何?…うるさくて全然聞こえないよ」などと言っているが、電車の中で一番うるさいのは電話で話をしている本人だ。また、これからちょうど電車に乗ろうとしているところなのに「ごめん、たった今、駅おりたところ。もうすぐ着くよ」などと言っているのも聞いたことがある。

今まで、電話は*限られた時間と場所からしかかけられなかった。しかしいつでも、どこからでもかけられる携帯電話は会話の*スタイルを大きく変えた。自分の都合のいいときに、話したい相手とだけ話す。そして、一度電話をかけだすと次々にだれかと話していたくなるらしい。ある*調査によると、高校生がふだん携帯電話で話をする友達は一〇〇人以上もいるそうだ。携帯電話はいつもだれかと*つながっていたいという、若い人たちの気持ちに*ぴったりなのだろう。

携帯電話	*mobile phone*	スタイル	*style, way*
～にとって	*for*	調査	*survey*
ファッション	*fashion*	つながる	*be joined*
限られた	*limited*	ぴったり	*exactly*

QUESTIONS

1. 携帯電話によって会話のスタイルはどのように変わったと言っていますか。

2. あなたは携帯電話が若い人に人気のある理由は何だと思いますか。

BUSY NEWS

Mobile Phones

A few days ago I was on the train and got quite a shock when the girl standing next to me suddenly burst out laughing as if she were with a friend. In fact she was just speaking on her mobile phone.

For young people these days a mobile phone is not just a cool fashion accessory, but something indispensable for their lifestyle. Usually what is actually said on the phone is pretty insignificant. Generally they say things like "Now I'm on the train but I can't hear a thing it's so noisy," when in fact they are making the most noise on the train. Then, even though they're just about to get on the train, I've heard people say, "Sorry, I just got off the train. I'll be there in a minute."

Until now the time and the place where telephone calls could be made was limited. But now mobile phones, which can be used anytime and anywhere, have changed the way people talk to each other. You speak to precisely the person you want to speak to, only when it suits you to speak to them. Then, if you start to call, it seems that you get the itch to go on and talk to the next person and the next. According to a survey, high school students generally speak to over 100 friends on their mobile phones. I suppose mobile phones are exactly what young people want, with their desire to feel joined and connected to other people all the time.

L E S S O N

19 And So That's Why It Had Such Big Teeth

SENTENCE PATTERN 1

~わけです

A：あの歯、大きいですね。何を食べていたんでしょうか。
Those teeth are big. What do you think it used to eat?

B：ほかの*きょうりゅうを食べていたそうですよ。
Presumably, it ate other dinosaurs.

A：なるほど。大きいわけですね。I see. That's why they're so big.

Does your language have a special way of expressing the feeling of having suddenly understood something that was a mystery, as if a fog had just lifted?

きょうりゅう *dinosaur*

PRACTICE

I

1. Listen to the tape while following the pictures below. Write the missing part ① in the space provided.

2. Practice the dialogue while listening to the tape. Take special care with your pronunciation and speak at the same speed as the tape.

① ______________________________

PRACTICE

II

どうしたんでしょう
What could have happened?

STUDENT A

You work at JBP Computers and have been puzzled by the following things recently. You decide to ask Student B, who you think will be able to help you understand what has been going on. Use the dialogue at the bottom of the page as an example.

ex. ビジーさんが最近、楽しそうなのはどうしてだろう。

部長が最近、*ぴりぴりしているのはどうしてだろう。

会社のカフェテリアの料理が急においしくなったのはどうしてだろう。

吉田さんが最近、とてもねむそうなのはどうしてだろう。

STUDENT B

You also work at JBP Computers and have learned the following information from colleagues. Answer Student A's questions. Use the dialogue at the bottom of the page as an example.

本社から*ちょうさの人が来る。

ex. ビジーさんは小林さんとけっこんすることになった。

吉田さんは子どもの*テレビゲームがおもしろくて、夜中までやっている。

最近「レストランローマ」からカフェテリアに新しいシェフが来た。

ex.

A：ビジーさんは最近、楽しそうなんですが、どうしたんでしょう。みんなもどうしたんだろうって、*ふしぎがっているんです。何かあったんでしょうか。

B：ビジーさんなら、小林さんとけっこんすることになったらしいですよ。

A：なるほど。だから、楽しそうなわけですね。

ぴりぴりする　*be nervous, be on one's toes*
ちょうさ　*investigation*
テレビゲーム　*video game*
ふしぎがる　*find mysterious, be puzzled*

SENTENCE PATTERN 2

～というわけです

4と9を使(つか)わないようにしているというわけです。
And this means that we make a point of not using 4 and 9.

PRACTICE

1. Read the following dialogue and answer the questions.

ビジー：　日本(にほん)では4と9はよくない数字(すうじ)だと言(い)われているそうですね。このあいだ、病院(びょういん)に行(い)ったら、4号室(ごうしつ)と9号室がありませんでした。どうしてですか。

先生(せんせい)：　日本で4と9の数字が*きらわれるのは日本語の音(おと)から来(き)ています。4は「shi」と*発音(はつおん)されますから、「死(し)」と同(おな)じ音になります。9は「ku」と発音されますから「苦(くる)しい」の「ku」と同じ音になってしまいます。病院では「死」とか「苦しい」という言葉(ことば)は*タブーなので4と9を使わないようにしているというわけです。

ビジー：　なるほど。そういうわけですか。

きらう　*dislike*
発音する　*pronounce*
死　*death, dying*
苦しい　*pain, agony*
タブー　*taboo, not tolerated*

① 日本ではどんな数字がよくない数字だと言われていますか。

② どうしてその数字がきらわれているのですか。

③ あなたの国(くに)にも同じようにきらわれている数字がありますか。

Communication

1. Talk about the photographs.

① 下の写真の袋はいつどのように使われるか知っていますか。

1

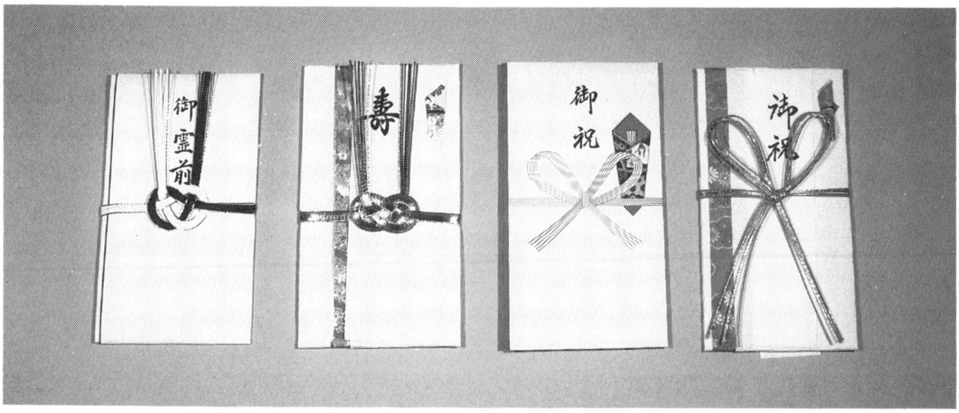

② 下の写真は新入社員が研修中に*地引きあみを引いているところです。どうしてこんなことをしているのかわかりますか。

2

袋　*envelope*
地引きあみを引く　*to pull a dragnet*

STUDENT A

1. Ask Student B about the special money envelopes. When, why, and how are they used?

2. Tell Student B about the new-employee training at McDonald's Japan. Feel free to use your own words when talking, but make sure that you communicate all the information that is supplied.

日本では新しく入社した社員におもしろい研修をさせている会社があります。たとえば日本マクドナルド株式会社では新入社員に地引きあみを引かせる研修をしています。ハンバーガーの会社ですからこの研修は*じっさいの仕事には関係がありません。では何のためにこのよう研修をするのでしょうか。地引きあみはひとりでは引けません。全員でひとつの地引きあみをひかなければなりません。つまり、この研修は協力することの大切さを知るための研修というわけです。

STUDENT B

1. Ask Student A about the aim of the new-employee training at McDonald's Japan.

2. Tell Student B about the special money envelopes. Feel free to use your own words when talking, but make sure that you communicate all the information that is supplied.

日本では、結婚式のとき、*そう式のとき、あかちゃんが生まれたとき、お見まいのときなど、袋にお金を入れておくる習慣があります。この袋にはいろいろなしゅるいがあって、いつ、どんな袋を使うか決まっています。結婚式やそう式のときはリボンの*むすび方が特別で、一回むすんだらかんたんには*ほどけません。つまり、結婚式やそう式は一回だけで、*くり返さないようにしたいというわけです。

じっさいの *actual*
そう式 *funeral*
むすぶ *tie (a knot)*
むすびかた *knot*
ほどく *become loose*
くり返す *repeat*

BUSY新聞

*汗をかいた後のビールがおいしいわけ

They say that if you have one after finishing a job or after exercise, a well-chilled beer has a wonderfully special taste. Why so?

日本では仕事の帰りやスポーツをした後、人々が集まって飲むのはたいていビールだ。日本人は外国人ほど酒に強くないが、それでも一人で一年間に*大ビン八八本のビールを飲むというからおどろきだ。

仕事やスポーツの後で飲むビールはどうしておいしいのだろうか。これには二つの*理由がある。運動をすることと、汗をかくことだ。運動をすると*脳の中から体の*つかれを忘れさせ、気分をよくする*物質が出てくる。いい気持ちになったところでビールを飲むのだから、おいしいわけである。それからたくさん汗をかくと*血液の中の*水分が減り、もっと水が飲みたくなる。ビールを飲むことはこの体の*欲求を満たすことになるので特別においしいというわけだ。もちろん、ビールでなくてもほかの飲み物でもいい。

専門家の話によると運動や汗をかくのは仕事やスポーツでなくてもよいそうだ。体を動かさなくても、*緊張した後はちゃんと汗をかいているという。ようするに、エキサイトするなら夫婦ゲンカでもいいわけだ。しかし夫婦ゲンカの後でビールを飲んでも、やはりおいしいのかどうか。

汗をかく	*work up a sweat*	物質	*substance*
大ビン	*big bottle (of beer)*	血液	*blood*
理由	*reason*	水分	*water*
脳	*brain*	欲求を満たす	*satisfy a physical desire*
つかれ	*fatigue*	緊張する	*get tense*

QUESTIONS

1. 運動すると脳からどんな物質が出てくるのですか。

2. あなたは夫婦ゲンカの後で飲むビールもおいしいと思いますか。

Busy News

"There's a Reason Why Beer Tastes So Good After You Work Up a Sweat."

In Japan when people get together after work or after sports they generally drink beer. Although the Japanese have a low resistance to alcohol compared to non-Japanese, on average they still consume a surprising 88 big bottles a year.

Why is it that the beer you drink after work or sports should taste so good? There are in fact two reasons. When you exercise, you sweat, and also the brain produces substances that dim your awareness of physical fatigue and make you feel good. Consequently the beer tastes good, because you're drinking it when you're already feeling good. Then again, when you sweat, the water levels in your blood diminish, and you want to consume liquids. By drinking beer you satisfy this physical desire, hence the sense that it tastes particularly good. Of course, it doesn't have to be beer. Any drink would do!

According to specialists, it is quite possible to sweat without taking any exercise or doing any sports, because, if you get tense, your sympathetic nerve will be stimulated and you can sweat without even moving. In short, to get excited and achieve the same results even a marital tiff will do the trick. However, I suspect that even if you have a beer after a quarrel, it may not taste that good ....

20 Akira Kurosawa, Movie Director

クロサワ

Akira Kurosawa, the movie director who made a whole series of masterpieces including *Rashomon, Seven Samurai,* and *Ran* over a fifty-year period was highly regarded abroad as well as in Japan. It is well known that he had a major influence on directors from all over the world, such as Francis Ford Coppolla, George Lucas, and Steven Spielberg.

READING

世界のクロサワ

「黒沢明」という名前は世界でもっともよく知られている日本人の名前かもしれない。一九九八年に八八歳で亡くなるまで映画監督として「羅生門」や「七人の侍」など三〇本の映画を作った。海外でも高い評価を得て多くの賞をもらったが、黒沢の映画の何が世界中の人々を感動させたのだろうか。スケールの大きさ、映像の美しさ、シナリオの面白さ、もちろんこれらも黒沢の映画のすばらしさだろう。

黒沢は完全主義者と言われていた。どんなに小さくてもごまかしや妥協を絶対に認めなかった。「天国と地獄」という映画で新幹線の中から身の代金を落とすシーンがあった。犯人が橋の下でその金が落とされるのを待っているところをカメラで撮っていたが、どうしてもある家の屋根がじゃまになった。すると、黒沢は住んでいる人がいるのにその家の屋根をたのんで壊してしまったそうだ。また、映画の中で使われた薬戸だなの引き出しは、開けられることはなくてもちゃんと中にほんとうの薬が入れてあったという。いくら時間と費用がかかっても、最後まで自分の考えを大切にする黒沢は「天皇」と呼ばれていた。このようにきびしい黒沢の仕事のやり方は映画会社や俳優たちに理解されず、難しい関係になったこともある。

しかしふだんの黒沢はやさしくて、とてもじょう談の好きな人だった。そしてだれよりも映画が好きで、撮影の前の日はまるでピクニックに行く前の子供のようだったそうだ。

黒沢はほんとうに映画を愛し、映画作りを楽しんだ人なのだろう。最後の作品「まあだだよ」の中で年寄りの先生が言っていた。「自分がほんとうに好きなものを見つけてください。見つかったら、その大切なもののために努力しなさい。君たちは、努力したい何かを持っているはず。きっと、それは君たちの心のこもった立派な仕事になるでしょう」。映画こそ黒沢が見つけたほんとうに好きなものだった。その大切な映画のために、黒沢はいっしょうけんめい努力した。そんな黒沢の生き方が世界中の人々を感動させたのではないだろうか。だからこそ、黒沢は「世界のクロサワ」になったのだ。

黒沢明　*Kurosawa Akira*
映画監督　*movie director*
羅生門　Rashomon
七人の侍　Seven Samurai
評価　*high respect*
賞　*prize*
感動する　*be touched*
スケール　*scale*
映像　*image*
シナリオ　*scenario*
完全主義者　*perfectionist*
ごまかし　*trick*
妥協　*compromise*
天国と地獄　Heaven and Earth
身の代金　*ransom money*
シーン　*scene*
犯人　*criminal*
屋根　*roof*
天皇　*emperor*
きびしい　*demanding*
ふだん　*usually*
撮影　*filming*
ピクニック　*picnic*
愛する　*love*
まあだだよ　Madadayo *(no, not yet)*
きっと　*surely*
心のこもる　*sincere*

QUESTIONS

1. この文を書いた人は、映画監督の黒沢明が世界中の人々を感動させた理由は何だと言っていますか。

2. あなたは映画が好きですか。今まで一番感動した映画は何ですか。それは、どんな映画でしたか。

The World-Famous Kurosawa

"Akira Kurosawa" is probably the most famous Japanese name in the world. Until his death in 1998 at the age of 88 Kurosawa had directed some thirty movies including *Rashomon* and *Seven Samurai*. Highly respected abroad, Kurosawa had received many prizes, but what was it about his films which so touched people all over the world? It must have been the marvellousness of his films with their sheer scale, their visual beauty, and the interest of the script.

Kurosawa was said to be a perfectionist who would never accept any compromise, however small. In the movie *Heaven and Earth* there was a scene in which ransom money is dropped from a bullet train. Kurosawa had been filming the criminal waiting under a bridge for money to be dropped, but, no matter what he did, there was a house of which the roof always got in the way. So Kurosawa—even though there was someone actually living in the house at the time—asked permission and knocked the roof down. Then there was also the story that when a medicine chest was used in a film of his, the drawers—even though they were never actually to be opened—had to be filled up with all the appropriate drugs. Kurosawa was nicknamed "The Emperor" because no matter how much time it took, or how much it cost, he would always follow through his ideas without compromise. Kurosawa's demanding and fastidious way of working was sometimes misunderstood, and there was often friction between him and movie companies and actors. However, when he was not working, he was a very good-natured, joke-loving fellow. He loved movies so passionately that the day before shooting started he was like a child about to go on a picnic!

Kurosawa really loved movies, and he really enjoyed making them. In his last work *Madadayo* an old teacher comments "You must find the thing that you really love best. When you find that thing, work hard on it. For you young people there is something out there that you really want to do, really want to work on. When you find it, it will become the basis for some splendid and emotionally-satisfying achievement." For Kurosawa, movies were, of course, the thing that he loved. For his beloved movies, Kurosawa worked like a man possessed, and I suspect it was this way of living his life that so impressed people all around the world. And that's why Kurosawa of Japan became Kurosawa the world-renowned director.

CHECK 5

1. Choose the correct expression from the two alternatives provided in parentheses.

（犬の*クローン）

佐藤：　子どものころ、クローンの話は本で①（たまに／めったに）読んだことがありますが、このごろニュースでよく聞きますね。

ビジー：　ちょうど今、それについて新聞で読んでいた②（とき／ところ）です。自分が飼っている犬のクローンをつくってもらう③（ために／ように）３おく円を研究所にきふした人の話です。

佐藤：　犬のクローンに３おく円も？

ビジー：　④（すごい／ひどい）*金持ちらしいから、そういう人⑤（には／では）３おく円は⑥（たいしたことない／たいしたことある）んじゃないですか。

佐藤：　そうかもしれませんね。ところで、犬のクローンってむずかしいんですか。

ビジー：　ええ、*牛や*ひつじ⑦（ぐらい／ほど）かんたんじゃないらしいですよ。

佐藤：　でも、いろいろな技術がどんどん進んでいますから、近い将来ペットのクローンが安くつくれる時代が来るんでしょうか。ビジーさんのうちの犬のジョンも、クローンをつくってもらったらどうですか？

ビジー：　いやですよ。ジョンのコピーなんて⑧（すっかり／まるで）工場でつくられたものみたいで、いい感じ⑨（がしません／になりません）。

佐藤：　⑩（それで／それに）、地球がペットのコピーでいっぱいになっても困りますからね。

ビジー：　ええ、今でもだいぶこんでいますからねえ。

クローン　*clone*
金持ち　*wealthy person*
牛　*cow*
ひつじ　*sheep*

2. Choose the correct expression from the two alternatives provided in parentheses.

(ホテルで)

グリーン： もしもし、110号室ですが。明日の朝、*ルームサービスをお願いします。

フロント： かしこまりました。110号室のグリーン様ですね。ご注文は？

グリーン： コーヒーとサンドイッチを①（めしあがりたい／いただきたい）んですが。

フロント： 何時に②（もってまいりましょうか／もっていらっしゃいますか)。

グリーン： 6時ごろ、お願いします。それから、今からワイシャツのクリーニングをたのみたいんですが……。

フロント： お客様の③（ご出発／お出発）は何時でしょうか。

グリーン： 7時にはここを出たいと思っているんですが。

フロント： それでは、ただ今、係の④（かた／もの）がすぐにとりに⑤（うかがいます／いらっしゃいます)。ワイシャツは明日の朝、お食事といっしょに⑥（お届けいたします／お届けになります）が⑦（よろしい／けっこう）でしょうか。

グリーン： はい、それで⑧（よろしい／けっこう）です。あっそうそう、今晩*イタリアの*サッカーリーグのゲームを放送すると聞いたんですが、何チャンネルですか。

フロント： ちょっとお待ちください。⑨（お待ちしました／お待たせしました)。7時から5番のチャンネルで⑩（ごらんになれます／お目にかかれます)。

グリーン： どうもありがとう。あれっ、もう10時だ。終わっちゃったよ。

ルームサービス *room service*
イタリア *Italy*
サッカーリーグ *soccer league*

3. In JAPANESE FOR BUSY PEOPLE III you met a number of expressions which used the word よう. Read the examples below and check that you understand their meaning.

LESSON 1

外資系の会社は女性の間で人気があるようです。

あの医者はひょうばんがいいようです。

先月ドイツから来た部長は日本語が上手なようです。

服装はサラリーマンのようです。

みんな若くて、大学生のようなふんいきです。

今日は春のようにあたたかいですね。

毎日、山のように仕事があります。

LESSON 3

酒屋に電話して、ビールを20本もって来るように言ってください。

LESSON 10

新幹線ができてから、東京、大阪間を3時間ほどで行けるようになりました。

日本のサラリーマンは、むかしにくらべると長く休むようになりました。

LESSON 12

なるべく早くれんらくするようにします。

LESSON 14

出かけようとしたとき、電話がかかって来ました。

LESSON 17

やくそくの時間におくれないように、少し早くうちを出ました。

Circle the most appropriate expression from the alternatives given in parentheses.

①

小林：　いつさいふをわすれたのに気がついたんですか。

ビジー：　バスにのってお金を（(a)払おうとしたときなんです(b)払うようにしたときなんです(c)払うようなときなんです）。

②

吉田：　JBPコンピューターの吉田ですが、鈴木さんをお願いします。

取引先：　ただ今、鈴木は出張中で来週の月曜日にもどりますが……。

吉田：　そうですか。じゃ、もどられたらこちらに（(a)電話するようにしてください(b)電話するようにします(c)電話するように伝えてください）。

③

渡辺：　東京の地下鉄は朝のラッシュが大変だと聞いていますが、田中さんは毎日どうしているんですか。

田中：　私ですか。そうですね。なるべくラッシュの前に（(a)うちを出るようです(b)うちを出ようとしています(c)うちを出るようにしています）。

④

加藤：　今日もざんぎょうですか。

中野：　ええ、もうつかれちゃってうちに帰ると（(a)死ぬように(b)死んだように(c)死なないように）ねていますよ。

⑤

吉田夫人：　お仕事をしながら日本語の勉強をずっと続けていらっしゃるそうですね。

ビジー：　はい、最初は大変でしたが、おかげさまで、このごろはかなり（(a)話すようにして(b)話せるようになって(c)話すようになって）毎日が楽しくなりました。

吉田夫人：　それはよかったですね。これからも、がんばってください。

4. In JAPANESE FOR BUSY PEOPLE III you met a number of adverbs which if used correctly can help you add more flavor and nuance to what you want to say in Japanese. Below we have reproduced the example sentences from the text and added a dialogue so that you can check that you understand how each adverb is used correctly in context.

①

ちっとも～ない (LESSON 1)

学生の服装は制服のようで、ちっとも個性的じゃありませんね。

だいぶ (LESSON 10)

新幹線の開通にともなって、サラリーマンの出張のようすもだいぶかわりました。

かなり (LESSON 10)

サラリーマンの中には、転勤をめいじられ、事情によって家族とはなれて生活している人がかなりいます。

大いに (LESSON 10)

新幹線はその後、九州方面、東北方面、そして新潟方面にものび、各地の発展に大いに役立っています。

吉田：新しいお宅を建てていらっしゃるとうかがいましたが、もうだいぶできたんですか。

加藤：そうですねえ。あと３週間ぐらいしたら引越せると思います。でも*予算の関係で最初の設計とはかなりちがったものになってしまいました。

吉田：そうなんですか。でも新しい家は気持ちがいいでしょう。ご家族で大いに楽しんでください。

加藤：いや、*ローンのことを考えるとちっとも楽しくないですよ。ははは。

予算　*budget*
ローン　*loan*

②

めったに～ない (LESSON 8)

作(つく)った米(こめ)をほとんど大名(だいみょう)にとり上(あ)げられて、のうみんはめったに米のご飯(はん)が食(た)べられなかったと言(い)われています。

たまに (LESSON 17)

今(いま)でも、たまに山(やま)にのぼります。

夫(おっと)：	いつも洋服(ようふく)ばかりで、めったに着物(きもの)なんか着ないきみが今日(きょう)はどうしたの？けっこんしきでもあるの？
つま：	あら、私(わたし)でもたまに着物を着ることもあるわ。そんなにへんじゃないでしょ？
夫：	ううん、ちっともへんじゃないよ。とってもすてきだよ。ところで、その着物、見(み)たことがないんだけど前(まえ)に着たことがあったかなあ？
つま：	あれ、*ボーナスで着物を買(か)うってあなたに言わなかったかしら？

ボーナス bonus

③

そろそろ (LESSON 6)

会議は３時からですから<u>そろそろ</u>つくえやいすをならべておいてください。

すぐに (LESSON 12)

夕食の後<u>すぐに</u>勉強を始めるようにしています。

加藤夫人： あら、もう５時だわ。<u>そろそろ</u>失礼いたします。

中野夫人： まだよろしいじゃないですか。お時間、だいじょうぶでしょう？今、コーヒーをいれますからどうぞゆっくりなさってください。

加藤夫人： そうですか。ありがとうございます。じゃあ、コーヒーをいただいたら、<u>すぐに</u>失礼いたします。ところで、奥様、駅前のお米屋さんのおばあさんのことなんですけど、お聞きになりましたか。

（となりの部屋で）

中野太郎： うーん、また長くなりそうだな。

---

④

なるべく (LESSON 2)

今、シーズン中でこんでいますので、なるべく早くごれんらくください。

できるだけ (LESSON 12)

じゃ、外出せずに待っていますから、できるだけ早くお願いします。

ぜったいに (LESSON 14)

ぜったいに遅れないと言ったのに、まだ来ませんね。

かんごふ：	明日、いのけんさがありますから、今晩食事はなるべく８時ごろまでにすませるようにしてください。
ビジー：	何を食べてもいいんですか。
かんごふ：	ええ、何をめしあがってもいいですが、９時をすぎたらできるだけがまんして水も飲まないでください。
ビジー：	ちょっとぐらいなら、ねる前にウィスキーを飲んでもいいですか。飲むとよく眠れるんですよ。
かんごふ：	ぜったいにだめです。

⑤

うっかり (LESSON 5)

あのことをうっかりしゃべっちゃいました。いけなかったんですね。ごめんなさい。

あいにく (LESSON 13)

お送りするつもりでしたが、あいにく車の調子が悪くて失礼いたしました。

A：カナダ旅行のじゅんびはできましたか。

B：ええ、それがパスポートを新しくとるのをうっかりわすれていたんです。

A：すぐ、手続きしたんでしょ？

B：ええ、それがあいにく休みの日で役所が開いていなかったんですよ。間に合わなかったらどうしようかと心配しましたが、今日もらうことができてたすかりました。

A：この前、メキシコに行ったときもそんな話をしていませんでしたか。

B：あれは、トラベラーズチェックでした。

A：このつぎは何でしょうね。

ANSWERS & ENGLISH TRANSLATIONS

LESSON 1

SENTENCE PATTERN 1–1 〜ようです
PRACTICE II

1. ① るすの　ようです
   ② でかけていないようです
   ③ ケーキを　やいているようです

PRACTICE III

1. ① My daughter has seemed a bit strange recently. Suddenly she's become stylish and pretty. On weekends, she often prepares a box lunch for two people before going out. She seems to have found a boyfriend.

   ② Recently, X has seemed a bit strange. He makes a lot of mistakes at work, and he often comes late to meetings. He's borrowed money from many people, and sometimes he gets telephone calls from credit card companies. He seems to be having problems of some kind.

SENTENCE PATTERN 1–2 〜ようです
PRACTICE

① ような　　② ように　　③ (a) よう　(b) ように

SENTENCE PATTERN 2 〜そうです
PRACTICE I

① (a) あった　(b) まだ　わかっていない
② (a) ストだ　(b) とばない
③ (a) きている　(b) わるくなる

2. ① ほっかいどうで　じしんが　ありましたが、くわしいことは　まだ　わかっていない
   ② あしたは　ひこうきがいしゃが　ストなので、ひこうきは　あさから　とばない
   ③ きゅうしゅうの　ちかくに　たいふうが　きているので、てんきは　わるく　なる

PRACTICE II

① (a) にちようびは　やすみだ　(b) 9じから　5じまでだ
② (a) かじだ　(b) 30ぷん　おくれる
③ (a) さむい　(b) あめが　ふる
(c) かさと　コートを　もっていった　ほうがいい

COMMUNICATION 1

2. ①「ドラキュラ」という　はなの　しゃしんです。
   ② にほんごが　わからないんですが、「monkey」って、にほんごで　なんと　いうんですか。
   さるって　えいごで　「monkey」ですか。

3. ① は　*ぞうの　あしの　うらの　しゃしんです。
   ぞうのあしのうら　sole of an elephant's foot

   ② は、おさけを　つくっている　しゃしんです。

COMMUNICATION 2

Student A

The man in photograph ① is a toy doctor. He fixes old and broken toys. These days, if a toy gets broken, many people just buy a new one right away. According to this toy doctor, though, many children still bring him broken toys every day. While there are many different kinds of broken toys, he says that most are high-tech.

Student B

Photograph ② shows a hearing dog. A hearing dog is a dog that helps people who are hard of hearing. Deaf people cannot hear alarm clocks, and they don't know when someone comes to their front door because they cannot hear the doorbell. When that happens, the hearing dog lets its master know that a bell is ringing. Acting as his master's ears is the job of the hearing dog.

LESSON 2

SENTENCE PATTERN 1 〜はずです
PRACTICE I

1. ① とめられる　② はいれる　③ まにあう

2. ① あいている　② ではない　③ しらない

PRACTICE II

1. ① この　ちかくの　はずなんですが。
② ちずに　よると　この　へんに　あるはずなんですが。
③ たしかに　さいふに　いれたはずなんですが。

PRACTICE III

① だれも　いない　② だれも　きていない　③ かないではない

SENTENCE PATTERN 2 〜で
PRACTICE I

① たいふう　② かじ　③ まんいん　④ インフルエンザ

PRACTICE II

1. ① (a) きょうは　かいしゃを　やすむ
(b) かぜで　ねつが　ある

② (a) ずめんを　おくるのが　おくれる
(b) こしょうで　コンピューターが　つかえない

③ (a) きょうじゅうに　とうきょうに　かえれない
(b) たいふうで　ひこうきが　とんでいない

2. ① ぶちょう。こばやしさんから　でんわが　ありました。
かぜで　ねつが　あるので、きょうは　かいしゃを　やすむそうです。

② ぶちょう。ビジーさんから　でんわが　ありました。
こしょうで　コンピューターが　つかえないので、ずめんを　おくるのが　おくれるそうです。

③ ぶちょう。さとうさんから　でんわが　ありました。
たいふうで　ひこうきが　とんでいないので、きょうじゅうに　とうきょうに　かえれないそうです。

COMMUNICATION 1

1. ① (○)

2. ① ばしょは　ぜったい　しっているはずです。　きのう　ちずを　わたしました。
② きょうは　ざんぎょうは　ないはずです。　ひまだと　いっていました。

COMMUNICATION 2

Model Answer

B：いいえ、きのう　でんわで　くると　いっていましたから、くるはずです。
A：ばしょが　わからないのかもしれませんよ。もう　いきませんか。
B：まえに　ここで　あったことが　あるので　わかっているはずです。
A：じゃ、きたくないのかもしれません。もう　いきましょうよ。
B：きのう　でんわで　たのしみにしていると　いっていたから　ぜったいに　くるはずですよ。
もう　すこし　まちましょう。

LESSON 3

SENTENCE PATTERN 1
PRACTICE I

1. Before Leaving Home

・Check whether the lights have been turned off.
・Check whether the answering machine has been set.
・Check whether you have your wallet.
・Check whether your shoes are clean.
・Look in a mirror to check whether your clothes match.

After Leaving Home

・Worry whether you locked the door.
・Worry whether you turned off the air conditioner or heater.
・Worry whether you shut the windows.

2. ① つくれるか　どうか　　② ふえているか　どうか

PRACTICE II

1. ① だれと　とりひきさきを　まわるか
② どこに　あいさつに　いくか
③ どんな　りょうりが　すきか

2. ① どこに　いくか　　② だれに　たのむか

PRACTICE III

① いまから　ホテルの　グレードが　かえられるか　どうか
② ひとりべやを　もうしこむと　どのぐらい　たかくなるか
③ ほけんりょうが　ツアーの　ひように　はいっているか　どうか
④ とうじつ　なんじまでに　くうこうに　いかなければならないか

PRACTICE IV

1. ① Mr. Yoshida: I'm scheduled to go skiing in Hokkaido with my entire family tomorrow. My wife and children have never been to Hokkaido, so they're looking forward to the trip. But the planes haven't been flying for the past three days because of a strike, and I'm a little worried about whether we'll be able to go.

② Mr. Bijii: I'm thinking of taking a Japanese test in December. My teacher says that I should pass because I've studied a lot. But I don't know very many kanji, so I'm a little worried about whether I'll pass.

③ Mr. Sato: Tomorrow I'm going on a business trip to our American branch. Until now I've always gone with our division chief, but this time I have to go alone and give a presentation. This will be the first time I've ever given a presentation, so I'm a little worried about whether I can do a good job.

2. ① (a) かぞくぜんいんで　ほっかいどうに　スキーに　いく　よていです。
(b) みっかまえから　ストで　ひこうきが　とんでいないので、りょこうに　いけるか　どうか しんぱいしています。

② (a) にほんごの　しけんを　うけようと　おもっています。
(b) かんじを　あまり　おぼえていないので、(ごうかくするか　どうか) しんぱいしています。

③ (a) アメリカししゃに　いきます。
(b) プレゼンテーションを　するのは　はじめてなので、(プレゼンテーションが　うまく　できるか どうか) しんぱいしています。

SENTENCE PATTERN 2
PRACTICE

1. ① あしたの　かいぎに　おくれないように
② しゅっちょうの　ひようが　いくら　かかるか　しらべるように
③ おおさかししゃに　つく　じかんを　れんらくするように

2. ① (a) こばやしさんが　ビジーさんに (あした　すこし　はやめに　くるように) つたえます。
(b) ビジーさんが　あした　すこし　はやめに　きます。

② (a) こんどうさんが　ビジーさんに (かいぎの　ひつような　しりょうを　そろえるように) つたえます。
(b) ビジーさんが　かいぎに　ひつような　しりょうを　そろえます。

COMMUNICATION 1

① (a) ○　② (b) ○　③ (a) ○

COMMUNICATION 2

Model Answers

1. ① A：もしもし、〜ですが、さとうさん　おねがいします。
B：さとうさんは　いま　がいしゅつちゅうですが。
A：そうですか。では、もどったら、かいぎは　3じからだと　つたえてください。
B：わかりました。そう　つたえます。

② A：もしもし、〜ですが、さとうさん　おねがいします。
B：さとうさんは　いま　せきを　はずしていますが。
A：そうですか。では、もどったら、かいぎの　しりょうは　もうできているか　どうか　きいてください。
B：わかりました。

③ A：もしもし、〜ですが、さとうさん　おねがいします。
B：さとうさんは　でんわちゅうですが。
A：そうですか。では、でんわが　おわったら、かいぎの　まえに　しりょうが　ひつようなので、2じまでに　とどけるように　つたえてください。
B：わかりました。そう　つたえます。

2. ① A：もしもし、やまだですが、しゅじん／つまを　おねがいします。
B：やまださんは　いま　でんわちゅうですが。
A：そうですか。では、でんわが　おわったら、こどもが　びょうきなので　わたしは　びょういんに　いくと　つたえてください。
B：わかりました。そう　つたえます。

② A：もしもし、やまだですが、しゅじん／つまを　おねがいします。
B：やまださんは　いま　せきを　はずしていますが。
A：そうですか。では、もどったら、しゅじん／つまに　いま　びょういんに　こられるか　どうか　きいてください。
B：わかりました。

③ A：もしもし、やまだですが、しゅじん／つまを　おねがいします。
B：やまださんは　いま　がいしゅつちゅうですが。
A：そうですか。では、もどったら、しゅじん／つまに　かえりに　びょういんに　むかえに　くるように　つたえてください。
B：わかりました。そう　つたえます。

LESSON 4

SENTENCE PATTERN 1　～そうです
PRACTICE II

1. ① はやそう　② はやそう　③ こわそう　④ やさしそう　⑤ かかりそう

PRACTICE III

2. ① さき　② おわり　③ あがり　④ いそがしくなり

PRACTICE IV

1. ① This happened when I went to a company party. The president's speech was so long and boring that I got sleepy. As I listened to it, I had a hard time keeping myself from yawning.

   ② This happened when I went to a classical music concert with a friend. Unfortunately, I had a terrible cold. During the concert, I had a hard time keeping myself from sneezing.

SENTENCE PATTERN 2　～く／にする　～く／になる
PRACTICE

① (a) なりました。 (b) し　(c) なった　(d) しました。　(e) なりました。
② (a) なった　(b) する　(c) なって　(d) なった

SENTENCE PATTERN 3　～らしいです
PRACTICE

① はっぴょうする　② おもしろい　③ かわる

COMMUNICATION

1. ① (a) こんでいる　(b) サッカー　(c) じょせい　(d) ある　(e) おもしろそうだ
② (a) サッカーチームの　サポーターだと　おもっていました。
(b) ひこうきが　キャンセルに　なったので　ゲートの　まえで　ひとが　まっていることが　わかりました。

Check 1

1. あいだ　せんじつ　さっき　ありました　はず　によると　おくれている
そういえば　とどきましたか　たしかに

2. ① うれしそう　ように　なるそう
② ように　おもそう
③ そう　あきらめていたよう　よさそう

LESSON 5

SENTENCE PATTERN 1–A ～てしまいます
PRACTICE I

1. ① なくして ② わすれて ③ しんで

PRACTICE II

1. ① こしょうしてしまったんです ② かかってしまいました ③ おそく なってしまいました
④ おこってしまった ⑤ かぜを ひいてしまった

PRACTICE III

1. ① The other day, I mistook a police car for a taxi. It was dark out and I couldn't see very well. I flagged down a car thinking it was a taxi, but it turned out to be a police car. I was really surprised when a policeman got out of the car.

② The other day, I took the wrong train and ended up an hour late to an appointment. A train was just pulling in when I reached the station platform, so I jumped on. But it was the train going in the opposite direction. I was scheduled to meet my friend outside, so she had to stand there for an hour. It was really inexcusable of me.

SENTENCE PATTERN 1–B ～てしまいました
PRACTICE

① おくって ② よんで ③ のんで

SENTENCE PATTERN 2 ～てみます
PRACTICE I

① (a) うんてんして (b) うんてんして
② (a) すわって (b) すわって

PRACTICE II

1. ① Now that it's springtime, I decided I wanted some new shoes. The other day, when I happened to walk by a shoe store, I noticed some shoes that looked good for walking. They had a nice design, too. When I tried them on, they fitted perfectly. These shoes I'm wearing now are the ones I bought then.

② I've had some free time recently, so I decided to start studying something. When I was reading the newspaper the other day, I noticed an advertisement for an economics seminar that looked useful. The lecturer was well-known. When I went to the seminar, though, it was so boring that I fell asleep.

COMMUNICATION

1. **Problem ①**

The other day when I was watching television, there was a program about Japanese drums. The performance was fantastic and looked like a lot of fun, so I decided that I wanted to try it myself. I decided to get in touch with the group that was performing, so I jotted down their name. I lost the paper, though, and I've forgotten the name of the TV station, so I can't contact the group. What should I do?

Advice a

If I were you, I would look for a newspaper from the day you saw that program. Newspapers carry TV listings. Just check the listings and then call the TV station. You can find newspapers at the library.

Advice b

If I were you, I would look for Japanese drum groups on the Internet. If you can't find the group that you're looking for, contact another drum group and ask them about other organizations. On the Internet, you should be able to find somebody who knows.

Model Answer

わたしが　あなただったら、ほんやに　いって　にほんの　おんがくの　ほんを　さがしてみます。その　グループが　みつからなかったら、その　ほんの　かいしゃに　でんわして　といわせれば　いいと　おもいます。

Problem ②

I have an acquaintance who likes fishing. Whenever he goes fishing, he always brings us fish that he caught. The first time he gave us some fish, I said that everyone in our family likes fish, so ever since he has brought us a lot of fish every week. At first everyone here was happy to eat the fish, but now they don't seem to want to eat it very much. Sometimes I even throw the fish away, though I feel sorry about it. What should I do?

Advice a

Freshly caught fish tastes good and is good for you, so it's too bad that you don't need it. If I were you, I would ask a friend who likes to cook for different ways of preparing fish. You should increase your cooking repertoire. I'm sure your family will then be happy to eat the fish.

Advice b

If I were you, I would give the fish to a friend who likes them. It's wasteful to just throw the fish away. It's hard to get freshly caught fish, so whoever you give them to is sure to be grateful.

Model Answer

わたしが　あなただったら、さかなを　くれるひとに　はっきり　ことわります。ざんねんだけど　いそがしくて　さかなを　りょうり　する　じかんが　ないと　いえば　そのひとは　おこらない　はずです。

LESSON 6

SENTENCE PATTERN 1　～ておきます
PRACTICE I

1. ・I make all my hotel reservations.
   ・I decide what I'm going to see during my trip.
   ・I buy some traveler's checks.
   ・I change some of my country's money into the currency of the country I'll be visiting.
   ・I study the language of the country I'll be visiting.
   ・I read guidebooks to find out about special food and souvenirs of the country I'll be visiting.
   ・If I have friends in the country I'll be visiting, I contact them.
   ・I arrange for a tour guide.
   ・I read a lot about the history of the country I'll be visiting.

2. **Model Answer**

   トラベラーズチェックを　つくっておくと　べんりですよ。

PRACTICE II

1. ① Generally, when people buy new clothes, either they decide before they go to the store what kind of clothes they're going to buy, or they decide after they go to the store. I usually decide what kind of clothes I'm going to buy before I go to the store.
   ② When they have to give a speech at a wedding, some people write out a draft of the speech by the day before the wedding, while others think about the speech only after they arrive at the place where the wedding will be held. If I don't write out what I'm going to say in advance, I have trouble sleeping the night before.

PRACTICE III

1. ① れいぞうこに　いれておいたんです
2. ① かみに　かいておいたんです　　② ノートに　かいておきます

SENTENCE PATTERN 2 〜てあります
PRACTICE I

① ならべて　② しいて

PRACTICE II

① **Model Answers**
・はい、かってみたいと　おもいます。いそがしときや　びょうきのとき　べんりですから。
・いいえ、かってみたいと　おもいません。あまり　おいしくないだろうと　おもいます。

② **Model Answer**
ぎゅうにくが　きれいに　ならべてあります。やさいや　とうふが　きってあります。だしが　よういしてあります。

PRACTICE III

1. ① いまが　あたためてあって、シチューと　サラダが　つくってあるのに　きが　つきました。
② **Model Answers**
・へやが　きれいに　そうじしてあったら、うれしいです。
・ばんごはんが　つくってあったら、うれしいです。

COMMUNICATION

1. ① クリスマスツリーの　したに　おいておきました。
② いいえ、たなかさんと　おくさんです。
③ あかい　はこと　あおい　はこが　おいてありました。
④ あおい　はこに　たろうくんへと　かいてあったので、わかりました。

2. こどもたちへの　プレゼント　／　おい　／　あかい　はこと　あおい　はこ　おい　／　かい　／　ゆうこちゃんへと　かい　／　ねこの　ししゅうが　し

LESSON 7

SENTENCE PATTERN 1 〜ても
PRACTICE I

① (a) あめだったら　(b) あめでも
② (a)（やきゅうをする　ひとが）すくなかったら　(b)（やきゅうをする　ひとが）すくなくても
③ (a) まよったら　(b) まよっても

PRACTICE II

2. Model Answer
わたしは　Cさんの　いけんに　さんせいです。うみの　うえなら　きを　きらなくても　ヘリポートが　つくれるので、いいと　おもいます。

SENTENCE PATTERN 2 〜てほしいです
PRACTICE I

- I miss greenery because there's so little of it. I wish there were more parks.
- I wish people wouldn't smoke in train stations and restaurants.
- I wish people wouldn't tell me that I speak Japanese well.
- Japanese streets are too narrow. I wish they would widen them.
- I cannot stand morning rush hour. I wish they would add more trains.
- I wish people wouldn't use their cell phones on trains and in restaurants.
- All the Japanese people around me speak English, so my Japanese doesn't get any better. I wish they would speak to me in Japanese as much as possible.

PRACTICE II

1. ① There's something I want to say to my company. We don't have enough vacation time, and our salaries are too low. I want them to lengthen our vacations and raise our salaries.

   ② There's something I want to say to the people who live next door. They often have parties until late at night, and it's so noisy I can't sleep. Yesterday, they kept making a racket until morning. I wish they would stop having parties so late.

   ③ There's something I want to say to my husband. He still has a lot of books and toys that he's kept ever since he was a child. He never throws anything away. Our place is very small, so I wish he would get rid of those things.

SENTENCE PATTERN 3 〜てもらいます
PRACTICE I

① みちを　おしえてもらった　② かみを　きってもらった　③ しょうかい　してもらった

PRACTICE II

1. ① Soon after I came to Japan, a friend took me to a sumo tournament. She told me about the history and rules of sumo, so I enjoyed it very much. Ever since, I always watch sumo as soon as it comes on TV.

   ② When I had a problem with a toothache, a friend recommended a really good dentist to me. The dentist was very nice and spoke English, so I was quite relieved. Ever since, I always go to that dentist whenever I have a sore tooth.

SENTENCE PATTERN 4 〜ていきます／きます
PRACTICE I

① (a) へってきました。　(b) へっていくだろう
② (a) ふえてきました。　(b) ふえていくだろう

PRACTICE II

① パンを　たべるひとが　ふえてきましたから。
② ふえていくだろうと　いっています。
③ さいきんは　ダイエットを　する　ひとたちの　あいだで　ごはんの　にんきが　でてきましたから。
④ **Model Answer**
わたしの　くにでは　あさごはんに　シリアルを　たべる　ひとが　ふえてきました。これからも　ふえていくだろうと　おもいます。

COMMUNICATION

1. ① (a) みどりが　へってきた。　(b) おおきい　ビルが　ふえてきた。
(c) しらない　ひとが　ふえてきた。　(d) スポーツクラブを　つくってほしい。
(e) わかい　ひとと　はなす　ひを　つくってほしい。

LESSON 8

SENTENCE PATTTERN passive forms
PRACTICE I

① おこなわれる	② つかわれる	③ わらわれる	④ ひらかれる
⑤ おされる	⑥ こわされる	⑦ つくられる	⑧ しなれる
⑨ たのまれる	⑩ よばれる	⑪ ふられる	⑫ とられる
⑬ しかられる	⑭ なぐられる	⑮ あつめられる	⑯ ほめられる
⑰ たてられる	⑱ しらべられる	⑲ ゆにゅうされる	⑳ もってこられる

PRACTICE II

1. ① (a) ビジーさんを　ほめ　　(b) ぶちょうに　ほめられ
   ② (a) ビジーさんを　さそい　　(b) ぶちょうに　さそわれ
   ③ (a) ビジーさんを　わらい　　(b) ぶちょうに　わらわれ
   ④ (a) ビジーさんを　ちゅういし　　(b) ぶちょうに　ちゅういされ

2. ① えいごの　せんせいに　よく　まちがいを　なおされたからです。
   ② スペインごの　せんせいに　よく　まちがいを　なおされたから　じょうずに　なったと　おもっています。

3. ・I didn't like it when my mistakes were corrected by the teacher when I was speaking in class.
   ・My mistakes were corrected by the teacher in class, so my Japanese improved.
   ・I didn't like it when my mistakes were corrected by my classmates.
   ・I was happy to be praised by the teacher in class.
   ・I was praised by the teacher in class, so my Japanese improved.

PRACTICE III

1. ① (a) たてられ　　(b) ひらかれ
   ② (a) たてられ　　(b) ひらかれ
   ③ (a) たてられ　　(b) したしまれ
   ④ (a) つくられ　　(b) かざられ
   ⑤ (a) つくられ　　(b) りようされ　　(c) よばれ

3. ① (a) つくられ　　(b) のまれ　　(c) いわれ　　(d) ゆしゅつされ
   ② (a) つくられ　　(b) たべられ　　(c) ゆにゅうされ
   ③ (a) しょうかいされ　(b) いわれ
   ④ (a) かかれ　　(b) かきなおされ　(c) よまれ

PRACTICE IV

1. ① わかい　おとこに　バッグを　とられました。
   ② つまに　ブランデーを　のまれました。
   ③ うしろの　ひとに　でんしゃの　なかで　せなかを　おされました。
   ④ となりの　ひとに　あさ　はやく　こられました。
   ⑤ ひしょに　やめられました。

2. ・On crowded trains, I've had my feet stepped on.
   ・I've had burglars break into my home.
   ・I've become angry because someone in my family threw away something important.
   ・I've had my passport stolen when traveling abroad.
   ・I've had my Japanese praised by a friend.
   ・I've had problems with salesmen calling at my home.
   ・I've had small children start crying after I spoke to them.
   ・I've been rained on when I didn't have an umbrella, so I got soaked through to the bone.

COMMUNICATION

1. ① びわこで　<u>ひらかれました</u> (L3)
   びわこで　<u>おこなわれています</u> (L4)
   メンバーによって　<u>かんがえられます</u> (L5)
   きょりによって　<u>きめられます</u> (L7)
   ちからを　あつめて　<u>つくられた</u> (L10)
   ② 1997ねんに　ひらかれました。
   ③ 7がつすえに　ひらかれます。
   ④ ひこうきの　デザインと　とんだ　きょりによって　きめられます。
   ⑤ そらを　とびたいと　おもっている　ひとなら　だれでも　さんかできます。

LESSON 9

SENTENCE PATTERN causative forms
PRACTICE I

1. ① つくらせる ② いかせる ③ あそばせる ④ いそがせる
⑤ またせる ⑥ たしかめさせる ⑦ やめさせる ⑧ とどけさせる
⑨ そうたいさせる ⑩ しゅっきんさせる ⑪ むかえに こさせる

2. ① ロボットを(に) むかえに こさせます。
② ロボットを てがみを かかせます.
③ ロボットを アイロンを かけさせます。
④ ロボットを くるまを あらわせます。
⑤ ロボットを まどを ふかせます。
⑥ ロボットを りょうりを つくらせます。
⑦ ロボットを そうじを させます。

PRACTICE II

1. ・Make the new recruits write a report every day.
・Make the new recruits learn how to give proper greetings.
・Make the new recruits remember the names of the companies we do business with.
・Make the new recruits do Zen meditation.
・Make the new recruits practice telephone manners.
・Make the new recruits clean the office.
・Make the new recruits play baseball or other sports that involve teamwork.
・Make the new recruits visit the companies we do business with together with their section leaders.

PRACTICE III

2. A: If my child said that he wanted to travel alone for a month, I would let him go, because I want my children to experience many things. If I let him have a lot of different experiences beginning in junior high school, then he will grow up able to make his own decisions. I think that the most important thing is to let children decide things for themselves.

B: Even if my child says that he wants to travel alone for a month, I would not let him. A junior-high-school student is too young to travel alone for a month. He doesn't know what things are dangerous, and he can't make the right decisions. I think that the most important thing is to not let one's children do anything dangerous.

① はい、いかせます。
② こどもの ころから じぶんで はんだんさせることが いちばん たいせつだと おもっています。
③ いいえ、いかせません。
④ こどもの ころは あぶないことを させないことが いちばん たいせつだと おもっています。

3. **Model Answers**
・こどもが よる ピザやで アルバイトしたいと いったら、させます。じぶんで はたらいて、じぶんで おかねを つくる けいけんは たいせつだと おもいます。
・こどもが よる ピザやで アルバイトしたいと いっても させません。よるの アルバイトは あぶないので、もっと あんぜんな アルバイトを させます。

PRACTICE IV

1. ① わたしに はらわせてください。 ② わたしに はらわせてください。
③ わたしに ごちそう させてください。

2. ① にほんごの レッスンを うけさせて ください。にほんごで ビジネスが したいんです。
② らいげつ おきなわで ひらかれる セミナーに しゅっせき させて ください。これからの しごとに たいせつな セミナーだと おもうんです。

③ しゅうに　ふつか　5じに　かえらせてください。ビジネススクールに　いって、べんきょう　しなおしたいんです。

COMMUNICATION

1. ① もうどうけんに　どんな　ことを　させているのでしょうか。(L 3)
もうどうけんを　あそばせない（L 5)
たべものを　もらっても　たべさせない（L 7)
ひだりがわを　あるかせる　(L 9)
もうどうけんを　とまらせる　(L 10)
もうどうけんに　はんだんさせる　(L 13)
はんだんさせるのは　たいへんです　(L 14)
トレーニングを　させているのでしょうか　(L 18)
かんさつさせるのだそうです。　(L 19)
あるいたら　あるかせて、　(L 20)
まっていたら　またせるのだそうです。(L 20)
② こうさてんを　わたっても　いいか　どうか　はんだんさせる　トレーニングです。
③ もうどうけんに　こうさてんに　いる　ひとを　かんさつさせます。ひとが　あるいたら、あるかせて、まっていたら　またせます。
④ もうどうけんを　あそばせない。
たべものを　ほかの　ひとから　もらっても　たべさせない。
あるく　ときは　トレーナーの　ひだりがわを　あるかせる。
こうさてんの　まえで　もうどけんを　とまらせる。

LESSON 10

SENTENCE PATTERN A　〜ようになります
PRACTICE I

1. ① かいしゃの　かえりに　かいものが　できるように
② まちで　えいがが　みられるように
③ えきまえに　くるまが　とめられなく

PRACTICE II

1. ① Two months have passed since I moved to this town. At first I didn't know where anything was in town, but lately I've come to know the town better. I also have more friends in the neighborhood now, so I can ask them for advice.
② Three months have passed since I started working for this company. At first I didn't know how to do my job, so I had to ask the people around me about everything. Lately, though, I've become able to do my work without asking questions. I've also got used to the commute, and I don't get very tired anymore.
③ Three years have passed since I began skiing. At first I couldn't even stand up straight when I put on skis, but now I can control my speed pretty well. I'm now able to turn freely on any slope, so skiing has become more fun.

SENTENCE PATTERN B　〜ようになります
PRACTICE

2. ① (3)　(2)　(1)
② (3)　(4)　(1)　(2)

Check 2

1. ① きてみ　② おいてある
③ みてきます／みてみます　④ きを　つけている
⑤ ふとってきた／ふとってしまった　⑥ てつだってもらい
⑦ うりきれてしまっ　⑧ おくってほしい／おくってもらいたい

3. ① とどけさせます　② してもらって　③ たべさせて　④ みてもらったら　⑤ あけられて

LESSON 11

SENTENCE PATTERN ～てくれます ～ていただきます／てくださいます
PRACTICE I

1. ① まいしゅう ざっしを とどけてくれ ② みまいに きてくださっ
③ うちあわせに きてくださっ

PRACTICE II

1. ① おしえていただいた ② かってもらう ③ つれていってもらっ ④ してもらった

PRACTICE III

① (a) おおばやし (b) おたくに まねいていただい
(c) おくさまに にほんりょうりを たくさん つくっていただい

COMMUNICATION

1. ① 2 ② 1 ③ 1 ④ 2

2. (a) はやし (b) おせわさまに なっ (c) つれていっていただい
(d) いろいろな かたに しょうかいしていただい (e) ニューヨークの クリスマスを たのしむ
(f) おれいまで

LESSON 12

SENTENCE PATTERN 1 ～ようにします
PRACTICE

- I make a point of jogging every morning.
- I make a point of swimming in the pool three times a week.
- I make a point of walking to work.
- I make a point of going to bed before 12 o'clock at night.
- On weekends, I make a point of going places that have a lot of greenery.
- I make a point of eating a lot of vegetables in order to get enough vitamins.
- I make a point of doing stretching exercises for 30 minutes before I go to bed at night.
- I make a point of not thinking about work on weekends.
- I make a point of not using elevators or escalators.
- I make a point of not drinking too much coffee or alcohol.

SENTENCE PATTERN 2 ～なくて
PRACTICE

1. ①—(d) ②—(e) ③—(a) ④—(f) ⑤—(c)

2. **Model Answers**
① おくれてしまった ② わからないことばを しらべることが できない
③ しんぱい している

SENTENCE PATTERN 3 ～ないで
PRACTICE I

- I learn kanji by writing them many times.
- I read quietly without reading aloud.
- Even if there's a word I don't know, I read to the end without looking it up in a dictionary.
- As much as possible, I study without using English in class.

・Whenever possible, I always memorize the dialogues before going to class.
・I practice the dialogues until I can say them without looking at the text.

PRACTICE II

1. ① When I chose my present job, I first consulted with many different people before deciding. You can learn a lot of things if you ask other people for their opinions. I think it's a good idea to consult with as many people as possible before deciding on a job.

② When I chose my present job, I didn't consult with anybody before deciding. Everyone has different ways of thinking and different values. I think it's a good idea to think for yourself as much as possible when choosing a job and to make your own decision.

COMMUNICATION

2. ① しごとに　しゅうちゅうすることが　たいせつです。でも、しゅうまつは　できるだけ　しごとのことを　かんがえずに、あそんだり　ほんを　よんだりするように　していました。

② わかい　ころから、いつも　いまの　じぶんに　なにが　できるか、なにが　できないか　かんがえるように　していました。

③ つまらなくても、ひとつの　しごとを　つづけるように　することが　たいせつです。

④ できるだけ　おおきいことを　かんがえるように　することと、ながい　しやで　かんがえるように　することに　きを　つけていました。

⑤ しごとで　いちばん　たいせつなのは、にんげんかんけいなので、せんぱいや　こうはいと　よくコミュニケーションを　とるように　していました。そして　せっとくするときは　2かいで　せっとくするように　しました。

LESSON 13

SENTENCE PATTERN　お／ご～になります　お／ご～します
PRACTICE I

1. ① まいります　② いらっしゃいます　③ おっしゃいます
④ なさいます　⑤ いたします　⑥ めしあがります
⑦ はいけんします

2. ① もうします　② いらっしゃいましたか　③ まいりました
④ すんでいらっしゃいますか　⑤ すんでおります　⑥ めしあがれますか
⑦ りょうりを　なさいますか　⑧ いたしません

PRACTICE II

① およりに　なり　② およみに　なり　③ おでかけに　なります　④ おつかいに　なります

PRACTICE III

① おあずかりします　② おとりします　③ おおくりします　④ おもちします

PRACTICE IV

1. ① どう　なさいましたか。　② おかけに　なってください。
③ おもち　しましょうか。　④ おもちに　なっていますか。
⑤ おやすみに　なってください。　⑥ なんでも　おっしゃってください。

2. ① おすきな　ものを　おとりください。　② めしあがってください。
③ おつかいください。　④ あけていただけませんか。
⑤ とってくださいませんか。

COMMUNICATION 1

1. ① だいがくで　べんきょう　しました。
② この　かいしゃに　はいれましたから／にほんで　しごとを　することが　できるように　なりましたから。

2. (a) カナダから　まいりました　(b) いろいろと　わからないことが　あります
(c) みなさまに　おしえていただきたい

3. Model Answers
(a) アメリカから　まいりました　スミス
(b) だいがくの　とき、いちど　にほんに　あそびに　きました。それで　とても　にほんが　すきになりました。みなさんと　いっしょに　しごとを　するのを　たのしみに　しています。
(c) まだまだ　にほんごが　じょうずではありません
(d) いろいろ　おしえていただきたい

COMMUNICATION 2

1. ① やまださんです。　② けっこんしきの　パーティーです。
③ いいえ。だいがくで　しりあいました。

2. (a) ただいま　ごしょうかいいただいた
(b) でございます
(c) おめでとう　ございます
(d) おまねきいただきまして、ありがとう　ございました
(e) どうぞ　いつまでも　おしあわせに

Check 3

1. ① はじめた　② あつまって　③ が　④ みないで
⑤ なくて　⑥ して　⑦ こんど　⑧ もらえませんか
⑨ その　⑩ たのしみに　しています

3. ① あつまり　あつめ　② おち　おとし　おち　③ きまっ　きめ
④ こわし　こわれ　⑤ さがら　さげる

4. ① かいておいて　かいてあります　② いれてある　いれておいた　③ あいていて　あけておいた

LESSON 14

SENTENCE PATTERN 1 〜のに
PRACTICE I

1. ① Tanaka-san and Bijii-san are learning to play tennis.
Coach: If you practice every day, you'll get better at playing tennis.
Two months later:
Tanaka: I'm better at tennis now, because I've been practicing every day.
Bijii: That's nice for you. I'm no better at tennis even though I've been practicing every day.

② Tanaka-san and Bijii-san are going to go buy tickets for a rock concert.
Mariko: I think you'll be able to buy the tickets if you go and line up outside Playguide by eight o'clock the day they go on sale.
A few days later:
Tanaka: I managed to buy one because I queued up outside Playguide in Shibuya at half past seven.
Bijii: That's good for you. I couldn't get hold of any although I was at Playguide Shinjuku from seven o'clock.

2. · When it rains although the sky is bright and clear.
· When an automatic door does not open even though you are standing in front of it.
· When leaves fall from trees even though it is spring.
· When the roads are crowded although it is one o'clock in the morning.
· When you see someone wearing sunglasses even though it is raining.

PRACTICE II

1. ① かったばかりな　② だめだと　おもっていた　③ なんども　れんしゅした

PRACTICE III

2. ① 2ねんまえから　ピアノを　ならっている
② なかなか　じょうずに　ならないんです
③ しごとの　あとで　れんしゅう　している
④ じょうずに　ならないんです

SENTENCE PATTERN 2　～ようとしたとき
PRACTICE

1. ① ケーキを　だそう　② おかねを　はらおう

2. ① (a) ケーキを　だそうとした
② (a) おかねを　はらおうと　した、　(b) さいふが　ない　ことに　きが　ついたんです

COMMUNICATION

2. A
I'm a 21-year-old student. I'm having problems with my roommate, K. She hates cleaning up. Every day I tell her that the person who uses the kitchen should clean up afterwards, but she never does. I like to go to bed early so I ask her to be quiet after 10 o'clock, but she keeps listening to music and watching TV until around midnight. And on weekends I want to relax, but her friends always come over to hang out. It's a real problem.

Counsellor
I understand very well how you feel. Living with a roommate must be difficult in many ways. But put yourself in K's position for a moment. Sometimes, when she's tired from work, she might want to clean up but not be able to. She may know that it's better to go to bed early, but maybe she wants to relax before going to bed by watching TV or listening to music. I know it must be hard to have a lot of guests on weekends, but maybe K is unable to turn them away even if she wants to.

And there's one more thing. Maybe K has some things that she would like to say to you. How about having a good talk with her again?

2. ① ルームメートの　Kこさんの　ことで　なやんでいます。
② Kこさんが　だいどころを　なかなか　かたづけないし、よる　おそくまで　おんがくを　きいたり、テレビを　みたり　しているからです。しゅうまつは　ゆっくり　したいのに、いつも　Kこさんの　ともだちが　あそびにくるからです。
③ Kこさんと　よく　はなしを　したら　どうですかと　いっています。

LESSON 15

SENTENCE PATTERN 1　～ことにします
PRACTICE I

① うける　ことに　しました。② かわない　ことに　しました。③ さんかする　ことに　しました。

PRACTICE II

1. ① (a) はい。つれていく　ことに　しました。
   (b) みんなで　いっしょに　くらしたいからです。
   ② (a) かわない　ことに　しました。
   (b) いえに　いる　じかんが　すくないからです。

SENTENCE PATTERN 2　〜ことに　なりました
PRACTICE I

① せんたくものは　ベランダに　ほしては　いけないことに　なりましたので、よろしく　おねがいします。
② じてんしゃは　ろうかに　おいては　いけないことに　なりましたので、よろしく　おねがい　します。
③ あきびんは　あきびんと　かいてある　はこに　いれることに　なりましたので、よろしく　おねがいします。
④ かんりにんは　にもつを　あずからないことに　なりましたので、よろしく　おねがいします。

PRACTICE II

1. ① A: It was the day after tomorrow wasn't it, that we were supposed to go to the Edo Museum?
   B: Yes, it was.
   A: Well actually, I have to go to Hong Kong on a three-day business trip from tomorrow.
   B: Oh I see. Shall we change it to next week then?
   A: I'm sorry, is that all right?

   ② A: It was Thursday evening wasn't it, that we were supposed to go on *hanami*?
   B: Yes, it was.
   A: Well, I've been asked by my boss to attend a party at one of our clients' on that Thursday.
   B: Oh. Shall we make it Friday then?
   A: Yes please, could we do that?

COMMUNICATION

1. ① はい、かわってきています。
   ② ふえてきています。
   ③ かいしゃによっては　はやく　たいしょくする　ひとには　たいしょくきんを　おおく　しはらうように　なりましたから。
   ④ あたらしく　みせを　はじめたり　かいしゃを　つくったりします。

2. ① きっさてんを　はじめようと　おもっています。
   ② ていねんより　まえに　やめると、たいしょくきんが　たくさん　もらえるように　なりました。

LESSON 16

SENTENCE PATTERN 1　〜たまま
PRACTICE I

- I have got out of a car and locked the door while the engine was still running.
- I have put on clothes while still wearing pajamas.
- I have slept until morning with the television still on.
- I have come home still wearing the name tag from a party.
- I have gone out wearing clothes that still had a dry cleaner's tag or a price tag on them.
- I have continued holding an umbrella up while walking even though the rain had stopped.
- I have washed clothes with money still in the pockets.
- I have got into the bath with my watch still on.
- I have taken pictures while the lens cover was still on the camera.
- I have fallen asleep while standing up on a train.

PRACTICE II

① このままで　いいです。　② いいえ、そのままで　どうぞ。
③ いいえ、そのままで　けっこうです。

SENTENCE PATTERN 2　plain imperatives
PRACTICE I

2. ① ひを　けせ　② あわてるな　③ そとに　でるな　④ がんばれ　⑤ いそげ　⑥ うごくな

PRACTICE II

① がんばれ　② かえってこい

SENTENCE PATTERN 3　〜とおりに

① みつもりしょどおりに　② かいてあるとおりに　③ れんしゅうしていたとおりに

COMMUNICATION

1. やまだ　すぐ　わすれる　まちだ　まちがいが　おおい　きむら　すぐ　びょうきに　なる
おがわ　ミス　すくない／しごと　はやい／らいげつ　かいしゃ　やめる

2. • A boss who, without reading the manual, tells me to show him how to use his computer even though I'm in the middle of work.
• A boss who tells me to drink alcohol even though I don't want to.
• A subordinate who, even though I told him to tell me immediately if there are any work problems with customers, waits until the problems get out of hand before telling me.
• A receptionist who chats with other company people while making guests wait.
• A child who doesn't, despite what I told her to do, put away the things she got out.
• A husband/wife who stays on the phone for a long time with the TV switched on.
• A husband/wife who leaves his/her clothes lying around without putting them away.
• A building superintendent who nags me to be quiet and not play the piano at night.

Check 4

1. ① したとき　② おぼえていた　③ ことにした　④ のに　⑤ しながら
⑥ とちゅうで　⑦ ぜったいに　⑧ いったい　⑨ とおり　⑩ もう

2. ① きいたのに　きいても　② ふべんでも　ふべんなのに
③ やすかったのに　やすくても　④ にほんごの　せんせいなのに　にほんごの　せんせいでも

LESSON 17

SENTENCE PATTERN 1　〜ように
PRACTICE I

1. • When I get up in the morning, I take a cold shower to wake myself up, even in the winter.
• Before I leave home in the morning, I always check my date book to make sure that I don't make any mistakes about that day's schedule.
• Whenever I'm asked to take a phone message, I always write it down so I don't forget.
• I always let my colleagues know my work schedule in advance.
• Before going to bed, I always take a bath to relax after the tiring day.

2. ① なおるように　② いいてんきに　なるように／あめが　ふらないように

PRACTICE II

1. ① (a) ひとを　よぶ　ちからが　あります。
   (b) おきゃくさんに　おおぜい　きてもらえるように　おいてあります。

   ② (a) しょうがつの　がんたんから　みっかまで　たべます。
   (b) あたらしい　としの　はじめから、しょくじの　じゅんびを　しなくても　いいように、つくって　おきます。

SENTENCE PATTERN 2　～ために
PRACTICE I

1. ①—(e)　②—(d)　③—(f)　④—(b)　⑤—(a)

2. **Model Answers**
   ① にほんごを　べんきょうする
   ② おおきい　いえを　かう
   ③ ともだちと　テニスを　する／やすく　かりられる　テニスコートを　さがしています。

PRACTICE II

1. ① しゅうにゅうを　えるために　はたらいている　ひとが　いちばん　おおいです。
   ② フィリピンです。

2. A: I work in order to make money. Without money, I can't live in a nice apartment, I can't travel, and I can't go do fun things with my friends.
   B: I work in order to create a better world. I believe that after we become adults we have a responsibility to society.
   C: I work in order to use my abilities. If my work is worthwhile, then every day is enjoyable.

PRACTICE III

1. ① ように　② (a) ために (b) ように　③ ように　④ (a) ために (b) ために　⑤ ように

SENTENCE PATTERN 3　～れる・られる（けいご）
PRACTICE I

1. ① かわれる　② よまれる　③ あわれる　④ はなされる
   ⑤ とられる　⑥ でられる　⑦ きめられる　⑧ つづけられる
   ⑨ あつめられる　⑩ とめられる　⑪ せつめいされる　⑫ がいしゅつされる
   ⑬ あいさつされる　⑭ もってこられる

PRACTICE II

1. ①—C　②—A　③—C　④—A　⑤—B　⑥—A　⑦—B　⑧—C

2. ① (a) りょこうを　すると　いっています。
   (b) かいがいに　いくと　いっています。
   ② (a) りょこうを　すると　いっています。
   (b) こくないに　いくと　いっています。
   ③ (a) 5ねんぐらい　にほんに　いました。
   (b) じゅどうを　ならったり、いろいろな　ところを　りょこうしたり　しました。

COMMUNICATION

1. ① てんじの　ボランティアを　しています。
   ② びょうきで　めが　みえなくなってしまった　ともだちを　たすけたいと　おもったからです。
   ③ はい。えいごを　おしえています。
   ④ テキストを　ぜんぶ　おぼえていきます。

2. おいそがしい　／　おじかん　とっていただきまして　／　おやくに　たちます　／　ボランティアを　されている　／　おききしました　／　ボランティアを　しております　／　めのみえない　かた　／　はじめようと　おもわれた　／　そのかた　／　なにを　されている　／　おはなし　／　きかせていただき

LESSON 18

SENTENCE PATTERN 1　speech levels

PRACTICE I

2. ① でなければならないのに　② いれておきましたよ
③ はやく　ごはんを　たべてしまってください　④ はやく　でかけましょう

PRACTICE II

① (a)　② (b)　③ (a)　④ (b)

SENTENCE PATTERN 2　～ところです
PRACTICE II

2. ① ついた　② あいた　③ でてくる　④ おりる　⑤ はじまる

COMMUNICATION

1. ① (a) T　(b) F　(c) T　② (a) T　(b) T　(c) F

LESSON 19

SENTENCE PATTERN 1　～わけです
PRACTICE I

1. ① だから、あんなに　じょうずな　わけですね。

SENTENCE PATTERN 2　～というわけです
PRACTICE

1. ① 4と　9が　よくない　すうじだと　いわれています。
② 4は　「shi」と　はつおんされて、「し」と　おなじ　おとに　なるし、9は　「ku」と　はつおんされて「くるしいの　く」と　おなじ　おとに　なってしまうからです。

COMMUNICATION

1. **Student A**
In Japan, some companies have interesting ways of training their new employees. For example, at McDonald's Japan they make the new employees pull large fishing nets onto the beach. This hamburger company's actual business has nothing to do with fishing nets, so why do they have that training? The reason is that one person cannot pull a large fishing net by himself. Everyone must pull the net together. Thus the purpose of the training is to show the importance of cooperation.

Student B
In Japan, there's a custom of giving money in an envelope when attending weddings or funerals, when a baby is born, and when visiting someone in the hospital. These envelopes come in many different types, with the specific type determined by when and how it will be used. On envelopes intended for weddings and funerals, the ribbon is tied in a special way so that once it has been tied it cannot be untied easily. The purpose is to show that a wedding or funeral should take place only once and never be repeated.

Check 5

1. ① たまに　② ところ　③ ために　④ すごい　⑤ には　⑥ たいしたことない
⑦ ほど　⑧ まるで　⑨ が　しません　⑩ それに

2. ① いただきたい　② もってまいりましょうか　③ ごしゅっぱつ　④ もの
⑤ うかがいます　⑥ おとどけいたします　⑦ よろしい　⑧ けっこう
⑨ おまたせしました　⑩ ごらんになれます

3. ① (a)　② (c)　③ (c)　④ (b)　⑤ (b)

TAPE SCRIPT

LESSON 1

SENTENCE PATTERN 1–1　～ようです
PRACTICE II (page 3)

ピンポンピンポンピンポン

ビジー：　るすの　ようですね。
こばやし：でかけているのかもしれません。
ビジー：　ドアが　あいています。

*ビジーさんと　こばやしさんは　いえの　なかに　はいりました。

ビジー：　やはり　でかけていないようですね。
こばやし：そうですね。

こばやし：いい　におい。
ビジー：　ケーキを　やいているようですね。

みんな：　ビジーさん。たんじょうび、おめでとう。

SENTENCE PATTERN 2　～そうです
PRACTICE II (page 8)

① Recorded Information

おでんわ　ありがとうございます。JBPショップの　*えいぎょうじかんは　げつようびから　どようびの　ごぜん　9じから　ごご5じまでです。*ごようの　かたは　*えいぎょうじかんないに　もういちど　*おかけなおしください。

におい　*smell, aroma*
えいぎょうじかん　*opening hours*
ごようの　かた　*person with an inquiry*
えいぎょうじかんない　*during opening hours*
おかけなおしください　*please call back later*

② Station Announcement

*おいそぎのところ、たいへん　*ごめいわくを　おかけしております。
となりの　えきが、かじです。でんしゃは　30ぷんほど　おくれる*みこみです。*くりかえします。でんしゃは　30ぷん　おくれます。

おいそぎのところ　*when you are in a hurry*
ごめいわくを　おかけしております　*(we are sorry) to inconvenience you*
みこみ　*expect*
くりかえします　*repeat*

③ Weather Forecast

それでは　あしたの　てんきを　*おつたえします。あしたの　*きおんは　10どぐらいでしょう。おはなみには　ちょっと　さむいかもしれません。よるに　なってから　あめが　ふりますので、おはなみに　でかける　ばあいは、　コートと　かさを　もっていった　ほうが　いいでしょう。

おつたえします　*tell, report*
きおん　*(air) temperature*

COMMUNICATION 1 (page 9)

2. こばやし：これ、なにに　みえますか。
ビジー：　にほんごが　わからないんですが、「monkey」って、にほんごで　なんと　いうんですか。
こばやし：さるですか。
ビジー：　さる？　さるって　えいごで　「monkey」ですか。
こばやし：そうですよ。さるは「monkey」です。でも、さるのように　みえるけど、さるじゃ　ありません。
ビジー：　じゃ　なんだろう。
あ！わかった。でも、また　にほんごが　わからないんですが、「bat」って　にほんごで　なんですか。
こばやし：こうもりです。
ビジー：　こうもりのように　みえます。
こばやし：ざんねんだけど、こうもりじゃないんですよ。
ビジー：　え〜〜。ほんとうは　なんですか。
こばやし：ほんとうは、これは　はななんですよ。
ビジー：　はなですか。おもしろい　はなですね。にほんの　はなですか。
こばやし：いいえ、*エクアドルの　はなです。「ドラキュラ」という　なまえだそうですよ。ドラキュラのように　みえるでしょう。

エクアドル　*Ecuador*

LESSON 2

SENTENCE PATTERN 1　〜はずです
PRACTICE II (page 17)

1. リンダ：ありませんね。
ビジー：このちかくの　はずなんですが。
リンダ：おかしいですね。
ビジー：ちずによると、このへんに　あるはずなんです。
ビジー：あった。
ビジー：あれ、きっぷが　ない。
おかしいなあ。たしかに　さいふに　いれたはずなんですが。
ビジー：あ、あった。やっぱり　はいっていました。
リンダ：よかった。

SENTENCE PATTERN 2　〜で
PRACTICE II (page 20)

ex. かわださんは　JBPコンピューターに　でんわを　します。

かわだ：もしもし、かわだです。おはようございます。すみませんが、あさの　かいぎに　おくれます。ぶちょうに　つたえてください。
ひしょ：どうか　しましたか。
かわだ：じこで　でんしゃが　うごいていないんです。
ひしょ：それは　たいへんですね。ぶちょうに　そう　つたえます。

① こばやしさんは　JBPコンピューターに　でんわを　します。

こばやし：おはようございます。こばやしです。
ひしょ：　おはようございます。
こばやし：すみませんが、きょうは　かいしゃを　やすみます。かぜで　ねつが　あるんです。ぶちょうに　つたえてください。
ひしょ：　わかりました。おだいじに。

② ビジーさんは　おおさかししゃから　とうきょうほんしゃに　でんわを　します。

ビジー：もしもし、ビジーですが。すみません。ずめんを　おくるのが　おくれます。
ひしょ：どうか　しましたか。
ビジー：こしょうで　コンピューターが　つかえないんです。ぶちょうに　つたえてください。
ひしょ：わかりました。そう　つたえます。

③ さとうさんは　きゅうしゅうの　くうこうから　とうきょうほんしゃに　でんわを　します。

さとう：もしもし、さとうですが。きょうじゅうに　とうきょうに　かえれないんです。
ひしょ：どうか　しましたか。
さとう：たいふうで　ひこうきが　とんでいないんです。ぶちょうに　つたえてください。
ひしょ：わかりました。つたえます。

COMMUNICATION 1 (page 21)

1. こばやし：さとうさん、ビジーさん、おそい　ですね。
さとう：　さきに　いきましょう。こないのかもしれません。
こばやし：いいえ、きのう　くると　いっていましたから、くる　はずです。
さとう：　ばしょが　わからないので、あきらめたのかもしれません。
もうすぐ　コンサートが　はじまりますよ。もう　いきませんか。
こばやし：でも、ばしょは　しっている　はずなんです。
きのう　ちずを　わたしましたから。
さとう：　じゃあ、しごとが　いそがしくて、ざんぎょうしているのかもしれません。
まにあいませんよ。いきましょう。
こばやし：いいえ、きょうは　ざんぎょうは　ない　はずです。
ひまだって　いっていました。
さとう：　わかりました。じゃあ、もう　すこし　まちましょう。

LESSON 3

SENTENCE PATTERN 1
PRACTICE IV

TALKING (page 30)

わたしは　らいげつ　にほんごの　スピーチを　する　よていです。　にほんごの　スピーチは　はじめてだし、まだ　にほんごが　じょうずではないので、うまく　できるか　どうか　しんぱいしています。

COMMUNICATION 1 (page 33)

① ビジーさんは　JBPの　よこはまこうじょうに　でんわを　します。

ビジー：　もしもし、ビジーですが、おちあいさん、おねがいします。
よこはまこうじょうの　ひと：いま、でんわちゅうですが。
ビジー：　じゃ、これから　しりょうを　ファックスで　おくると　つたえてください。
よこはまこうじょうの　ひと：わかりました。つたえます。

② さとうさんは　おおさかししゃに　しゅっちょうしています。とうきょうの　JBPに　でんわを　します。

さとう：　もしもし、さとうですが、ビジーさんは　いますか。
JBPの　ひと：　がいしゅつちゅうですが……。

さとう：　ビジーさんが　かえったら、わたしに　みつもりしょを　ファックスで　おくるように　つたえてください。

JBPの　ひと：　わかりました。つたえます。

③ ビジーさんは　おおさかししゃに　でんわを　します。

ビジー：　もしもし、ビジーですが、さとうさん、いますか。

おおさかししゃの　ひと：いま、せきを　はずしていますが。

ビジー：　じゃ、もどったら、さっき　わたしが　おくった　しりょうが　とどいたかどうか　きいてください。

おおさかししゃの　ひと：わかりました。

LESSON 4

SENTENCE PATTERN 1　～そうです

PRACTICE II (page 39)

ビジー：どちらの　れつが　はやいでしょうか。みぎの　れつの　ほうが　はやそうですね。

さとう：いいえ、ひだりの　れつの　ほうが　はやそうですよ。ならんでいる　ひとの　にもつが　すくないですから。

ビジー：でも　ひだりの　かかりの　ひとは、ちょっと　こわそうですよ。おこっているように　みえます。　みぎの　かかりの　ひとは　やさしそうです。

さとう：でも、ひだりに　ならんでいる　ひとは　ツアーのようだから、あまり　じかんが　かからないと　おもいますよ。それに　みぎの　れつの　ひとは　にもつが　とても　おおいです。

ビジー：そうですね。みぎの　れつの　ほうが　じかんが　かかりそうですね。ひだりに　ならびましょう。

PRACTICE IV

TALKING (page 42)

ひとりで　でんしゃに　のっていた　ときの　はなしなんですが、ともだちから　きいた　おもしろいはなしを　おもいだしたんです。わらいだしそうで　こまりました。

SENTENCE PATTERN 3　～らしいです

PRACTICE (page 44)

ex. A：となりの　ＡＢＣコンピューター、ちいさいけれど、きゅうりょうが　いい　らしいよ。

B：そんなに　よさそうに　みえないけど、ほんとう？

A：ほんとうか　どうか　よく　しらないけど、30さいで　1かげつ　200まんえんぐらい　もらうって　きいた。

B：200まんも！

① A：ＭＸしゃは　あたらしい　スポーツカーを　はっぴょうする　らしいですよ。

B：え、それで、いまの　モデルが　きゅうに　やすくなったんですね。

② A：きのう　えいがに　いったら、すごく　こんでいた。

B：なにを　みたの。

A：「しらない人」っていう　えいが。

B：どうだった？

A：すごく　おもしろかったよ。

③ A：こんど　ABしゃの　しゃちょうが　かわるらしいですよ。
B：え、どうして。まだ　なったばかりでしょう？
A：なにか　もんだいが　あったらしいですよ。
B：そうなんですか。

COMMUNICATION (page 45)

1. ビジー：　ゲートの　まえに　ひとが　たくさん　いますね。なんでしょう。
こばやし：サッカーチームの　サポーターの　ひとたちかもしれませんよ。きのうの　よるの　ニュースで　ブラジルに　しゅっぱつする　といっていましたから。
ビジー：　サッカーチームの　サポーター？
こばやし：ええ。サッカーせんしゅの　ファンの　ひとたち。
ビジー：　それで　あんなに　たくさん　ひとが　いるんですか。
こばやし：いま、にほんの　わかい　ひとたちの　あいだで　サッカーは　とても　にんきの　あるスポーツらしいですよ。
ビジー：　でも　おんなの　ひとが　たくさん　きていますよ。サッカーは　おとこの　スポーツでしょう？
こばやし：ビジーさん。ふるいですよ。いま、サッカーの　せんしゅは　えいがスターのように　にんきが　あるんですよ。それに　さいきん　じょせいの　サッカーチームも　ふえているらしいです。
ビジー：　そうなんですか。たしかに　サッカーは　だれにでも　できそうな　スポーツだし、おもしろそうですよね。
こばやし：あら！なにか　アナウンスを　しているわ。でも　よく　きこえない。

ビジー：　「ひこうきがキャンセル」って　いっているようですよ。
こばやし：ええ！たいへん！じゃあ、あそこに　たくさんいる　ひとたちは　みんな　ひこうきを　まっていたんですね。

LESSON 5

SENTENCE PATTERN 1-A　～てしまいます
PRACTICE II (page 52)

1. さとう：ビジーさん、こばやしさんと　ドライブに　いったそうですね。
ビジー：ええ、でも、たいへん　だったんです。
さとう：なにか　あったんですか。
ビジー：ふじさんに　いったんですが、ゆきが　ふっていたんですよ。
さとう：え、ゆきだったんですか。
ビジー：ええ、ゆきの　なかで　くるまが　こしょうしてしまったんです。なおすのに　1じかんもかかってしまいました。
さとう：それは　たいへんでしたね。
ビジー：ええ、かえりの　みちも　じゅうたいしていたので、かえるのが　おそくなってしまいました。こばやしさんは　おこってしまったし、わたしは　さむくて　かぜを　ひいてしまったし、ほんとうに　たいへんでした。

PRACTICE III
TALKING (page 54)

じつは　このあいだ、さいふを　おとしてしまったんです。ともだちと　レストランで　しょくじをした　あとで、　おかねを　はらおうと　したら、さいふが　ありませんでした。　おかねを　おろしたばかりだったし、カードも　たくさん　はいっていたので、ほんとうに　こまりました。

SENTENCE PATTERN 2
PRACTICE II

TALKING (page 58)

このあいだ　スーパーに　いったら、めずらしい　やさいが　あったんです。おいしそうだったので、かって　たべてみたら、まずかったんです。ぜんぶ　すててしまいました。

LESSON 6

SENTENCE PATTERN 1　〜ておきます
PRACTICE II

TALKING (page 65)

はじめての　ばしょに　いく　とき、まえもって　ちずで　よく　しらべておく　ひとと、とうじつちかくに　いってから、さがす　ひとが　います。　わたしは　まえの　ひに　よく　ちずを　みて、いきかたを　メモしておきます。

PRACTICE III (page 66)

1. A：ビールがない！ばんごはんの　ときに　のもうと　おもって　2じかんぐらいまえに　れいぞうこにいれておいたんですが。
   B：すみません。わたしが　のんでしまいました。

2. A：メモがない！ともだちの　でんわばんごうを　かみに　かいておいたんですが……。
   B：すみません。ごみだと　おもって、すててしまいました。
   A：いいんです。これからは　ノートに　かいておきますから。

LESSON 7

SENTENCE PATTERN 2
PRACTICE II

TALKING (page 79)

じつは　つまに　ちょっと　いいたい　ことが　あります。　わたしは　りょこうに　いったら、　とまった　ホテルの　パンフレットを　かならず　いえに　もってかえって　コレクションしています。でも、つまは　この　コレクションが　きにいらないようで、　すててほしいと　いつも　いっています。　わたしには　たいせつな　コレクションなので、　わかってほしいんです。

SENTENCE PATTERN 3
PRACTICE II

TALKING (page 82)

にほんに　きたばかりの　とき、となりの　いえの　ひとに　いろいろな　ことを　おしえてもらいました。ごみの　すてかたを　おしえてもらったり、いい スーパーや　レストランに つれていってもらったりしました。そのときから　にほんの　せいかつが　たのしく　なりました。

COMMUNICATION (page 85)

1. インタビューアー：やまださん、こんちには。やまださんは　ずっと　ここに　すんでいるそうですが、いまと　むかしとでは　ずいぶん　かわったでしょうね。
   やまだ：　はあ？
   インタビューアー：いまと　むかしとでは　ずいぶん　かわりましたか。

やまだ：　はい、はい。そうですねえ。むかしは　みどりが　おおくて　いい　まちでしたが、さいきんは　みどりが　へってきましたし。かわってしまいましたね。

インタビューアー：そうですか。むかしは　みどりが　たくさん　あったんですね。

やまだ：　ええ、それに、おおきい　ビルも　だんだん　ふえてきましたし。まえは　しっているひとばかりでしたが、いまは　しらない　ひとが　どんどん　ふえてきて、ちょっとさびしいですね。

インタビューアー：やまださんは、まちが　どんどん　かわっていっても、このまちに　すみつづけたいですか。

やまだ：　はあ？

インタビューアー：やまださんは、まちが　どんどん　かわっていっても、この　まちに　すみつづけたいですか。

やまだ：　ええ。もちろんです。この　まちが　すきですからね。

インタビューアー：そうですか。このまちが　おすきなんですね。ところで、まちにして　ほしいことはありますか。

やまだ：　そうですねえ。わたしたちのような　おばあさんや　おじいさんでも　いくことの　できる　スポーツクラブを　つくってほしいんです。

インタビューアー：スポーツクラブですか。

やまだ：　ええ。それから、わかい　ひとと　はなす　ひを　つくってほしいですねえ。わかいひとの　かんがえかたも　きいてみたいし。

インタビューアー：それは　いい　かんがえですね。きょうは　どうも　ありがとうございました。Aまちから、とても　おげんきな　80さいの　やまだうめさんでした。

LESSON 9

SENTENCE PATTERN causative forms
PRACTICE IV (page 105)

A：わたしに　はらわせて　ください。

B：いいえ、いつも　おせわに　なっているので、わたしに　はらわせてください。

A：こちらこそ、いつも　おせわに　なっているので、わたしに　ごちそう　させてください。

B：じゃ、きょうは　ごちそうに　なります。

LESSON 10

SENTENCE PATTERN A
PRACTICE II

TALKING (page 114)

ピアノの　れんしゅうを　はじめてから、1ねん　すぎました。　はじめは　みぎてと　ひだりてとべつべつに　ひくのが　たいへんでしたが、さいきんは　ずいぶん　じゆうに　ひけるように　なったので、よろこんでいます。

LESSON 11

SENTENCE PATTERN　～てくれます　～ていただきます／～てくださいます
PRACTICE I (page 123)

2. Aさんと　Bさんが　かいしゃで　はなしています。Bさんは　さいきんまで　にゅういんしていました。

A：もう　すっかり　よく　なりましたか。

B：ええ、おかげさまで、すっかり　げんきに　なりました。　ともだちが　スープや　くだものを　なんども　もってきてくれたり、まいしゅう　ざっしを　とどけてくれたりして、うれしかったです。しゃちょうが　おみまいに　きてくださったし、とりひきさきの　ぶちょうが　うちあわせにきてくださったりして、もうしわけなかっです。

A：みんな　Bさんに　はやく　げんきに　なって　もらいたかったんですよ。

PRACTICE II (page 124)

よしだふじん：ビジーさん、よく　すもうを　みに　いくそうですね。

ビジー：　ええ、にほんに　くる　まえは　すもう　について　なにも　しらなかったんですよ。でもよしだぶちょうに　すもうを　みに　つれていっていただいてから　とても　すきに　なりました。

よしだふじん：いまは　しゅじんより　ずっと　くわしいと　ききましたよ。

ビジー：　ぶちょうに　ルールや　りきしの　なまえを　おしえていただいたので、いまでは　だいたい　わかるように　なりました。

よしだふじん：すもうの　チケットは　なかなか　かえないんでしょう。

ビジー：　じつは、さいきん　すもうの　ファンクラブの　ひとと　ともだちに　なったんです。それで　たのんで　チケットを　かってもらうことが　できるように　なりました。

よしだふじん：それは　いいですね。

ビジー：　このあいだは　すもうべやに　つれていってもらって、よこづなに　サインを　してもらったんです。

よしだふじん：へー。サインを。

COMMUNICATION (page 127)

1. やまだ：やあ、かとうくん。

かとう：やあ、やまだくん。

やまだ：げんき？

かとう：うん、やまだくん、ふゆやすみ、ニューヨークへ　いくんだって？

やまだ：そうなんだ。ともだちが　ニューヨークに　いるだろう？このあいだ　てがみを　くれて、ぼくが　いけば　あんないしてくれるって、いっているんだ。

かとう：ぼくも　いくんだ。ニューヨークの　してんちょうの　はやしさんが　てがみを　くださってニューヨークに　あそびに　くるように　いってくださったんだ。

やまだ：はやしさんの　アパートは　ひろくて　きれいらしいよ。

かとう：うん。そうらしいね。はやしさんは　とめてくださるって　いったけれど、えんりょして　ホテルを　よやくしたんだ。おもったより　たかくて　びっくりした。

やまだ：ぼくは　ともだちが　アパートに　とめてくれると　いっているので、とめてもらおうと　おもっているんだ。

かとう：それは、いいね。クリスマスの　ころは　*オペラや　ミュージカルが　たくさん　みられるし、スキーも　できるから　たのしみだね。

やまだ：そうだね。じゃ、ニューヨークで　また　あおうよ。

オペラ　*opera*

LESSON 12

SENTENCE PATTERN 3
PRACTICE II

TALKING (page 135)

わたしは　りょこうに　もっていく　ほんを　えらぶ　とき、ほんやに　つとめている　ともだちにきいて　きめます。ほんやさんなら、さいきん　どんなほんが　にんきが　あるか　よく　しっているからです。　ほんを　えらぶ　ときは、ほんに　くわしい　ひとに　きいて、きめるのが　いいと　おもいます。

LESSON 13

SENTENCE PATTERN お／ご〜になります お／ご〜します
PRACTICE IV (page 144)

1. パーティーに しゅっせきしている ひとが きぶんが わるそうです。ホテルの ひとが しんぱいして はなしかけています。

A：どうなさいましたか。
B：ちょっと、きぶんが……。
A：どうぞ あちらに おかけに なってください。
B：ありがとう。
A：おみずでも おもちしましょうか。
B：ええ、おねがいします。
A：おくすりは おもちに なっていますか。
B：ええ、ここに。
A：では、どうぞ ゆっくり おやすみに なってください。
B：ありがとう。
A：ごようが ありましたら、どうぞ なんでも おっしゃってください。
B：ありがとう。ちょっと やすませていただきます。

2. きょうは うちで パーティーです。たくさんの ひとが あつまって、たのしそうです。

① どうぞ おすきな ものを おとりください。
② よろしかったら、めしあがってください。
③ どうぞ。おつかいください。
④ すみませんが、ドアを あけていただけませんか。
⑤ すみませんが、しゃしんを とってくださいませんか。

COMMUNICATION 1 (page 146)

1. カナダから まいりました ジョン・スミスです。
だいがくで けいざいと にほんごを べんきょういたしました。ずっと にほんで しごとを してみたいと おもっておりましたので、このかいしゃに はいれて、たいへん うれしく おもっております。
いろいろと わからないことが ありますので、みなさまに おしえていただきたいと おもいます。どうぞ よろしく おねがいいたします。

COMMUNICATION 2 (page 147)

1. しかい： それでは やまださまに おいわいの スピーチを おねがいいたします。
やまだ： ただいま ごしょうかい いただいた やまだ でございます。
よしこさん、たろうさん、おめでとう ございます。
ほんじつは すばらしい けっこんしきに おまきいただきまして、ありがとう ございました。
よしこさんと たろうさんは だいがくを そつぎょうなさる まえから、けっこんの やくそくを なさっていたそうです。おふたりとも スポーツが とても おじょうずで、よくテニスや スキーに いらっしゃっていました。これから おふたりで、あかるく げんきな かていを おつくりになると おもいます。
どうぞ いつまでも おしあわせに。

LESSON 14

SENTENCE PATTERN 1 〜のに
PRACTICE II (page 156)

① ビジー： パソコンの ちょうしが わるいんですか。
こばやし： ええ、かったばかりなのに、また こしょうしたようです。

② ビジー：　しんじられない。だめだと　おもっていたのに、ごうかくしたんです。
　こばやし：おめでとう。

③ よしだ：　ビジーさん、どうしたんですか。げんきが　ありませんね。
　ビジー：　なんども　れんしゅうしたのに、スピーチが　うまく　できなかったんです。

COMMUNICATION (page 160)

わたしは　21さいの　がくせいです。ルームメートの　Kさんの　ことで　なやんでいます。Kさんは　そうじが　きらいなんです。「だいどころは　つかった　ひとが　かたづけましょう。」と　まいにち　Kさんに　いっているのに、Kさんは　なかなか　かたづけてくれないんです。　よるは　わたしは　はやく　ねたいから、10じ　いこうは　しずかに　してほしいと　いっているのに、Kさんは　12じごろまで　おんがくを　きいたり、テレビを　みたりしています。それから、しゅうまつは　ゆっくりしたいのに、いつも　Kさんの　ともだちが　あそびにくるので、こまっています。

LESSON 15

SENTENCE PATTERN 1
PRACTICE II (page 166)

このあいだ　ハワイに　ふねで　いった　ひとの　はなしを　ききました。　とても　たのしかったそうです。わたしも　ことしの　なつ　ハワイに　いきます。　わたしも　ふねで　いきたいと　おもいましたが、じかんが　かかるので、ふねで　いくか　どうか　まよいました。けっきょく　ながい　やすみが　とれなかったので、　ひこうきで　いくことに　しました。

SENTENCE PATTERN 2
PRACTICE II

TALKING (page 169)

A：ピクニックに　いくのは　こんしゅうの　にちようびですよね。
B：ええ、そうですよ。
A：じつは、　しゅうまつに　くにから　ははが　くる　ことに　なってしまったんです。
B：そうですか。じゃ、らいしゅうの　にちようびに　かえましょうか。
A：すみません。おねがいします。

COMMUNICATION (page 170)

A：さいきん、ていねんまえに　かいしゃを　やめる　ひとが　ふえてきたそうですね。
B：ええ、うちの　かいしゃの　おおたも　ながい　あいだ　まよっていたようですが、いよいよ　かいしゃを　やめて、きっさてんを　はじめる　ことに　したと　いっていました。
A：ええ？おおたさんが？まだ　ていねんまえですよね。
B：じつは　ことしから　うちの　かいしゃの　たいしょくきんの　システムが　ちょっと　かわったんですよ。ていねんは　60さいなんですが、50さいで　かいしゃを　やめる　ひとは、ていねんで　やめる　ひとの　3ばいの　たいしょくきんが　もらえる　ことに　なったんです。
A：へえ。それじゃ、これからは　ていねんまえに　やめる　ひとが　もっと　ふえるでしょうか。
B：さあ、どうでしょう。　おおたさんのように　ほかに　やりたい　ことが　ある　ひとは、はやく　やめるように　なっていくかもしれませんね。
A：そうかもしれませんね。

LESSON 16

SENTENCE PATTERN 1　～たまま
PRACTICE II (page 175)

① A：つくえの　うえを　かたづけましょうか。
　B：このままで　いいです。

② A：くつを　ぬいだほうが　いいですか。
B：いいえ、そのまま　どうぞ。

③ A：ふくろに　おいれしましょうか。
B：いいえ、そのままで　けっこうです。

SENTENCE PATTERN 2 plain imperatives
PRACTICE II (page 177)

ex. さとうさんは　びょういんで　おいしゃさんと　はなしています。

いしゃ：　だいぶ　よく　なりましたね。
さとう：　じゃ、そろそろ　おさけを　のんでも　いいですか。
いしゃ：　まだ、だめですよ。いま　おさけを　のんだら、また　わるく　なりますから、ぜったいに　のまないで　ください。いいですね。
さとう：　はあ、わかりました。

① さとうさんは　かいしゃで　じょうしの　ぶちょうと　はなしています。

さとう：　ぶちょう。じつは　こんど、あたらしい　プロジェクトの　たんとうしゃに　なったんですが、はじめてなので　しんぱいです。
ぶちょう：　さとうくんなら、しんぱい　しなくても　だいじょうぶだよ。
さとう：　そうでしょうか。
ぶちょう：　そうだよ。がんばってくれよ。
さとう：　わかりました。とにかく、がんばります。

② さとうさんは　おとうさんと　でんわで　はなしています。

ちち：　たくや、げんきか。
たくや：あ、おとうさん、げんきだよ。おとうさんは？
ちち：　わたしは　げんきなんだが、おかあさんが　たくやに　あいたがっている。すぐに　かえって　こられないだろうか。
たくや：かえりたいけれど、すぐには　ちょっと　むりだな。
ちち：　*たいした　ことは　ないんだが、おかあさんが　ちょっと　ぐあいが　わるいんだ。こんしゅうの　にちようびにでも　かえってきてくれれば。
たくや：え、おかあさんが。わかった。かえるように　するよ。

たいした　ことは　ない　*nothing much*

COMMUNICATION (page 179)

1. A：うちの　ぶかの　ことで　あたまが　いたいんです。なかなか　おもった　とおりに　いかなくて、こまっています。
B：なにか　しっぱいでも　したんですか。
A：おおきい　しっぱいでは　ないんだけど。ちいさい　ミスが　おおいんですよ。まいにち　ちゅうい　しているんです。
B：たとえば、どんな？
A：やまだくんは　たのんでおいた　ことを　すぐ　わすれるんです。きょうも　とりひきさきから　でんわが　あったのに、つたえるのを　わすれたし。かならず　メモを　かいて、わたしの　つくえの　うえに　おいておけって　いっているのに、わすれるんですよ。
B：なるほど。
A：まちだくんは　まちがいが　おおいんです。せんしゅうも　みつもりしょを　1まい　つくるのに　3かいも　かきなおさせたんです。まちがいが　ないか　どうか、かならず　かくにんしろと　いっているのに、いつも　そのまま　なんですよ。
B：こまりましたね。

A：きむらくんは　ちょっと　しごとが　いそがしくなると、すぐ　びょうきになって、かいしゃを　やすむんです。せんしゅうも　あたらしい　プロジェクトで　いそがしいのに、ふつかも　やすんだんです。

B：はあ、そうですか。たいへんですね。でも　がんばっている　ひとも　いるんでしょう。

A：ええ。おがわくんは　しごとも　はやいし、ミスも　すくないし、とても　たすかります。なにも　いわなくても、どんどん　しごとを　してくれるんです。

B：なるほど。そういう　ひとが　ひとりでも　いれば、たすかりますね。

A：でも、かのじょは　らいげつ、けっこんして　かいしゃを　やめてしまうんですよ。いったい　どうしたら　いいんでしょうね。

B：はあ。

LESSON 17

SENTENCE PATTERN 3　～れる　～られる（けいご）
PRACTICE II (page 191)

2. ①　インタビューアー：すみません。ちょっと　おうかがい　したいんですが。
つうこうにん：なんでしょうか。
インタビューアー：なつやすみは　どう　すごされますか。
つうこうにん：そうですね。りょこうに　いきます。
インタビューアー：りょこうは　かんがいに　いかれますか、こくないに　いかれますか。
つうこうにん：かいがいですねえ。
インタビューアー：もう　どこに　いかれるか　きめられましたか。
つうこうにん：ええ、カナダに　しました。
インタビューアー：もう　ホテルの　よやくを　されましたか。
つうこうにん：はい、もう　しました。
インタビューアー：そうですか。おいそがしい　ところ　ありがとう　ございました。

②　インタビューアー：すみません。ちょっと　おうかがい　したいんですが。
つうこうにん：なに？
インタビューアー：なつやすみは　どう　すごされますか。
つうこうにん：やっぱり、りょこうだね。
インタビューアー：りょこうは　かいがいに　いかれますか、こくないに　いかれますか。
つうこうにん：こくないだね。
インタビューアー：もう　どこに　いかれるか　きめられましたか。
つうこうにん：ほっかいどうが　いいね。
インタビューアー：もう　ホテルの　よやくを　されましたか。
つうこうにん：まだ、してないよ。
インタビューアー：そうですか。おいそがしい　ところ　ありがとう　ございました。

③　A：カーターさんが　ホンコンに　てんきん　されたそうですね。
B：そうなんですよ。さびしく　なりましたね。
A：カーターさんが　にほんに　こられたのは　いつでしたか。
B：たしか、5ねんぐらいまえでしたよ。
A：しごとも　よく　されたけれど、にほんの　せいかつも　じゅうぶん　たのしまれましたね。
B：じゅうどうも　ならわれて、しあいにも　でられたそうですよ。
A：いろいろな　ところへ　りょこうされたし、わたしたちより　ずっと　にほんの　ことを　ごぞんじかもしれませんね。

COMMUNICATION (page 192)

インタビューアー：きむらさん、きょうは　おいそがしい　ところ　おじかんを　とっていただきまして　ありがとう　ございました。

きむら：　いいえ、おやくに　たちますか　どうか。

インタビューアー：さっそくですが、きむらさんは　ボランティアを　されていると　おききしましたが。

きむら：　ええ、てんじの　ボランティアを　しております。

インタビューアー：てんじと　いいますと、めの　みえない　かたの　ために　つくられた　もじの　ことですね。

きむら：　はい、そうです。　めの　みえない　かたが　さわって　よむことが　できるんです。

インタビューアー：どうして　てんじの　ボランティアを　はじめようと　おもわれたんですか。

きむら：　じつは、ともだちが　きゅうに　めが　みえなくなる　びょうきに　なってしまったんです。めが　みえないのに、はたらく　ということの　たいへんさを　ちかくでみて、なにか　できることは　ないかと　かんがえました。

インタビューアー：そうですか。　そのかたは　いま　なにを　されているんですか。

きむら：　ともだちは　まだ　がっこうで　えいごを　おしえています。じゅぎょうちゅう　こまらないように、テキストを　ぜんぶ　おぼえていくそうです。それを　きいて、わたしも　ともだちの　ために　なにか　したいと　おもったんです。

インタビューアー：よく　わかります。　きょうは　とても　いい　はなしを　きかせていただき、ありがとう　ございました。

LESSON 18

SENTENCE PATTERN 1 speech levels
PRACTICE II (page 197)

① A：やまだ、もう　レポート　かいた？
B：ううん、まだだよ。しけんの　べんきょうしなきゃならないし、いそがしくて。きみだって、レポート　あるだろ？
A：うん、でも　せんしゅう　だしちゃったよ。
B：はやいなあ。

② A：ねえ、れい子、うちの　かいしゃの　あたらしい　ヨーグルト　すごい　にんきね。
B：ああ、ダイエットヨーグルトでしょ？　どこの　みせでも　うりきれで　かえないんですって。
A：そう。わたしは　さいきん　ともだちから　ダイエットヨーグルトが　ほしいって　でんわがあるの。
B：わたしもよ。わたしたちでも　かえないのにね。

③ A：かとう、あした　だいじな　とりひきさきに　いって、プレゼンテーション　するんだってね。
B：そうなんだ。おおきい　とりひきだから、しっぱい　しないと　いいんだけど。
A：きみなら　だいじょうぶだよ。じしんもって　やれよ。
B：そう　いってくれると　うれしいよ。

④ A：はやしさん、ひさしぶり。げんき。
B：ええ。おかげさまで。ねえ、きいて。わたし、むすこが　がっこうに　いっている　あいだに　しごとを　する　ことに　したの。
A：まあ、ほんとう？どんな　しごと？
B：ペットシッターなの。
A：ペットシッターって？
B：ペットを　さんぽ　させたり、たべものを　やったり　する　しごと。
A：たいへんじゃない？
B：ううん、ぜんぜん。どうぶつが　すきだから、たのしみなの。

COMMUNICATION (page 200)

① A：きむら、おそくなって、ごめん。
B：いいや、ぼくも　いま　きたところだよ。
A：ひさしぶりだな。げんきか。
B：まあね。きゅうに　よびだしてわるかったな。
A：いや、いいよ。でも、なんだよ、そうだんって。
B：うん、いま　かいしゃ　やめようか　どうか　なやんでるんだ。
A：なんでだよ。せんげつ　あったとき、こんど　きゅうりょうが　あがったって　よろこんでたじゃないか。
B：せんしゅう　ヘッドハンティングの　かいしゃから　でんわが　あってさ。がいしけいの　かいしゃで　はたらかないかって　きかれたんだ。
A：そうか。それで？
B：ホンコンしてんなんだよ。
A：にほんじゃないのか。
B：ああ、してんちょうの　ポストなんだよ。きゅうりょうも　すごく　いいんだ。
A：そうか。いい　はなしだと　おもうけど、がいしけいの　かいしゃも　たいへんだってきくから、よく　かんがえろよ。

② A：ようこ、おそくなって、ごめんね。まった？
B：いいえ、わたしも　いま　きた　ところよ。
A：ひさしぶり、げんき？
B：ええ、ごめんなさいね。きゅうに　よびだして。
A：いいのよ。ひまだから。でも、どうしたの。そうだんって、なに？
B：いま　かいしゃ　やめようか　どうか　まよってんの。
A：え〜、どうして？この　あいだ　しごと　たのしくなってきたって　いってたじゃない。
B：そうなんだけどね。せんしゅう　テレビで　ハリウッドの　スターに　なった　ひとの　インタビュー　みたの。そのひと　スターに　なるまえに　がっこうの　せんせいだったんですって。それで　こどもの　ころからの　ゆめ　おもいだしちゃって。
A：ああ、ジャズボーカリストに　なるって　ゆめ？
B：うん、アメリカで　べんきょうしたくなったの。
A：そう。かんたんなことじゃないから、よく　かんがえてね。

LESSON 19

SENTENCE PATTERN 1　〜わけです
PRACTICE I (page 204)

A：　グリーンさんですよ。　すごく　じょうずですね。
B：　ほんとうだ。プロみたいですね。
A：　どうして　あんなに　じょうずなんでしょう。
B：　じょうずすぎますよ。
C：　グリーンさんは　オリンピックに　でた　ことが　あるんですよ。
A／B：なるほど。だから、じょうずな　わけですね。

Japanese–English Glossary

10点　10 runs　180
10馬身　ten [horse's] lengths　162
122対0　122 to 0　180
1ヶ月後　one month later　35
1着　(set of clothes)　129
21世紀　twenty-first century　25
4億通り　400 million (ways)　109
6連勝　six consecutive victories　162
ＯＨＰ　overhead projector　142
ＶＩＰ　VIP　67

あ

あいする　愛する　love　162
あいにく　unfortunately　42
アイロンをかける　do the ironing　102
(～に)あう　meet with (disaster, accident, etc.)　185
あきびん　empty bottle　167
あくびがでる　あくびが出る　yawn　42
あげる　raise, put up　78
アジア　Asia　98
あせをかく　汗をかく　work up a sweat　209
あてな　あて名　addressee, addressed to　138
あみをせっとする　網をセットする　set a net　61
「ありときりぎりす」*The Ant and the Grasshopper* (*Aesop's Fables*)　80
あるひ　ある日　one day　35
アルミホイル　aluminum foil　68
アワリ・ゴルフクラブ　Awari Golf Club　12
アンケート　questionnaire　138
あんらくし　安楽死　mercy killing　162

い

いけ　池　pond　61
いけばなてん　生け花展　ikebana exhibition　56
いこう　以降　from, after　160
いぜんほど～ない　以前ほど～ない　... not as much as before　186
イタリア　Italy　215
いれかわる　入れかわる　be mixed up　171
いんしょう　image, impression　107
インターナショナルスクール　international school　15
インターネット　Internet　58
インタビュー　interview　85

う

ウィルス　virus　187
うかがう　hear (humble form)　148
うし　牛　cow　214
うしなう　失う　lose　117
うつ　打つ　to hit　12
うまくすすむ　make good progress　178
うりだし　売り出し　go on sale, be put on sale　155
うりだしちゅう　売り出し中　up for sale, on the market　138
うんてんめんきょしょう　運転免許証　driver's license　35

え

えいがかんとく　映画監督　movie director　212
えいきょう　影響　influence　72
えいぞう　映像　image　212
エンジン　engine　56

お

オーストラリア　Australia　35
オーブン　oven　159
おうえん　応援　support　180
おおきいみちにでる　大きい道に出る　get onto a big street　23
おおびん　大ビン　big bottle (of beer)　209
おきなわ　沖縄　Okinawa　106
おきもの　置物　ornament　186
おこる　angry, cross　39
おしゃれ　stylish, dressed up　4
おせちりょうり　おせち料理　special New Year food　186
おとしより　お年より　senior citizens　85
おふろにはいる　お風呂に入る　take a bath　193
おぼれる　drown　117
おもい　重い　serious　76
おもちゃ　toy　11
おもな　主な　main　116
おる　fold　185

か

かがみ　mirror　26
かぎられた　限られた　limited　201
かくにんする　make sure, check　26
かさをさす　open an umbrella　174
かざる　decorate　92
かじ　家事　housework　116
カスパロフ　Garry Kasparov　109
かためる　to harden　12
かちかん　values　135

かっこいい　nice, cool　150
かつ　勝つ　win　109
かてい　家庭　family　193
かねもち　金持ち　wealthy person　214
かぶ　stick, share, equity　41
かみさま　神様　God　183
かもりょう　カモ猟　duck hunt　61
カルテ　medical chart　171
カレーライス　curry with rice　121
かんがえ　考え　way of thinking　189
かんげきする　感激する　be deeply moved, be thrilled　35
かんこうきゃく　かんこう客　tourist　116
かんさつする　observe　107
かんしゃする　感謝する　appreciate, be grateful　125
かんじゃ　患者　patient　171
かんぜんしゅぎしゃ　完全主義者　perfectionist　212
かんそうき　drier　50
かんとく　監督　coach　180
かんどうする　感動する　be thrilled　117
かんどうする　感動する　be touched　212
かんどうてき　感動的　thrilling　97
かんばん　shop sign　23
かんりしょく　管理職　management　116
ガイドブック　guidebook　64
がくふ　楽譜　(musical) score　150
がまんできない　cannot stand　77
がんたん　元旦　New Year's Day　15

き

きかいか　mechanization　116
きがする　気がする　feel like　126
きがつく　気がつく　notice　35
きっと　surely　212
きになる　気になる　worry (about)　26
きびしい　demanding　212
きびしい　strict　107
きほん　基本　the basics　136
きまり　決まり　regulation　171
キャッチフレーズ　slogan　193
キャップ　(lens) cover /cap　174
きょうりゅう　dinosaur　203
きょうりょく　協力　cooperation, help　129
きょく　曲　(piece of) music　46
きょり　distance　97
きらう　dislike　206
きろく　record　97
きをぬく　気をぬく　relax　180
きんちょうする　緊張する　get tense　209
ぎじゅつ　技術　technology　86
ぎじゅつしゃ　技術者　technical expert　109
ぎゅうにゅう　milk　83
ぎょうせき　業績　(company) results　170

く

くさる　develop bedsores　162
くしゃみ　sneeze　42
くずれはじめる　begin to collapse　170
クッション　cushion　70
クラシック　classical (music)　42
クラスメート　classmate　91
くりかえす　くり返す　repeat　208
クリスマスイブ　Christmas Eve　70
クリスマスツリー　Christmas Tree　70
くるしい　苦しい　pain, agony　206
くるまがはしってくる　車が走って来る　a car comes　107
クレジットカード会社　credit card company　4
クローン　clone　214
くろさわあきら　黒沢明　Kurosawa Akira　212
ぐうぜん　by chance, coincidentally　120
グライダー　glider　189
グラフ　graph　103
グリーン　green　12
グレード　grade, level　28

け

けいえいしゃ　経営者　the management　193
けいけん　experience　103
けいじばん　message board　153
けいたいでんわ　携帯電話　mobile phone　182, 201
けつあつ　blood pressure　151
けつえき　血液　blood　209
ける　kick　98
けれども　but　84
けんせつ　建設　construction　76
ゲート　gate　45
げんこう　draft　65
「げんじものがたり」「源氏物語」*The Tale of Genji*　94
げんちしゅうごう　現地集合　meet on the spot, make your own way there　75

こ

コース　(golf) course　12
コーヒーメーカー　coffeemaker　15
こうこう　高校　high school　91
こうこく　広告　advertisement　57
こうし　lecturer　57
こうそくどうろ　高速道路　expressway, motorway　23
こうはい　後輩　(colleague who joined the firm after you)　136

こうもり　bat　9
こえをかける　声をかける　say something　193
こげた　burned　159
こころのこもる　心のこもる　sincere　212
こっかい　国会　the Diet　92
こっかいぎじどう　国会議事堂　Diet Building　92
こっせつ　骨折　fracture　162
このあいだ　the other day, recently　53
このたび　この度　recently　148
こめ　米　rice　83
ころがる　to roll　12
こわい　frightening, scary　18
こわれる　break　11
こんかい　今回　this time, (on) this occasion　29
コントロール　control　113
コンビニ　convenience store　23
コンロ　gas cooking stove　68
ゴール　finish line　162
ごまかし　trick　212
ゴルフじょう　ゴルフ場　golf course　61

さ

サーブ　serve　198
さいごに　最後に　ultimately　46
さいしゅうでんしゃ　最終電車　the last train　133
サイレンススズカ　Silence Suzuka (racehorse name)　162
サインをだす　サインを出す　give a sign　106
さぎょうちゅう　作業中　while at work　35
さそう　invite　18
さっか　作家　writer, author　94
サッカーボール　soccer ball　98
サッカーリーグ　soccer league　215
さつえい　撮影　filming　212
さとう　sugar　83
さほう　作法　manners (in tea ceremony)　125
さる　monkey　9
さわぐ　make a lot of noise　78
さわる　touch　150
さんかする　参加する　enter (a competition)　97
さんじゃまつり　三社まつり　"Sanja" Festival　92
さんせい　agree, be for something　76
サンタクロース　Santa Claus　70
ざぜん　Zen meditation　102

し

し　死　death, dying　206
シーン　scene　212
しあい　試合　game, match　19
シェークスピア　Shakespeare　92
しかい　司会　master of ceremonies, host　147
しく　lay out　67
ししゅう　embroidery　70
したしむ　love　92
しちにんのさむらい　七人の侍　*Seven Samurai*　212
シチュー　stew　69
しつこい　overbearing, stubborn　136
しどうする　指導する　give advice　148
シナリオ　scenario　109
しばふ　芝生　grass　12
しぶや　渋谷　Shibuya (place in Tokyo)　155
しめす　示す　indicate　86
しもん　fingerprint　150
しや　視野　field of vision　136
しゅうしんこよう　終身雇用　lifetime employment　170
しゅうちゅうちりょうしつ　集中治療室　intensive care (unit)　171
しゅうにゅうをえる　収入をえる　receive a salary　188
しゅじゅつ　手術　operation　162
しゅじゅつしつ　手術室　operating theater　171
しょう　賞　prize　212
しょうがい　障害　handicap　117
しょうひしゃ　しょうひ者　consumer　189
しょうひりょう　consumption　83
しょうゆ　soy sauce　129
しょくせいかつ　食生活　diet　84
しりあい　知り合い　friend　61
しんじゅく　新宿　Shinjuku (place in Tokyo)　155
しんせいひん　新製品　new product　189
しんせんな　新鮮な　fresh　86
しんぞう　心臓　heart　171
しんぱん　審判　umpire　180
しんぼくかい　しんぼく会　get-together　75
シンボル　symbol　92
しんぽする　進歩する　improve　109
じさボケ　時差ボケ　jet-lag　131
じしん　自信　(self-) confidence　117
じっさいの　actual　208
じどうてきに　自動的に　automatically　150
じびきあみをひく　地引きあみを引く　to draw a dragnet　207
ジャズボーカリスト　jazz vocalist　200
じゅんい　position, place　97
じゆうに　自由に　freely　113
じょうほう　information　41
じょうほうシステム　情報システム　information system　86
じょせいむき　女性むき　women's, for women　45
じんこうしば　人工芝　artificial turf　12
じんじぶ　人事部　personnel department　16

す

スイッチ　switch　15
すいでん　水田　rice paddy　61
すいぶん　水分　water　209
スキーウェア　skiwear　129
すきなひとができる　好きな人ができる　find a boyfriend/girlfriend　4
すぎる　pass　113
スケール　scale　212
すすめる　encourage　170
スタイル　style, way　201
ストレッチ　stretching exercises　132
ストレッチャー　stretcher, trolley　171
すな　砂　sand　12
すもうべや　すもう部屋　sumo stable　124
スロープ　slope　113
ずがいこつ　頭蓋骨　skull　98
ずぶぬれ　soaked through to the bone　96

せ

せいごかっけい　正五角形　pentagon　98
せいさんち　生産地　country of origin　86
せいひん　製品　product　129
せいろっかっけい　正六角形　hexagon　98
せきたん　石炭　coal　35
せきにん　responsibility　188
せきゆ　石油　crude oil, petroleum　12
せきをはずしております　席をはずしております　be away from one's desk　28
せっかく　(I took all the trouble to ...)　133
せっとく　説得　persuade　136
せなか　背中　back　2
セミナー　seminar, course　57
センサー　sensor　150
せんしゅ　選手　athletes　117
せんそうじ　浅草寺　Sensoji Temple　92
せんたくもの　洗濯物　laundry　167
せんでんする　宣伝する　advertise　157
せんとう　銭湯　public bath　193
せんぱい　先輩　(colleague who joined the firm before you)　136
ぜいかん　税関　customs　121
ぜんたい　全体　overall　188

そ

そうしき　そう式　funeral　208
そっと　quietly, softly　18
そのほかに　what else　108
ソフト　software　148
それいらい　それ以来　since then　97
そろえる　sort out　32

た

たいしょくきん　退職金　severance pay, golden handshake　170
たいせんする　対戦する　play a tournament　109
タイタニック　Titanic　46
タイムマシン　time machine　26
タグ　(price) tag　174
たすかる　to be a help　68
たすける　help, aid　11
たちば　立場　position, perspective　160
タブー　taboo, not tolerated　206
タラップ　landing steps　199
ダイエット　diet (for weight reduction)　84
ダイエットヨーグルト　diet yogurt　197
だいず　大豆　soy bean　86
だいよんコーナー　第4コーナー　fourth corner　162
ダイレクトメール　direct mail (DM)　138
だから　therefore　117
だきょう　妥協　compromise　212
だし　stock　68
だんせいむき　男性むき　men's, for men　45

ち

チームプレー　teamwork　102
チェス　chess　109
チェックする　check　150
ちほう　地方　region, area　35
ちゃいろ　茶色　brown　98
チャンピオン　champion　109
ちゅういする　注意する　caution, warn　90
ちゅうとう　中東　the Middle East　12
ちゅうねん　中年　middle-aged　46
ちょうさ　調査　survey　201
ちょうせん　挑戦　challenge　117
ちょうどうけん　ちょうどう犬　hearing dog　11

つ

ツアー　tour　28
ツアーガイド　tour guide　64
つうきん　通勤　commute　113
つかまえる　捕まえる　catch　61
つかれ　fatigue　209
(〜に)つく　is stuck on ..., is on ...　2
つけもの　漬物　pickles　86
つながる　be joined　201
つる　Japanese crane　185
つる　fishing　60

て

てにはいる　手に入る　get hold of　60
てれくさそうに　照れくさそうに　self-consciously　46

テレビきょく　broadcasting company　59
テレビゲーム　video game　205
テレビばんぐみ　テレビ番組　TV program　85
てんきよほう　天気予報　weather forecast　8
てんごくとじごく　天国と地獄　*Heaven and Earth*　212
てんじ　点字　braille　192
てんのう　天皇　emperor　212
ディープブルー　Deep Blue　109
でてくる　出てくる　appear, come out　70
でんわのうけかた　電話の受け方　telephone manner　102

と

とうきょうけいばじょう　東京競馬場　Tokyo Racecourse　162
とうきょうタワー　東京タワー　Tokyo Tower　92
とうきょうドーム　東京ドーム　Tokyo Dome　92
とうじつ　当日　(on) that day　28
とかい　都会　city　116
とこや　barber's shop　43
ところが　however　72
とち　土地　land　61
トップになる　take the lead　162
とどけもの　届け物　a delivery　167
トライアスロン　triathlon　117
トラベラーズチェック　traveler's checks　64
とり　鳥　bird　5
とりいそぎおれいまで　とり急ぎお礼まで　(letter ending; lit.: "Greetings in haste")　125
とりにんげんコンテスト　鳥人間コンテスト　Birdman Contest　88
トレーナー　trainer　107
トレーニングちゅう　トレーニング中　in training　107
ドームスタジアム　domed stadium　92
どうぶつ　動物　animals　148
ドクター　doctor　11
ドラキュラ　Dracula, vampire　9
ドレスうりば　ドレス売り場　dress floor　119
どんなに　however much　109

な

ながでんわ　長電話　on the phone for a long time　179
ながねぎ　長ネギ　green onion　86
なく　泣く　cry　117
なげたボールのかず　投げたボールの数　pitch count　180
なべ　pot　68
なみだがでる　なみだが出る　burst into tears　42
なやむ　worry about, be concerned about　160
なんみんキャンプ　refugee camp　104

に

にあう　似合う　suit (one), go together　26
におい　smell, aroma　2
にげる　逃げる　fly away　61
にている　似ている　be alike　171
〜にとって　for　201
にんげん　人間　human　9

ね

ネームカード　name tag　67
ねこ　cat　70
ねむる　眠る　sleep　162

の

のう　脳　brain　209
のうりょく　能力　abilities, skills　136
のうりょくをいかす　能力をいかす　make use of one's skills　188
のばす　伸ばす　stretch　193
のべさんおくにん　延べ3億人　over three hundred million people　98

は

は　歯　tooth　81
は　葉　leaf　155
はい　肺　lungs　171
はいしゃ　歯医者　dentist　81
ハイテク　high-tech　11
はしる　走る　run　61
はずかしい　shy, embarrassed　120
はだか　裸　be naked　193
はつおんする　発音する　pronounce　206
はなしかける　話しかける　speak (to a person)　96
「ハムレット」　*Hamlet*　92
ハリウッド　Hollywood　200
はりねずみ　hedgehog　43
ハンターバレー　Hunter Valley　35
はんたい　disagree, be against something　76
はんたいほうこう　はんたい方向　opposite direction　53
はんだんする　judge, decide　103
はんにん　犯人　criminal　212
バーレーン　Bahrain　12
バザー　bazaar　151
ばしょ　場所　location　23
バット　baseball bat　70
バランスがくずれる　lose balance　151
ばんぐみらん　番組らん　TV listings　59

ばんごうあんない　番号案内　information desk　182
パジャマ　pajamas　174
パトカー　police car　53
パネル　panel　98
パラリンピック　Paralympic Games　117

ひ
ひきわたす　引きわたす　hand over　171
ひげき　悲劇　tragedy　162
ひつじ　sheep　214
ひょうか　評価　high respect　212
びょう　秒　second　109
びわこ　琵琶湖　Lake Biwako　88
びん　bottle, jar, glass container　167
ピアノきょうしつ　ピアノ教室　piano lessons　46
ピクニック　picnic　212
ピザや　ピザ屋　pizzeria　104
ぴったり　a perfect fit　57
ぴったり　exactly　201
ピッチャー　pitcher　180
ぴりぴりする　be nervous, be on one's toes　205

ふ
ファスナー　zip　119
ファッション　fashion　201
ファンクラブ　fan club　124
ふく　服　clothes　65
ふくろ　袋　envelope　207
ふしぎがる　find mysterious, be puzzled　205
ふたりぶん　二人分　for two people　4
ふだん　usually　212
ふやす　increase　60
ぶっしつ　物質　substance　209
ぶひん　部品　component　97
ブラウン　brown　12
ぶんぼうぐ　文房具　stationery　129
プライド　self-respect　180
プラン　plan　48
プレート　plate　150
プレゼンテーション　presentation　29
プロ　professional　198
プログラム　program　67

へ
ヘアースタイル　hairstyle　5
ヘッドハンティング　headhunting　200
ヘッドホン　headphones　46
へび　snake　5
ヘリポート　heliport　76
べっそう　別荘　country house　18
ベランダ　veranda, balcony　167
ペット　pet　197
ペットボトル　PET (polyethylene terephthalate) bottle　129

ほ
ほうこうおんち　方向オンチ　(person who has) no sense of direction　23
ほうりつ　法律　law　129
ほけんりょう　ほけん料　insurance premium　28
ほす　dry　167
ほとんどのひと　ほとんどの人　most people　84
ほどく　become loose　208
ホラス・ウィルソン　Horace Wilson　94
ほんもの　本物　real　5
ボーナス　bonus　216
ボランティア　voluntary work　104
ポケット　pocket　174
ポリウレタン　polyurethane　98
ポルトガル人　a Portuguese　72

ま
まあだだよ　*Madadayo* (No, not yet)　212
まいにちのように　毎日のように　almost every day　138
まえもって　前もって　beforehand　65
まける　負ける　lose　180
ますいをかける　麻酔をかける　anesthetize　171
ますます　more and more　86
まずは、お礼まで　(Anyway,) thank you　148
まちがえる　間違える　mistake for　53
マット　mat　12
まどをふく　clean windows　102
マナー　manners　193
まよう　get lost　75

み
ミス　mistake　4
みちにまよう　道に迷う　lose one's way, get lost　23
みのしろきん　身の代金　ransom money　212
みみのふじゆうなひと　耳の不自由な人　hard of hearing, deaf　11
みやげもの　souvenirs　64
みりょく　attraction　116

む
むすびかた　knot　208
むすぶ　tie (a knot)　208
むらさきしきぶ　紫式部　Murasaki Shikibu　94

も

もうどうけん　もうどう犬　guide dog, seeing-eye dog 107
もえないごみ　nonburnable trash 167
もくてき　目的　objective 188
もったいない　wasteful 60
モデルチェンジ　model change 189
もれる　leak 138

や

やくにたつ　useful 57
やっと　at last, finally 189
やね　屋根　roof 212

ゆ

ゆうき　勇気　courage 117
ゆうしょうする　優勝する　win 162
ゆえんち　theme park 116
ゆとり　relaxation 136
ゆにゅうする　輸入する　import 35
ゆぶね　湯船　bathtub 193
ゆめ　夢　dream 162
ゆをながす　湯を流す　run hot water 193

よ

ようき　容器　container 129
よこづな　Grand Champion 124
よさん　予算　budget 216
よっきゅうをみたす　欲求を満たす　satisfy a physical desire 209
よぶ　invite, attract 186

ら

ライセンス　permit, license 189
ライト　lights 92
ラケット　racquet 198
らしょうもん　羅生門　*Rashomon* 212
ラベル　label 86

り

リーキ　leek 86
リサイクル　recycling 129
りじかい　理事会　(residents') committee 167
りゅうがく　留学　study overseas 104
りゆう　理由　reason 86

る

ルームサービス　room service 215
ルームメイト　roommate 160
ルール　rules, regulations 81
るすでん　るす電　answering machine 26

れ

れいじょう　礼状　thank-you letter 125
レジ　cash register, till 186
れつ　line, queue 39
レパートリー　repertoire 60
レポーター　reporter 199
レポート　report 41
レインボーブリッジ　Rainbow Bridge 92
れんらくをとる　make contact, reach 133

ろ

ローン　loan 216
ろうか　corridor 167
ロックする　lock 174
ロックミュージシャン　rock musician 199
ロボット　robot 100

わ

ワールドカップ　World Cup (soccer) 98
ワクチン　vaccine 187
わだいこ　和だいこ　Japanese drum 59
わらいだす　わらい出す　burst out laughing 42
ワンサイドゲーム　one-sided game 180

SOURCES

The following books, magazines, and newspapers were used as reference sources when compiling these learning materials.

Books

「Visual Sports '93」大修館書店

「企業トップ 32 人の人間学講座 20 代・30 代に私が学んだこと」海藤守著　実務教育出版

「英語で話す日本の謎Ｑ＆Ａ」講談社インターナショナル

Newspapers and Magazines

AERA

朝日新聞

ＮＨＫきょうの健康

サンデー毎日

JAF MATE

週間文春

日刊スポーツ

日経ビジネス

日本経済新聞

（改）コミュニケーションのための日本語 III
ワークブック
JAPANESE FOR BUSY PEOPLE III
THE WORKBOOK Revised Edition

1999年10月29日　第１刷発行

著　者　社団法人　国際日本語普及協会
発行者　野間佐和子
発行所　講談社インターナショナル株式会社
〒112-8652 東京都文京区音羽 1-17-14
電話：03-3944-6493

印刷所　株式会社　平河工業社
製本所　株式会社　国宝社

落丁本・乱丁本は、小社業務部宛にお送りください。送料小社負担にてお取替えします。

定価はカバーに表示してあります。

Printed in Japan
ISBN4-7700-2331-6